Tribe Memories
the first century
by Russell Schneider

League Park

> *"I believe in the Rip Van Winkle theory, that a man from 1910 can wake up after being asleep for seventy years, walk into a ball park and understand baseball perfectly."* **– former Baseball Commissioner Bowie Kuhn**

Moonlight Publishing
Copyright 2000
All rights reserved

ISBN 0 - 9672056 - 1 - 1

Front cover illustration by Tom Denny
Back cover illustration by Tom Denny
Stadium illustrations by Tom Denny
Layout and design by Moonlight Publishing
Photographs courtesy of
The Cleveland Indians
The Cleveland *Plain Dealer*

Manufactured in the United States of America
First printing March 2000

"I have discovered in 20 years of moving around a ball park that the fans' knowledge of the game is usually in inverse proportion to the price of the seats." – **former Indians owner Bill Veeck**

"Baseball is almost the only orderly thing in a very unorderly world. If you get three strikes, even the best lawyer in the world can't get you off." – **former Indians owner Bill Veeck**

"It breaks your heart. It is designed to break your heart. The game begins in the spring, when everything else begins again, and it blossoms in the summer, filling the afternoons and evening, and then as soon as the chill rains come, it stops and leaves you to face the fall alone." – **former Baseball Commissioner A. Bartlett Giamatti**

"The only way to get along with newspapermen is to be like Dizzy Dean. Say something one minute and something different the next." – **Hall of Fame outfielder and former Indians general manager Hank Greenberg**

"The greatest thrill in the world is to end the game with a home run and watch everybody else walk off the field while you're running the bases on air." – **former Indians third baseman Al Rosen**

The Author

Tribe Memories, the First Century, was authored by Russell Schneider, whose byline as a sportswriter-columnist appeared in the Cleveland *Plain Dealer* for 32 years, and the memories collected here date back to 1901 when Cleveland's professional baseball team was a charter member of the American League.

Schneider covered the Indians on a daily basis from 1964-77 – a period considered to have been "the bad old days" - and continued to report their successes and failures until 1993, when he left the newspaper to do free lance writing.

Schneider played one season in the Indians minor league system (as a good field, light hitting catcher) before he and then-farm director Hank Greenberg correctly came to the realization that his future in baseball would be better served behind a typewriter than behind a mask.

And so, after graduating from Baldwin-Wallace College, Schneider found it easier (and was more successful) *writing* about curve balls, than trying to hit them. He also covered the Cleveland Browns from 1978-83, during their heyday as the "Kardiac Kids," was an investigative reporter and wrote a sports column for the *Plain Dealer*.

A Marine Corps veteran, Schneider and his wife Kay raised three children, Eileen, whose husband, Eric Raich, pitched for the Indians in 1975-76; Russell Jr., who played a major role in the editing, design and production of this book; and Bryan, who is employed by the *Plain Dealer* in a management position.

Other books by Schneider:
Frank Robinson, the Making of a Manager (1976)
Lou Boudreau, Covering All The Bases (1993)
The Cleveland Indians Encyclopedia (1995)
The Glorious Indian Summer of 1995
The Unfulfilled Indian Summer of 1996
The Boys Of The Summer of '48 (1998)
The Best of the Cleveland Browns Memories (1999)

Dedication and Acknowledgments

There are many to whom this book should be – and is – dedicated, and appreciation extended, beginning, as always, with my wife, best friend and severest critic, Kay; and to my eldest son and partner in this endeavor (and others), Rusty, for his editing, design and production of Tribe Memories, the First Century; and to Tom Denny, for his outstanding artwork on the front and back covers; and to Joe Simenic, a dear friend, remarkable researcher and great baseball fan; and to the players and other personnel of the Indians of the past who created the memories collected in this book; and, most assuredly, to the fans, whose devotion to the Blues, Bronchos, Naps and Indians throughout the first century of professional baseball in Cleveland has been outstanding, making the franchise one of the best in professional sports; and, last but certainly not least, to Bob DiBiasio, Indians vice president/public relations, Bart Swain and Curtis Danburg for their assistance, and the use of their files and photographs.

Introduction

Some would call it a labor of love, and in many respects it was for me, recalling the memories – even the unpleasant ones – that have accumulated over a lifetime as a fan of the Indians, when Lou Boudreau was the "Boy Manager," and Bill Veeck was the "Barnum of Baseball."

In those days, when major league baseball truly was as much a sport as it was a business, the deeds of the Indians too often were more lamented than exulted, except in 1948, when Boudreau and Veeck became civic heroes. That was the year the Indians won the second pennant and World Series of their existence.

It was then, too, that the characters on the team – not the *character* of the players - commanded almost as much attention as the games they won and lost, rather than the amount of money the stars were paid, or when they'd be free to auction their services to the highest bidders, and nobody employed an agent to represent them.

Were those "old" times better? In some ways, yes. Unequivocally.

In other ways, based on the Indians' success (or lack of same) on the field, no. Also, unequivocally.

From 1901, when the American League – and this collection of memories – began, through the mid-1970s, when players won the right to become free agents and salaries escalated to frenzied and outrageous heights, the Indians won only three pennants in seven decades.

But since then, as dollar signs became as prominent on sports pages as batting averages, the Indians went from being a weak, "have not" franchise to one of the best in the major leagues, on the field and at the box office, winning five consecutive division championships and two pennants in the final five years of the 1900s.

Through it all, the good as well as the bad times since Ban Johnson founded the American League and Cleveland's professional baseball team was called the "Blues," a multitude of memories have accumulated. Many of them follow, including, admittedly, some we'd just as soon forget. They are listed, in no particular order, in the index at the end of this book.

Russell Schneider
Cleveland, Ohio
March 2000

"Sometimes sportswriters write what I say and not what I mean." – **retired third baseman Pedro Guerrero**

"The trouble with baseball is that the person who know how to bat and field best is sitting in the bleachers or in the press box." – **Anonymous**

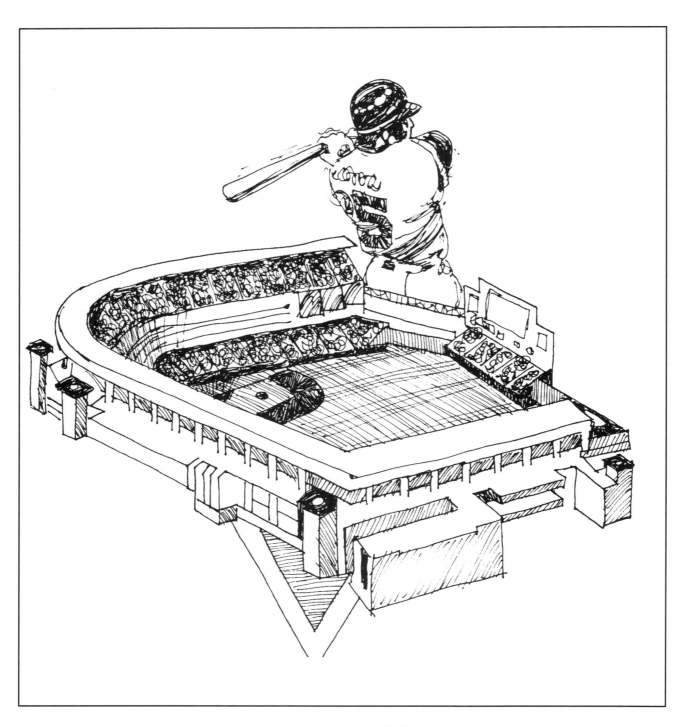

Jacobs Field

When he surfaced as the then-prospective new owner of the Indians, Lawrence J. Dolan – better known as "Larry" from the time he was a football star at St. Ignatius High School in the late-1940s – made two points perfectly clear.

First, he would be the sole owner and chief executive officer by purchasing 100 percent of the club for $323 million.

And, second, that John Hart would continue to make all the player personnel decisions, as he had done so well since 1991 when he was named general manager of the Indians.

"If it ain't broke, don't fix it," was Dolan's attitude.

"The players we hire and those we retain will be up to John and his baseball people," Dolan emphasized on Nov. 4, 1999, when the pending sale was announced.

Larry Dolan

Dolan also paid tribute to Richard E. Jacobs, who had owned the Indians since 1986 when he and his late brother, David, bought the franchise for a reported $45 million.

"Dick is my greatest asset and my greatest liability," Dolan said. "He's an asset because of all the outstanding things he's done for this organization and this city. But he's a liability because he's going to be a tough act to follow."

Major league club owners approved Dolan's purchase of the team on Jan. 19, 2000, and the deal was officially consummated on Feb. 7, 2000, in a vote of shareholders, though that was merely a formality because Jacobs controlled the vast majority of outstanding shares.

Dolan, born in Cleveland in 1931, is an alumnus of Notre Dame University, an ex-Marine and father of six children, a partner in the Chardon-based law firm of Thrasher, Dinsmore and Dolan, and co-owner (with his older brother Charles) of Cablevision, a television cable provider.

An avid Indians fan from the time he was a catcher on the Cleveland sandlots playing for the "Variety Post" team in the American Legion Class E-Unbacked Division in 1946, Dolan's favorite then – and still is – Lou Boudreau.

"My idol was always Lou Boudreau ... it never occurred to me to be Bill Veeck," Dolan said of his longtime interest in, and devotion to the former Indians player-manager. A few days later Boudreau, 83, who makes his home in Frankfurt, Ill., called Dolan to offer his congratulations. It was a gesture that thoroughly thrilled the 14th owner of the Cleveland franchise which was a charter member of the American League when it was founded in 1901 by Byron Bancroft "Ban" Johnson.

"There is a proud legacy here, and there has been for many, many decades," Dolan said. "Dick (Jacobs) and his organization have developed and operated an outstanding franchise. I am honored to follow in his footsteps. Dick has done for this city in the 90s what Bill Veeck did in the 40s."

Veeck owned the Indians from June 1946 through November 1949, having purchased the team for a reported $2.2 million. Previous owners were Charles W. Somers, James Dunn, and Alva Bradley, who sold to Veeck. Since 1949, and prior to the Jacobs brothers, the Indians were owned by groups headed by Ellis Ryan, Myron H. Wilson, William R. Daley, Gabe Paul, Vernon Stouffer, Nick Mileti, Alva T. Bonda and F. J. "Steve" O'Neill.

'I trust Charlie implicitly'

It was a long time coming and, when the opportunity finally arrived, there never should have been any doubt that Charlie Manuel would get the job – or that he deserved to become the 37th manager of the Indians.

Charlie Manuel

The then-55 year old, career baseball man was hired Nov. 1, 1999, to succeed Mike Hargrove in the wake of the Tribe's fifth consecutive American League Central Division championship, but also a second straight failure to reach the World Series.

Under Hargrove, who replaced John McNamara as manager on July 6, 1991, the Indians won two pennants, but each time lost in the World Series, to Atlanta in 1995, and to Florida in 1997. His won-lost record of 721-591 is second-best in franchise history (to Lou Boudreau's 728-649).

Manuel, the Tribe's hitting coach from 1988-89 and 1994-99, managed in the minor leagues for eight years, for the Indians from 1990-93, and the Minnesota Twins from 1983-87. His teams compiled an overall 647-622 record, and he was named Manager of the Year in the Pacific Coast League in 1992.

When he was introduced as the new Indians Chief, Manuel, in his folksy, West Virginia drawl, expressed his appreciation.

"This is the utmost compliment anyone can give me," he said, then promised, "I'm not going to say I'll do everything in my power to get us where we want to go, because I'll do more than that."

His appointment should not have been a surprise, considering the unequivocally-stated high regard in which Manuel was held by General Manager John Hart.

When Manuel was developing the Tribe's best prospects at Colorado Springs of the P.C.L. and Charlotte of the International League, Hart said, "Charlie is a remarkable baseball man. He can do it all, as a manager, a coach, a scout. You name it, Charlie can do it. He has helped everybody we've sent to him … I trust Charlie implicitly."

Manuel had a long playing career as an outfielder, beginning in 1963 when he was signed by Minnesota. He made it to the Twins in 1969, went back to the minor leagues from 1973 to 1975 when he finished the season with the Los Angeles Dodgers. In 242 major league games he compiled a .198 batting average

From 1976 through 1981, Manuel played for the Yakult Swallows and Kintetsu Buffaloes in Japan where he clubbed 192 homers in six seasons, including 48 in 1980 which was, at that time, an American home run record for Japanese baseball. He also was the first American to win the Most Valuable Player award in Japan, in 1979 when he batted .324 with 37 homers and 97 RBI.

Manuel began his managerial career in 1983 at Wisconsin Rapids of the (Class A) Midwest League, was promoted by the Twins to (Class AA) Orlando of the Southern League in 1984 and 1985, and to (Class AAA) Toledo of the International League in 1986, and Portland of the P.C.L. in 1987.

Named to Manuel's coaching staff were former Twins teammate Ted Uhlaender, former Chicago Cubs manager Jim Riggleman, former Boston coach Grady Little, and former Anaheim pitching coach Dick Pole. Three Tribe coaches were retained: Luis Isaac, Clarence Jones and Dan Williams.

History was made on the afternoon of April 24, 1901 when Ollie Pickering stepped to the plate for the Cleveland Blues.

Pickering, an outfielder who would hit .309 that season, lofted the second pitch from Roy Patterson of the Chicago White Sox to center field.

It was caught by William Hoy, a deaf mute who was cruelly nicknamed "Dummy," and just like that the American League was underway.

That first game, played in Chicago's South Side Park, was won by the White Sox, 8-2, and might have been a portent of the future for Cleveland's professional baseball franchise that subsequently changed its name to "Bronchos" in 1902, to "Naps" in 1903, and to "Indians" in 1915.

The league had been formed by a former sportwriter, Byron "Ban" Johnson.

Cleveland and Chicago had the honor of playing that first game by accident - or perhaps better stated, an act of God.

Ban Johnson

The American League's other opening day games all were rained out: Detroit at Milwaukee, Philadelphia at Washington, and Baltimore at Boston.

It isn't difficult to identify the goat of Cleveland's first defeat in the American League, based on newspaper accounts at the time.

It was a slightly-built, 31-year old pitcher named Bill (Wizard) Hoffer, who would win three games and lose eight for the Blues in 1901, his only season in the American League.

"Wizard Hoffer slipped up yesterday in his effort to mystify umpire Connolly," as the Cleveland *Press* reported that first game.

"For two innings Hoffer aimed the ball at the tin gutters on the roof of the grandstand. After each pitch he would appeal with his eyes to the umpire, as if to say, 'See that strike?'

"But Connolly only shook his head and sent White Stockings to first on gifts. Beginning with the third inning, Hoffer was as puzzling as of old (when he'd pitched with some success in the National League), but the damage had already been done."

The account of the game in the Cleveland *Plain Dealer* was no more charitable.

Under a subhead that reported, "Hoffer's Wildness Lost the Game," the *PD* said: "(Manager James) McAleer's men had two disastrous innings today, the first and second, then steadied down and played hardball, but Comiskey's aggregation had turned into the home stretch and the game was won and lost.

"Hoffer could not control the ball in those two innings, apparently unable to get it far below the shoulder (though) he steadied wonderfully in the third and pitched good ball the remainder of the game."

Then the unidentified *PD* sportswriter reported, "The season opening game was a great success," perhaps because of the "enormous crowd, variously estimated at from 10,000 to 15,000."

The Blues did not fare well that first season, finishing seventh with a 54-82 won-lost record, after which McAleer was fired and replaced by William Armour.

Three seasons later the team climbed to respectability, finished second in 1908, and won Cleveland's first pennant in 1920.

The season of dreams

At precisely 11:02 p.m., Sept. 8, 1995, a foul ball off the bat of Baltimore's Jeff Huson landed in the glove of Indians third baseman Jim Thome at Jacobs Field, and thousands – make that *several hundred thousands-* of baseball fans in Cleveland went crazy.

John Hart

As an elated Tom Hamilton, the radio play-by-play voice of the Indians shouted into his microphone: "The season of dreams has become reality in Cleveland."

Huson's foul ball was the final out in the Tribe's 3-2 victory over the Orioles, clinching the championship of the American League's Central Division.

It vaulted the team constructed by General Manager John Hart and led on the field by Manager Mike Hargrove into major league baseball's postseason playoffs for the first time in 41 years, since 1954, when the Indians last won a championship.

"I cried, thinking of all we'd gone through to get to where we are," said catcher Sandy Alomar Jr., one of only four players who were wearing Cleveland uniforms in 1991, when the Indians lost a franchise record 105 games. The others: pitcher Charles Nagy, outfielder Albert Belle and second baseman Carlos Baerga.

The Indians went from clinching the division title to go 14-7, winning 100 games for only the second time in club history.

They swept Boston in the best-of-five Division Series, and beat Seattle in six games for the pennant, their fourth since becoming a charter member of the A.L. in 1901.

But then the Tribe fell victim to Atlanta's outstanding pitching staff in the World Series, losing to the Braves, four-games-to-two. The finale was a heart-wrenching, 1-0, loss administered by Tom Glavine that was finalized on the wings of a sixth inning homer by David Justice off southpaw Jim Poole.

The Indians were beaten by the Braves, 3-2, in the opener of the World Series on a two-hitter by Greg Maddux. They wasted numerous opportunities against Glavine and three relievers in losing the second game, 4-3. Back in Jacobs Field for Game 3, the Indians rallied for a 7-6 victory on an 11th inning, run-producing single by Eddie Murray in a 4-hour, 9-minute marathon. Ryan Klesko homered to overcome solo shots by Belle and Manny Ramirez as Atlanta won the fourth game, 5-2. Orel Hershiser kept the Indians alive in Game 5, as Belle and Thome homered for a 5-4 victory.

But then Glavine and Justice halted the Indians comeback in Game 6.

(Ironically, two years later Justice would come to the Indians, with center fielder Marquis Grissom in a trade with the Braves for center fielder Kenny Lofton and pitcher Alan Embree.)

However, that loss to the Braves, ending the Indians' quest for their third world's championship – which they previously won in 1920 and 1948 – did not diminish the ardor of the fans. Two days after the final game more than 50,000 people attended a rally in downtown Cleveland in honor of their fallen, but still loved heroes.

Hargrove told the crowd, "We can't guarantee we'll ever get to do this again, but if hard work, pride and talent gets you back and wins the World Series, this bunch of guys will do it for you."

And, speaking for the players, Omar Vizquel flat-out promised, "We'll be back. We'll be in the World Series again."

Jacobs Field, which has been the Indians' home since 1994, is recognized throughout baseball as one of the best and most functional ball parks in the country.

It covers 12 acres in downtown Cleveland, bounded by Ontario St. on the west, East 9th St. on the east, Prospect Ave. on the north, and Carnegie Ave. on the south. It was designed by Hellmuth, Obata & Kassabaum, Inc., and constructed by the Gateway Sports and Entertainment Complex at a cost of $169 million, funded through the sale of Gateway Bonds, the Cuyahoga County 15 year luxury tax on alcohol and cigarette sales, private investments and pre-paid leasing on luxory seating.

Jacobs Field replaced the Cleveland Municipal Stadium where Indians home games had been played for 61 years (although, from 1932, when the Stadium opened on July31, through 1946, some home games continued to be played at League Park).

The Stadium, constructed at a cost of $2,640,000, had a seating capacity for baseball of 74,483 although 80,184 fans jammed into the mammoth, "C" shaped structure for the July 31 opener, won by Philadelphia, 1-0.

Actually, that first game was only the second major event to be held in the Stadium; the first was a professional boxing match between heavyweight champion Max Schmeling and Young Stribling on July 3, 1931. A crowd of 36,936 saw Schmeling win on a 15 round technical knockout.

Before the Stadium came into existence, professional baseball in Cleveland had five homes, the best known of which was League Park, located at Lexington Ave. and East 66th street.

It was a cozy, intimate park that seated 27,000 fans. League Park opened on May 1, 1891 for a game in which the Cleveland team, then called the "Spiders," and legendary Cy Young beat Cincinnati, 12-3, in front of a crowd estimated at 9,000.

The name was changed to "Dunn Field" in 1916, in honor of James Dunn, then owner of the Indians, but was re-named League Park in November 1927 when Alva Bradley bought the franchise.

Professional baseball was first played in Cleveland in 1869 by a team called the "Forest Citys" on a field known as "Case Commons" at East 38th Street, between Scovill and Community College Avenues.

In 1871 the Forest Citys, then in the National Association, played in a park located at East 55th Street and Central Avenue, but the franchise folded a year later and it was not until 1879 that professional baseball returned to Cleveland in the National League.

The new team, the "Spiders," played at a field between Cedar and Carnegie Avenues, near East 46th Street, through 1884 when that franchise also folded.

The Spiders were resurrected in 1889 and played at the East 46th Street park for two more years, until it was destroyed in 1890 by lightning and the team's owner, Frank DeHaas Robison constructed "National League Park," which eventually was shortened to League Park.

Several noteworthy events took place at League Park before the Indians moved in 1947 to the Stadium to play all their games.

Among them was baseball's only unassisted triple play in a World Series game, by Indians' second baseman Bill Wambsganss on Oct. 10, 1920, in an 8-1 victory over the Brooklyn Dodgers as the Indians won the world's championship. Babe Ruth struck his 500th career homer over the high (40 feet) but close (290 feet down the foul line) right field fence off Willis Hudlin on Aug. 10, 1929.

And it also was at League Park that Joe DiMaggio hit safely in his 56th consecutive game on July 16, 1941, the day before his streak was stopped at the Stadium.

'A milestone event in... sports'

It outlived its "magnificence" a long time ago and was demolished in 1996, two years after the Indians moved out of the Cleveland Municipal Stadium and into Jacobs Field.

But back there in 1932, when it opened for baseball on July 31, the Stadium was called "a magnificent structure, the ultimate athletic facility in the country."

Connie Mack

And that first game in the Stadium, against the Philadelphia Athletics, was called "a milestone event in middle western sports" by the late Franklin Lewis, former sports editor of the Cleveland *Press,* in his 1949 history of the Indians.

"Cleveland strutted at the mere mention of the world's largest baseball plant," when it was built at a cost of $2,640,000, Lewis wrote. "Every seat in the new stadium had been sold for weeks in advance of the opener as Cleveland put on its celebrating clothes and rushed to the lake front. The pregame ceremony was as impressive as the game itself.

"Baseball's brass shone beneath the omnipresent sun as (Baseball Commissioner) Judge Landis, (American League President) Will Harridge, A's President Tom Shiba, Ohio's Governor George White, who pitched the first ball, and the Mayor of Cleveland, Ray T. Miller, who caught it (were in attendance).

"Connie Mack (owner and manager of the A's) took the public address microphone and thanked (Indians owner) Alva Bradley and (General Manager) Billy Evans for their roles in providing the Indians, and all of baseball with such a magnificent structure.

"There was naught but cheers that day, cheers sent up by a shirt-sleeved audience of 80,184, of whom 76,979 paid their way in. These included the thousands in the center field bleachers who blocked the vision of batters so that the final score of 1-0, with the A's winning, was not unexpected.

"Lefty Grove nosed out Mel Harder ... who pitched eight innings and gave up five hits. The A's pushed across a lone run in the eighth on a pass to Max Bishop, a sacrifice by Mule Haas, and (Mickey) Cochrane's sharp grounder that went past Harder into center for a single. But, despite the Indians loss, it was a great day."

The pitchers, especially, loved the new park. Though the left and right field foul poles were 320 feet from the plate, the bleachers were 436 feet away to left and right center, and 445 feet to dead center.

As Babe Ruth said the first time he played in the Stadium, "You need a horse to play the outfield in this place."

It wasn't until 1947 that Bill Veeck installed a temporary fence, making the dimensions of the playing field fairer to the hitter.

That first year the fence was moved in and out, depending upon the caliber of the Indians' opposition for each game, though the practice was subsequently outlawed in 1948.

Bradley, who'd bought the Indians in 1927, a few months before a bond issue was passed to finance construction of the Stadium, was thrilled by the opener, and especially the crowd. "We'll fill the place often, every Sunday," he predicted.

However, as Lewis pointed out, "Alas ... not for another 16 years (1948) was the Stadium to be overflowing again with a population the size of the city of Binghamton, New York."

The end of the 'Old Gray Lady'

The count on Mark Lewis went to 2-and-2 and 72,390 fans stood as one in anticipation.

Some cheered, but most were silent. The date was Oct. 3, 1993.

Jose DeLeon wound up and flung a wicked slider that broke low, on the outside corner of the plate. Lewis swung mightily, hoping, perhaps, to drive the ball into virgin territory – the center field bleachers – but hit nothing but air.

Umpire Larry Barnett punched his right fist into the sky, finalizing a 4-0 victory by the Chicago White Sox over the Indians.

And with that, baseball in Cleveland's Municipal Stadium – a.k.a. "The Old Gray Lady by the Lake" – ended after 62 years.

Cleveland Stadium

The Stadium then became the exclusive home of the Cleveland Browns of the National Football League, but only temporarily. It was torn down when the original Browns re-located to Baltimore as the Ravens, and a new stadium was constructed for the new Browns franchise that came into existence in 1999.

That loss by the Indians in the final game at the Stadium was charged to Charles Nagy, whose record fell to 2-6 (he spent most of the season on the disabled list after undergoing shoulder surgery). Jason Bere was the winner, boosting his record to 12-5.

It was the Indians' third loss in a row at the hands of the White Sox. They won the opener of the final series, 4-2, on Oct. 1, as Alex Fernandez raised his record to 18-9 with relief help from Scott Radinsky and Roberto Hernandez, handing Mark Clark his fifth loss in 12 decisions. The White Sox won again by a 4-2 score, this time in 12 innings on Oct. 2, with the victory credited to Chris Howard, the fifth of six Chicago pitchers, with the loss charged to Jeremy Hernandez, working in relief of Bill Wertz and Dave Mlicki.

The final home run at the Stadium was struck by Albert Belle, who smashed his 38th of the season, a solo shot off DeLeon in the eighth inning of the game on Oct. 2. It also was Belle's 129th RBI of the season, most in the major leagues in 1993.

Appropriately, it was then 83-year old Mel Harder who took the mound to conclude the closing ceremonies at the Stadium by tossing a ball to a young sandlot player behind the plate, with retired Tribe catcher Ray Fosse at the boy's side.

On July 31, 1932, it was Harder, then a 22-year old right-hander for the Indians, who pitched the opener at the Stadium, losing, 1-0, to the Philadelphia Athletics and future Hall of Famer Lefty Grove.

Fitting, too, was the presence of 90-year old Bob Hope in the final game ceremonies. Hope was born and raised in Cleveland and, in the late-1940s, was a minority owner of the Indians in partnership with Bill Veeck, who bought the franchise in 1946.

Hope sang a version of his famous "Thanks for the Memories" trademark song to the approval of the fans on hand for the finale who raised the Indians season attendance to 2,177,908, third most in franchise history.

It ended an era that included only two championship seasons by the Indians, 1948, when they beat the Boston Braves in the World Series, and 1954, when they were swept by the then-New York Giants.

It also set the stage for the beginning of a *winning* era at Jacobs Field, the Indians' new home into which they moved in 1994.

7

A most perfect beginning

Appropriately befitting the occasion, Dennis Martinez's first pitch split the plate, umpire Larry Barnett bellowed, "Strike one!" and precisely at 1:21 p.m., April 4, 1994, Jacobs Field and the Indians' 94th season in the American League came to life.

Eddie Murray

Catcher Sandy Alomar Jr. tossed the ball into the Tribe dugout to be saved among other souvenirs of the historic game, played against the Seattle Mariners, and Martinez settled down to the business of winning his first game in a Cleveland uniform.

He didn't, but the Indians prevailed nonetheless, and the day that began so perfectly, ended that way, although there was ample reason for concern through much of the sun-drenched proceedings.

The memorable occasion was witnessed by a capacity crowd of 41,459 fans, along with President Clinton, who threw out the ceremonial first pitch.

One pitch after Martinez's first offering, Rich Amaral grounded to Carlos Baerga for the first out, though the next three Mariners reached safely - Edgar Martinez, who was hit by a pitch, and Ken Griffey Jr. and Jay Buhner, both of whom walked.

Moments later the first run in Jacobs Field scored on Eric Anthony's sacrifice fly, before Tino Martinez popped to Manny Ramirez in short right field to end the uprising.

Randy Johnson, then the Mariners' 6-10 southpaw who would flirt with a no-hitter through seven innings, walked Tribe leadoff batter Kenny Lofton, but no matter. Lofton was caught stealing and, after Omar Vizquel also walked, both Baerga and Albert Belle grounded out to end the first inning.

The first hit and home run in Jacobs Field came in the top of the third, struck by Anthony off a 1-and-0 pitch. It was drilled 352 feet into the Mariners bull pen in right field, giving Seattle a 2-0 lead.

The Indians finally got their first hit in the eighth inning, a single by Alomar with Candy Maldonado (who had walked) aboard, and nobody out.

It apparently unnerved Johnson, whose next pitch to Ramirez was wild, advancing both runners into scoring position. They came home on Ramirez's double against the facing of the left field bleachers, tying the score, 2-2.

It remained that way as the game went into extra innings, after both starting pitchers had been replaced in the ninth, Johnson by Tim Davis, and Martinez by Jose Mesa, who was making his debut as a reliever.

Mesa survived a threat in the ninth and went to the showers in the 10th, in favor of Derek Lilliquist, after Griffey led off with a single. Then, with two outs, pinch hitter Keith Mitchell singled to score Griffey, giving the Mariners a 3-2 lead.

But the Indians re-tied the score in their half of the 10th against reliever Kevin King. He walked Ramirez, who then came home on a double by pinch hitter Jim Thome.

The Indians won it in the 11th when Eddie Murray doubled with one out, and took third as Paul Sorrento flied deep to Griffey. Alomar was intentionally walked and, five pitches later, Murray scored on a single by Wayne Kirby. The loss was charged to King, and the victory credited to Eric Plunk.

It was a perfect ending to what turned out to be a perfect beginning for the Indians and Cleveland's new field of dreams.

He was Public Enemy No. 1 in Cleveland, but three years later not only did Indians fans forgive Robbie Alomar, they fell madly in love with him.

And, in both cases, their emotions were well founded.

It all began three days before the 1996 season ended, as Alomar was leading the wild card Baltimore Orioles into the playoffs. During a heated argument, he spat in the face of umpire John Hirschbeck.

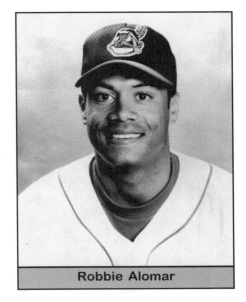

Robbie Alomar

American League President Gene Budig promptly suspended Alomar for five games. It would have – *should have* – made him ineligible for the Orioles first two games of the Division Series, against the Central Division champion Indians.

But Alomar appealed the suspension, enabling him to remain eligible in the postseason, and he became the Orioles' hero, all but single-handedly beating the Indians in the fourth and deciding game of the best-of-five series on Oct. 5.

The gifted second baseman singled off Jose Mesa with two outs in the ninth inning, driving in a tying run and sending the game into extra innings. Three innings later, leading off the 12th, Alomar homered, also off Mesa, and the Orioles won, 4-3, eliminating the Indians – and accentuating the fans hatred of him.

But all was forgiven in 1999, after the Indians signed Robbie to a four year, $32 million contract, and he went on to establish himself as a leading candidate for the A.L. Most Valuable Player award.

In his first season with the Indians, as they won their fifth consecutive A.L. Central Division championship, Robbie Alomar became the first player in the 99-year history of the franchise to hit 20 or more homers (24), score more than 100 runs (138), steal more than 30 bases (37), and drive in 100 or more runs (120).

Those 138 runs he scored were two fewer than the Indians team record set by Hall of Famer Earl Averill in 1931, and he is one of only 25 active major league players with a career batting average over .300 (.304 in 12 seasons).

Alomar also fielded spectacularly well, winning eight Gold Glove awards, and in teaming with shortstop Omar Vizquel gave the Indians arguably the best second base combination in baseball.

Little wonder that Tribe fans fell passionately in love with Robbie Alomar.

But his attributes are not limited to the physical variety. As Robbie was quoted in a *Plain Dealer* story upon joining the Indians: "I'm not only a player of the game, I'm a student of the game. I watch and learn," to which Jack McKeon, Alomar's former manager then with the San Diego Padres, readily agreed.

"You never had to tell him a thing," McKeon said. "He always knew what to do."

Robbie's major league career began with San Diego in 1988 and continued through 1990. He was traded (with Joe Carter) to Toronto (for Fred McGriff and Tony Fernandez), signed as a free agent with Baltimore in December 1995, and when his contract with the Orioles expired in 1998, Robbie joined his older brother, Sandy Jr., the Indians all-star catcher.

Which, again, brought smiles – instead of frowns – to the faces of Tribe fans.

The wizardry of the Bossards

It all started with Emil Bossard in 1936, and continued through four generations of the family that was known throughout baseball – beginning in Cleveland – as groundskeeping wizards.

Harold and Marshall Bossard, sons of the patriarch, followed in their father's footsteps in Cleveland. A third son, Eugene – better known as "Geno" - tended the grounds at old Comiskey Park in Chicago, where he was succeeded at new Comiskey Park by his son, Roger, who is still assisted by, not only his son, Brandon, but also daughter Brittany.

Emil Bossard

And Brian Bossard, who was Harold's son, tended the grounds at San Diego's Jack Murphy Stadium and also Yankee Stadium in New York before he died at the age of 40 in 1993.

According to a Sept. 21, 1998 article in *Sports Illustrated*, the groundskeeping experience of the Bossards at that time totaled more than 235 years of toil on baseball fields.

And the importance of their efforts can't be minimized, as expressed by Bill Veeck, who owned the Indians from 1946-49, and the White Sox from 1959-60 and again from 1975-80. He said a groundskeeper could help the home team win 10 to 12 games a year.

As written in *Diamonds, the Evolution of the Ballpark*, by Michael Gershman: "(Emil Bossard's) wizardry was to adapt Cleveland parks to the talents of individual Indians at any given time. The Bossards attended spring training every year to see how many pull hitters the Tribe featured, how many beat the ball into the dirt (and) how many good bunters were around. Then he started his unique brand of customizing.

"'This is a game of inches,' Bossard (who died in 1981 at age 88) would say. 'An inch is often the difference between a base hit and an out. We try to have the inches go our way.'

"He speeded up the field one day, slowed it down the next, built the foul lines up to aid the Indian bunters and slowed down hard grounders along third base to make the hops easier to field – whatever it took to give the Indians an edge."

The Bossards also implemented Veeck's since-outlawed practice of moving the interior fence at Cleveland's old stadium in or out, depending upon the visiting team's power - or lack of same. When the Yankees, with their long-ball hitters, came in, the Bossards surreptitiously moved the fences out. But when a weaker hitting team provided the opposition, the fences were moved, in the dead of night, closer to the plate to help the Indians.

Of course, there also was another way to help the home team, as revealed by Bob Feller in the book, *The Boys of the Summer of '48*, and confirmed by Marshall Bossard.

Feller and Bob Lemon, used to hide in the scoreboard at the old stadium with a high-powered telescope that Feller brought home from his World War II ship, the USS Alabama.

When either wasn't pitching, Feller or Lemon peered through the telescope, picking off the opposing catcher's signals, calling them out to Marshall or Harold who, in turn, signaled to the Indians' batters, telling them what kind of a pitch to expect.

As Feller said then, "All's fair in love and war – and when you're trying to win a pennant."

No doubt the Bossards would agree.

His wife was the famous one, but that didn't bother Don Rudolph.

Neither did the taunts directed his way from bench jockeys on opposing teams.

"She's good, and I'm proud of her," Rudolph said of his wife when he reported for spring training with the Indians in 1962. They had drafted Rudolph, a left-handed pitcher who, some said, reminded them of Whitey Ford.

As it turned out, Rudolph never approached Ford's degree of success as a pitcher - but then, Mrs. Ford never approached Mrs. Rudolph's degree of success, either.

Mrs. Rudolph, you see, was "Patti Waggin, the Coed With the Educated Torso." She was a stripper.

With her 37-23-36 dimensions and dancing ability, Patti Waggin was, by her husband's admission, "One of the three top performers in the business, along with Lily St. Cyr and Tempest Storm."

Unfortunately for Rudolph, he was never as good at pitching baseballs as his wife was at taking off her clothes on a burlesque stage. Rudolph was up and down with the Chicago White Sox in 1957 and 1958, was traded to Cincinnati in May 1959, and drafted by the Indians in December 1961.

Patti Waggin/Don Rudolph

But he didn't last in Cleveland long. A month into the 1962 season, Rudolph was traded with pitcher Steve Hamilton to Washington for outfielder Willie Tasby.

During the off-season, as Rudolph quipped in newspaper accounts at the time, he went from pitching to catching.

That is, he "caught" his wife's clothes off-stage as she stripped on-stage.

Actually, Rudolph was Patti's press agent, personal manager and No. I fan.

"Patti projects from the stage," Rudolph was quoted in a 1962 article in the Cleveland *Press*. "She makes every man in the audience feel that she is playing to him alone, and would like to date him."

Obviously, it didn't bother Rudolph. "Why should it?" he asked. "I consider her to be primarily a dancer. A modern dancer, and her dancing is the background for the production numbers she uses.

"And if you want to know how good she is, she was offered a movie contract by MGM and refused it. She also has several TV offers."

The pitcher and the stripper met when Rudolph was playing for Colorado Springs, which was then a Chicago White Sox farm team, in the Class A Western League, and she was Patricia Hardwick, dancing in a night club called the "House of Oscar."

"All the players used to visit the place but I wouldn't date any of them," said Patti. "Then one night Don showed up and it was different." A year later they were married.

While Patti's career flourished, Don's soon flattened out.

He was 7-19 for the lowly Senators in 1963, but won only one game in 1964 and was released. His major league career record was 18-32 in 124 games.

Rudolph started a construction company in Southern California in 1966.

But that didn't last long either. Two years later the husband of the famous Patti Waggin, the coed with the educated torso, was killed in an industrial accident.

The Tribe's greatest victory

It wasn't the greatest game ever pitched by a member of the Indians; it wasn't even a no-hitter.

But never in Cleveland baseball history did anybody ever pitch a more meaningful game, or one that was more pressure packed than Gene Bearden did in Boston on October 4, 1948.

Gene Bearden

That was the day the Indians faced and beat the Red Sox, 8-3, in an unprecedented, one game playoff for the American League pennant.

Bearden, a rookie, was the surprise choice of Manager Lou Boudreau to pitch the game that capped a rags-to-riches season for both the 6-3, 28-year old southpaw, and the Indians, who'd won only one pennant previously - and have won only three since then.

Bearden's record was 20-7 with a glittering 2.43 earned run average in 1948, and he went on to also win Game 3 of the World Series, and saved Game 6 as the Indians beat the Boston Braves four games to two.

Unfortunately, Bearden faded into obscurity almost as quickly as he burst into stardom, winning a total of only 25 games and losing 31 in five seasons following his heroics of 1948.

By 1954, Bearden was back in the minors after being traded to Washington and then to Detroit, St. Louis and the Chicago White Sox. He was out of baseball by 1957, with a less than sensational career won-lost record of 45-38.

Ah, but for that one season, the acquisition of Bearden from the Now York Yankees in the winter of 1946-47 represented one of the Indians' best deals.

Ironically, Bill Veeck, then owner of the team, initially wanted another pitcher, Spec Shea.

But the Yankees wouldn't part with Shea and offered Bearden instead, along with outfielder Hal Peck and pitcher Al Gettel, for catcher Sherman Lollar and second baseman Ray Mack.

Another factor in the Yankees' willingness – actually, even eagerness - to include Bearden in the deal undoubtedly was their concern for his physical condition.

Bearden suffered a fractured skull and a knee injury when his ship, the USS Helena, was sunk in the South Pacific during his service with the Navy in World War II. He was discharged with an aluminum plate in his head and a screw in his knee, and the resumption of his professional baseball career was very much in doubt.

But whatever problems those injuries might have caused, they were not evident in 1948. Bearden beat Washington, 6-1, on May 8, for his first major league victory, and won seven straight games in the stretch run in August and September, enabling the Indians to force the playoff.

Bearden was shaky at the start of that all-or-nothing playoff game, yielding a run on two hits in the first inning.

But thereafter he was masterful, and well supported as Boudreau hammered two homers and Ken Keltner one to lead the Indians' 13-hit assault.

The Red Sox got only three hits after the first inning and Bearden struck out six to win what certainly was his greatest game and - absolutely no doubt about it - the most meaningful one in the Indians' first century.

The Tribes's most devastating loss

There have been many losses that qualify as "heart-wrenching" in the long and storied history of the Indians since the Cleveland franchise became a charter member of the American League in 1901.

But the worst – because it meant so much – had to be the one administered by the Florida Marlins on Oct. 26, 1997, in Game 7 of the World Series.

The Indians were one out away from winning their first world championship in 49 years, since 1948, when they beat the Boston Braves.

They went into the bottom of the ninth inning clinging to a 2-1 lead behind ace reliever Jose Mesa. He had registered 103 saves in four seasons, including a major league high 46 in 48 chances in 1995, plus four in the Indians' nine victories in the postseason playoffs that enabled them to reach the final game in 1997.

Jaret Wright, then a precocious rookie who was 8-3 in 16 games after being promoted to the Indians on June 24, was making his second start against the Marlins after beating them in Game 4.

Tony Fernandez, then the Indians' second baseman, staked Wright to a 2-0 lead with a two-out, two-run single off Al Leiter in the third inning. The Marlins retaliated with a run in the seventh on a leadoff homer by Bobby Bonilla.

Jose Mesa

When Wright walked Craig Counsell with one out in the seventh, Paul Assenmacher took over and retired the next two batters, and turned the game over Mike Jackson in the eighth. Jackson set down the first two batters, and was relieved by Brian Anderson, who got pinch hitter Jeff Conine to foul out, ending the inning.

Then, with the Indians leading by a run – and as cases of champagne were being iced in their clubhouse - Mesa stalked out to wrap up the game in the ninth, but couldn't. He was greeted with a single to left center field off the bat of Moises Alou.

Bonilla fanned for the first out, but Charles Johnson slashed a single to right, sending Alou to third. Then, after Gregg Zaun ran for Johnson, Counsell lofted a sacrifice fly to Manny Ramirez in right field, scoring Alou with the tying run. Mesa got out of the inning by making Jim Eisenreich ground out, but the damage was done and the game went into overtime.

The Indians threatened in the top of the 10th as Tony Fernandez singled with one out, but died on base. The Marlins also were blanked in their half of the inning as Charles Nagy replaced Mesa, who'd relinquished a pair of singles with one out.

The end came in the 11th after the Indians were unable to score despite a leadoff walk to Matt Williams by Jay Powell who took over on the mound for Robb Nen.

Bonilla opened the 11th for Florida with a single off Nagy. Zaun popped out, but Counsell reached when his grounder went through Fernandez for an error, Bonilla taking third on the play.

Nagy then intentionally walked Eisenreich, loading the bases, and Bonilla was forced at the plate when Devon White grounded to Fernandez.

But Nagy couldn't get the third out – Edgar Rentaria singled to center to score Counsell with the game-winning run for Florida's 3-2 victory – writing the final chapter on the most heart-wrenching loss in the history of the Cleveland franchise.

The 'Cleveland Cry Babies'

Paris fell to the Germans in World War II on June 13, 1940, but the next morning the Cleveland *Plain Dealer* featured another story on Page One: The Indians rebellion against Manager Oscar Vitt.

It cost them the 1940 pennant, and earned a nickname they came to despise: "Cleveland Cry Babies."

Hal Trosky

Vitt had lost the respect of the players, who felt the rebellion was necessary to keep their pennant hopes alive, Mel Harder said in a story published 24 years later.

According to Harder, "It was the way Vitt operated. He would pat you on the back one minute and criticize you behind your back the next. He was two-faced (and) it finally got to some of the players.

"We had a good ball club – Bob Feller, Hal Trosky, Jeff Heath, Lou Boudreau, Ken Keltner and a lot more – and they thought we had a good chance to win the pennant. But they didn't feel we could do it with Vitt managing."

Though Trosky was called the "ring-leader" by Franklin Lewis in his 1949 history of the Indians, he didn't attend the meeting in owner Alva Bradley's office asking that Vitt be fired. Trosky's mother had died and he'd gone home to Norway, Ia.

Others who also missed the meeting were Boudreau and Ray Mack, who'd recently been called up from the minors; Roy (Beau) Bell, because he'd just been acquired in trade; and "one or two others, notably Roy Weatherly, (who) backed away from participation," according to Lewis. "You're either with us or against us," Weatherly was told by his teammates, to which he reportedly told them, "Just count me out."

Bradley listened to the complaints of the players, but took no action, other than to admonish the players. After the story of the rebellion got out, Bradley convinced the players to sign a statement in which they backed off from their request to get Vitt fired.

When the season ended, Bradley admitted he was wrong in not taking immediate action against Vitt.

"We should have won the pennant ... our real trouble started when a group of ten players came to my office (and) made four distinct charges against (Vitt) and asked for his dismissal," Bradley wrote in a memo to the team's directors.

Bradley's memo, published in the Cleveland *News* in 1951, also said: "The four charges made against Vitt, on investigation I have made, were 100 per cent correct."

Significant, too, was what Bradley told the players in their meeting with him: "If this story ever gets out, you'll be ridiculed the rest of your life." They certainly were the rest of that season.

On Sept. 19, upon arriving by train in Detroit for a series with first place at stake, the Indians were greeted by 5,000 Tiger fans, many of them pushing baby carriages and shouting "Cry Babies!"

Exactly one week later the Tigers came to Cleveland for the final three games of the season. They trailed by two and needed to sweep the series to win the pennant.

But they didn't; a rookie named Floyd Giebell beat Bob Feller, 2-0, on a home run by Rudy York in the opener of the three-game series and it was all over.

Nine days after the season ended, Bradley fired Vitt, who never managed again.

The Tribe's 1940 Pricetag: $1,848,000

In the wake of what then-Indians owner Alva Bradley called the "melancholy mess" of the 1940 season, several directors advocated selling the franchise.

They were disillusioned by the troubles that had surfaced in the players' failed rebellion against Manager Oscar Vitt, earning them the nickname, "Cleveland Cry Babies."

The attempted mutiny was a major factor in the Indians losing the pennant that season as they finished second by one game to Detroit.

Bradley, an unassuming man who later admitted he should have fired Vitt when the players demanded that he do so, established what he considered the realistic value of the franchise, but found nobody able to come up with the money.

Alva Bradley/Oscar Vitt

Bradley's price was $1,848,000 – slightly more than $1.8 million! – which was a huge sum then, but a far cry from what major league baseball teams are worth today.

Consider, for example, that the Indians were purchased by Richard and David Jacobs for $45-million in 1986, and sold in January 2000 to Lawrence Dolan for $323-million.

But it was differenct back there on Sept. 9, 1940, when Bradley wrote the following letter to Joseph C. Hostetler, then secretary of the Indians.

"Dear Joe: At the last meeting of the directors it was suggested that I write you a letter giving you what I thought would be the market price on the ball players we have on the Cleveland club, and I am enclosing the list which I think would be a fair value for our players.

"To this can be added $250,000 for all of the material we have in the minor leagues, which I would say would be about the price that they have cost us. I think, also, that to this figure you can add $600,000, which I think would cover the value of our park and the American League franchise."

Bradley's pricetag on the 32 players then on the roster totaled $998,000 - but only $598,000 if Bob Feller were not included.

Feller, then an upcoming star, was the highest-valued player at $400,000.

But after Feller there was a large dropoff in the pricetag Bradley put on his players - Lou Boudreau, Ken Keltner and Ray Mack were valued at $75,000 each; Hal Trosky at $40,000; Roy Weatherly at $30,000; Mel Harder, Al Milnar and Rollie Hemsley at $25,000 each; Jeff Heath and Clarence Campbell at $20,000 each; and Joe Dobson, Al Smith and Russ Peters at $15,000 each.

Five players, including Johnny Allen, who already had won 117 games for the Indians, were considered by Bradley to be worth $10,000 each. The others were Mike Naymick, Roy Bell, Ben Chapman and Del Jones.

Ten players were considered to be worth $7,500 each, including catcher Frankie Pytlak and pitcher Harry Eisenstat.

And finally, an outfielder named Millard (Porky) Howell, whose major league career consisted of seven at-bats with two hits in 11 games for the Indians in 1941, was valued by Bradley at $3,000 - which today wouldn't even buy the contract of a batboy.

Baseball's first black manager

A thousand thoughts raced through Frank Robinson's mind as he sat alongside Ted Bonda and Phil Seghi in front of a hundred or so reporters at baseball's second "breakthrough" event.

The first was 28 years earlier, when Jackie Robinson broke baseball's color barrier as a player for the Brooklyn Dodgers.

Frank Robinson

Then, on October 3, 1974, the Indians hired Frank Robinson as major league baseball's first black manager.

Certainly, among Robinson's thoughts that day were a recollection of what happened to him in Ogden, Ut. in 1953, when he began his professional baseball career.

"We don't serve niggers here," Robinson was told when he tried to buy a ticket at the local movie theater.

Certainly, too, Robinson thought of his namesake.

"If I had one wish I was sure would be granted, it would be that Jackie could be here, seated alongside me today," Frank said after the cameras and tape recorders were turned off.

It was a great time for Robinson and the Indians, though it didn't start that way - and didn't finish so great either.

Robinson was acquired, ostensibly as a player, Sept.5, 1974, in a waiver deal with California. Seghi said then, "I think (Robinson) can help us because we still have a chance to win (the pennant) this year."

Quickly though, Robinson was embroiled in a confrontation with the Indians ace pitcher and highest paid player, Gaylord Perry.

The very first day Robinson wore an Indians uniform, he and Perry nearly came to blows in an argument in the clubhouse over which player deserved to paid more money. It was Perry's remark - "I want to make one dollar more than (Robinson)" - that set off the near-fight.

They were separated by then Manager Ken Aspromonte, whose job would soon be given to Robinson.

Animosity between Perry and Robinson smoldered thereafter, though both tried to keep it hidden, and two months into the 1975 season Perry was traded to Texas.

The end of Robinson's managerial career in Cleveland wasn't pleasant either. He was fired June 19, 1977.

In retrospect, Robinson's 2 ½ year record was neither very bad, nor very good. Under him in 1975 the Indians finished 79-80, fourth by 15 1/2 games, they were 81-78, fourth by 16 games in 1976, and 26-31, in fifth place, eight games out of first place when he was fired.

Overall, Robinson's winning percentage in Cleveland was .496 (186-189). Only two of the eight men who managed the Indians since Robinson – Dave Garcia (1979-82), and Mike Hargrove (1991-99) – have better winning percentages. Garcia's was .503 (247-244) and Hargrove's was .549 (721-591).

If Robinson had a problem with the Indians – other than Perry – it was his inability to understand why his players didn't have the same determination to excel that he did.

And excel he did.

In a 21-year playing career with Cincinnati, Baltimore, Los Angeles, California and the Indians, Robinson hit .294 with .586 homers, and was elected to the Hall of Fame in 1982.

It was called the eighth "most significant game" of all-time by *The Sporting News*, and Cleveland fans voted it "the most memorable moment in Indians history."

It was the most memorable moment for Frank Robinson, too.

Hollywood couldn't have written a better script than Robinson did on April 8, 1975, in front of an Opening Day crowd of 56,204 fans at the Stadium.

Making his debut as the Indians player-manager - and baseball's first black manager - Robinson homered in his first at-bat off New York Yankees right-hander Doc Medich.

As the Tribe's designated hitter batting in the second position, Robinson took Medich's first two pitches for called strikes by umpire Nestor Chylak.

He fouled off the next two, watched two more pitches sail wide of the plate for a 2-and-2 count, then hit another foul ball.

Medich's eighth pitch was another strike - or would have been if Robinson had not made contact.

The ball jumped off his bat and arched high and deep over the left-center field fence.

The fans knew in an instant that it would be a home run, and rose as one to celebrate the implausible event.

George Hendrick/Frank Robinson

So did the Indians, who swarmed out of the dugout to greet Robinson as he toured the bases.

One of the first to embrace Robinson was Gaylord Perry, who'd feuded with the new manager ever since Robinson had joined the team seven months earlier, though both tried to keep their hostility toward each other hidden. And, after the game, won by the Indians, 5-3, Robinson was the first to greet and embrace Perry, the winning pitcher.

Robinson's homer, the 575th of his career – he finished with a total of 586 – was a "called shot" by General Manager Phil Seghi, it was revealed later.

"Phil suggested this morning," Robinson related after the game, "'Why don't you hit a homer the first time you go to the plate?' I told him, 'You've got to be kidding.'"

Seghi confirmed his "suggestion" to Robinson, but said, "I never dreamed he'd do it … though I should have. Knowing Frank, I shouldn't be surprised by anything about the man's ability to rise to an occasion."

Robinson admitted he could hardly believe what happened as he trotted around the bases. "By the time I got to third base, I thought to myself, 'Wow, will miracles never cease?'"

It was, Robinson said, "The single most satisfying thing that happened, other than winning. Right now I feel better than I have after anything I've done in baseball. Take all the pennants, the awards, the World Series, the All-Star games, and this moment is the greatest."

Unfortunately, the rest of Robinson's tenure as the player-manager was not as glorious as that memorable moment on Opening Day.

Later in 1975, Robinson suffered an injury to his right shoulder that hampered, not only his throwing, but also his hitting and he appeared in only 49 games that season, batting an uncharacteristic .237. He played in 36 games in 1976 and hit .224, ending his 21 year playing career with a batting average of .294 and 2,943 hits. He was inducted into the Hall of Fame in 1982.

Feller's momentous decision

It was in a meeting in the Terminal Tower in the spring of 1936 that Bob Feller's name was first mentioned in Cleveland.

"Gentlemen, I've found the greatest young pitcher I ever saw," C.C. (Cy) Slapnicka began his remarks to the directors of the Indians.

C.C. Slapnicka/Bob Feller

Then Slapnicka, assistant to Indians owner Alva Bradley, cleared his throat and embellished his original superlative.

"I suppose this sounds like the same old stuff to you, but I want you to believe me. This boy that I found out in Iowa will be one of the greatest pitchers the world has ever known."

If Slapnicka wasn't 100% accurate in his prediction, he certainly came close - and also certainly would have come closer if it had not been for World War II.

Feller spent 44 months in the Navy. He enlisted two days after Pearl Harbor was attacked and the war began in 1941, and missed almost four full seasons of what would have been the prime time of his career.

As it was, "Rapid Robert," as Feller was aptly nicknamed, won 266 games (and lost 162), hurled three no-hitters and 12 one-hitters, and struck out 2,581 batters in 3,827 innings.

April 16, 2000 is the 60th anniversary of his first no-hitter, the only one ever pitched on Opening Day, as Feller beat the Chicago White Sox, 1-0, in 1940.

He was elected to the Hall of Fame in 1962, his first year of eligibility, and has become an institution in Cleveland.

As testament to Feller's integrity - to the great relief of the Indians - he rejected an opportunity to become a free agent in 1936, which would have allowed him to sign with any team in baseball.

It would have been a financial bonanza for Feller and his parents, even though bonuses were non-existent then and baseball salaries were miniscule compared to what today's "can't-miss" prospects are paid.

Commissioner Kenesaw M. Landis was prepared to make Feller a free agent because the Indians were guilty of breaking a rule then in effect that prohibited major league clubs from directly signing amateur players.

That first contract Feller and his father signed was written on a scrap of paper and dated July 22, 1935. It claimed to be with the Indians' farm club at Fargo, N.D. though Landis didn't see it that way.

It specified, "The Fargo club agrees to allow Robt. Feller to visit his folks at any time during the 1936 season, also to invite Robt. Feller's folks to visit him at Fargo during the summer of 1936 at the expense of the Fargo baseball club.

"The Fargo club has no objection to Robt. Feller playing basketball at any time," and concluded, "For a consideration of one dollar paid to Robt. Feller this agreement is declared valid."

But Landis, after a lengthy investigation, invalidated the agreement, calling it a "cover up" deal.

When Landis indicated he might separate the young pitcher from the Indians, Feller told the commissioner, "I don't want to play any place else. I want to play for Cleveland."

Which he did. Long and spectacularly well.

And he is still a prominent member of the Cleveland community, and continues to work in a public relations capacity for the Indians.

They would have been a sensational one - two punch if, instead of being classic opponents, Hal Newhouser and Bob Feller had been teammates with the Indians when both were in their prime.

Instead, they didn't join forces until 1954, and by then Newhouser was trying to make a comeback and Feller was only two years away from retirement.

Newhouser won 207 games, many of them against Feller in a 15 year career with Detroit that began in 1939 when he still hadn't observed his 19th birthday.

Nicknamed "Prince Hal," Newhouser won the American League's Most Valuable Player award in 1944 and 1945, the only pitcher to be accorded that honor twice. He led the A.L. in victories four times, in 1944 with 29, 1945 with 25, 1946 with 26, and in 1948 with 21. Newhouser also was the earned run champion twice, in 1945 with 1.81, and in 1946 with 1.94.

Newhouser was released by the Tigers in July 1953, after he pitched in seven games, losing his only decision; and that winter came knocking on the Indians' door.

Certainly, Hank Greenberg and Al Lopez, the Indians Chiefs, were interested. They needed a left-handed spot starter-reliever, and Newhouser would be ideal - if he could still pitch.

Hal Newhouser/Bob Feller

Newhouser proved in spring training that he was sound, and signed an Indians contract two days before the 1954 opener.

"I know the Indians are taking a gamble with me, and I certainly hope that I'm able to do the ball club some good," Newhouser said in a Cleveland *Plain Dealer* story on April 12. "My arm feels good and I'm ready to work any place, either the bull pen or as a starter, whatever Lopez wants me to do."

Newhouser made 26 appearances, all but one in relief, and responded with seven victories, seven saves and a 2.51 ERA. He was charged with two losses as the Indians, who won an American League record 111 games and the pennant, finished eight games ahead of the New York Yankees.

Thrilled by his success, Newhouser reported for spring training the following season and declared, "They'll have to cut the uniform off me before I'll quit."

Which, it turned out, the Indians did.

Newhouser opened the season with the Tribe, but his arm problems surfaced again. He pitched only 2 1/3 innings in two games and then it was over. The old magic was gone.

Newhouser was finished at 34 with career totals of 207 victories, 150 losses and a 17 year earned run average of 3.06.

He was elected to the Hall of Fame by the Veterans Committee in 1992, after being bypassed earlier in the general elections by members of the Baseball Writers Association of America, which left a bad taste in Newhouser's mouth.

"The Hall of Fame is everybody's goal, and I made a living off a lot of the players who are in there," Newhouser was quoted in a 1973 story, 19 years before he was elected. "My credentials are there, but there's nothing more I can do now."

But there would have been so much more Newhouser could have done for the Indians had he been free join them before he did in 1954.

The pride of the Indians

He wasn't the winningest pitcher in the history of the Indians – only second to Bob Feller – but there's no doubt that to Mel Harder rightfully belongs the title, "Pride of the Indians."

Harder wore a Cleveland uniform with distinction for 36 years, 20 as a pitcher, from 1928-47, and 16 more as the Tribe's pitching coach, from 1948-63.

Mel Harder

The bespectacled right-hander from Beemer, Nebr. compiled a 223-186 won-lost record, and only Feller (266-223) was a bigger winner for the Indians.

What's more, Harder's 223 victories are more than the games won by 16 of the 55 starting pitchers enshrined in the Baseball Hall of Fame, including several who were more highly-publicized: Dizzy Dean (150), Sandy Koufax (165), Don Drysdale (209), Bob Lemon (207), Hal Newhouser (207) and Lefty Gomez (189).

In fact, Harder is tied for 60th place in all-time victories, and 71st in innings pitched (3,426 1/3), and only Walter Johnson and Ted Lyons pitched more years for one club.

Though Harder hurled for 20 seasons for Tribe teams that seldom were contenders, he is one of only 23 pitchers in baseball history to win 15 or more games eight times.

Adding to his impressive credentials, Harder appeared in four consecutive All-Star Games (from1934-37), and is the only pitcher to work 10 innings or more in the "Mid-Summer Classic" without allowing a run. He took over in the fifth inning of the 1934 game and became the winning pitcher after shutting out the National League the rest of the way, yielding only one hit through the final five innings.

That was the game in which the N.L.'s Carl Hubbell struck out five future Hall of Famers in succession (Babe Ruth, Lou Gehrig, Jimmie Foxx, Al Simmons and Joe Cronin).

What's more, two of baseball's greatest hitters, Joe DiMaggio and Ted Williams, called Harder the toughest pitcher they faced. DiMaggio, whose career batting average was .325, but only .180 against Harder, made the statement on a television interview, and Williams similarly credited Harder in his autobiography, *My Turn At Bat*.

Williams also was quoted by the Associated Press: "Mel Harder was a great pitcher. He had a great curve ball, great control, and the thing about Mel was that every one of his pitches did a little something. He was so tough to hit against."

Last but certainly not least in any endorsement of Harder is the fact that, after his 20 year active career ended, he was considered one of baseball's best pitching coaches.

Serving in that capacity for the Indians for 16 years, Harder transformed Bob Lemon from a weak-hitting (but strong armed) third baseman/outfielder into a future Hall of Fame pitcher.

Harder also is credited for the development of Mike Garcia and Herb Score, and other pitchers, and for teaching Early Wynn a curve that helped him win 300 games and get into the Hall of Fame. During the time Harder was the Indians pitching coach, 17 of his proteges became 20 game winners.

In 1961, Harder was elected by Cleveland's baseball writers as the Indians' "Man of the Year," an honor that usually is won by a player.

Little wonder Mel Harder long has been considered the "Pride of the Indians."

Two lamentable pitches

It happened seven decades ago, on July 31, 1932, but Mel Harder still vividly remembers the two pitches that cost him the game he considers to have been "the biggest thrill of my baseball career."

Both were fast balls, the first to Max Bishop, the second to Mickey Cochrane, and both were made in the eighth inning of a game against the Philadelphia Athletics.

It was the first game ever played in the newly-completed Cleveland Municipal Stadium, and 80,284 fans were on hand to see Harder, a 21-year old pitcher then in his third full season with the Indians, duel Lefty Grove, the Athletics' ace.

Harder walked Bishop, leading off the eighth inning, on a 3-and-2 count.

"I thought it was a strike," said Harder, "but Bishop had a reputation for having a good eye and the umpire - funny, I don't remember who he was - gave Bishop the benefit of the doubt and called it ball four."

The next batter, Mule Haas, sacrificed Bishop to second, and Cochrane singled for the only run of the game.

"It also was a fast ball that Cochrane hit," said Harder. "It was inside, a pretty good pitch, but he got a hit so it couldn't have been real good.

"Cochrane hit the ball just to the left of the mound. I just missed it by about six inches. It went between our second baseman, Bill Cissell, and the bag. Cissell came close, but he missed it and the run scored."

It was the only run of the game as Grove, who was elected to the Hall of Fame in 1947, shut out the Indians, 1-0.

"I wasn't supposed to pitch that day, Wes Ferrell was," said Harder. "But when Ferrell came to the park he said his arm was stiff so Peck (Manager Roger Peckinpaugh) told me I would start.

"It was a thrill, the biggest thrill of my baseball career to pitch in front of all those people in the first game in the Stadium. I would've liked to win, but I wasn't any more disappointed than any game I lost.

"There weren't any fences at the Stadium then and you had to hit a ball pretty good to get one over an outfielder's head. Batters would hit a ball real hard and it would go deep, but usually it was just an out.

"If an outfielder tried to cut off a ball hit in the gap and it got by him, it was a triple, maybe even an inside-the-park homer."

The rest of the Indians' lineup that day: Luke Sewell was Harder's catcher, Eddie Morgan, first base; Cissell, second; Johnny Burnett, shortstop; Willie Karnm, third base; Joe Vosmik, left field; Earl Averill, center; and Dick Porter, right.

Only two of the 50 players on those two teams are still alive: Harder and pitcher teammate Willis Hudlin.

It's also interesting to note that, in addition to Grove, three other Philadelphia players Harder faced in that inaugural game – Cochrane, Jimmie Foxx and Al Simmons, as well as Athletics owner/manager Connie Mack - are in the Hall of Fame.

Mack, a.k.a. "The Tall Tactician," managed the A's for 50 years from the time they entered the American League as a charter member in 1901 through 1950, led them to nine pennants, and was elected to the Hall of Fame in 1937. Cochrane entered with Grove in 1947, and Foxx in 1951.

Mel Harder

When 'Joltin' Joe' was stopped

It was a hot and humid night at the Stadium and 67,468 fans, which comprised the largest crowd to see a baseball game under the lights until then, would never forget it.

Neither could Joe DiMaggio.

Al Smith

The date was July 17, 1941.

When Al Smith took the mound for the Indians, DiMaggio had hit safely in 56 consecutive games, having broken the record that had been set 44 years earlier by Wee Willie Keeler.

The day before at League Park, where the Indians played some of their games, DiMaggio went 3-for-4 against Tribe southpaws Al Milnar and Joe Krakauskas. Those hits boosted DiMaggio's average to .408.

But this night was destined to be different.

Smith, 33, a southpaw whose record was 6-6, walked DiMaggio in the fourth, but blanked him in his first and third official at-bats. Then Jim Bagby Jr., a 24-year old right-hander, stopped the "Yankee Clipper" in the eighth - though both pitchers needed good plays in the field to end DiMaggio's record-setting spree.

"I can remember like it was yesterday the way Ken Keltner played me halfway out to left field and right on the line," DiMaggio recalled several years later. "People say that's what stopped me, but I've got another theory. It rained the night before, the ground was wet and the field was very slow.

"When I came up in the first inning, there was Keltner, playing right on the line and halfway to left field. He knew I wouldn't bunt because I hadn't during the entire streak. I didn't believe I should. I felt it had to be a real hit.

"I swung away and hit a ball right down the line. Keltner made a great stop, really in foul territory, that's how deep he was playing, and made the long throw to first base. He got me just like this," said DiMaggio, slapping his hands together twice in rapid succession. "I think I would have beaten it if the ground hadn't been so wet and slow."

DiMaggio walked on a 3-and-1 pitch in the fourth. He faced Smith again in the seventh and again was thrown out by Keltner. "If ever a play was duplicated, this one was a duplicate of the ball I hit in the first," he said. "It was just as close, too.

"In the eighth, after Bagby had come in to pitch, I hit to the left of Lou Boudreau with a runner on first. The ball took a bad hop and hit Boudreau in the chest, but he grabbed it and went to second to start a double play. That's how it ended, though we won the game, 4-3.

"I couldn't believe it was over. I was like a boxer who'd just been knocked out. It took me a day to got righted, to realize the streak was really over," said DiMaggio.

Maybe it took DiMaggio a day to got "righted," but he immediately started another streak, this one lasting 16 games. Thus, if it had not been for the wet field, or DiMaggio's fierce pride that wouldn't permit him to bunt, or Boudreau's recovery of the bad bounce in the eighth, the record streak might have been an incredible 73 consecutive games, instead of 56.

And the end would not have come in Cleveland.

The blunders that hurt DiMaggio

Back in 1941 the Indians had an outfielder named Larry Rosenthal, who – because of a base-running mistake - played an otherwise-overlooked key role on July 17, in the game that Joe DiMaggio's consecutive game hitting streak was stopped at 56 at the old Cleveland Stadium.

If it had not been for Rosenthal's blunder, DiMaggio might have received at least one more chance to extend the streak.

Joe DiMaggio

Rosenthal, who played in the major leagues from 1936-41 and 1944-45 for the Chicago White Sox, Philadelphia Athletics and New York Yankees, in addition to the Indians (45 games in 1941), was a pinch hitter representing the potential tying run in the ninth inning of that game.

With the Indians trailing the Yankees, 4-1, Rosenthal batted for Ray Mack after Gee Walker and Oscar Grimes opened the inning with singles off Lefty Gomez.

Rosenthal greeted reliever Johnny Murphy with a line drive to right-center field, between DiMaggio and Tommy Henrich. It was a triple that scored both runners, cutting the Indians' deficit to 4-3, still with nobody out.

As reported in Michael Seidel's book, *Streak, Joe DiMaggio and the Summer of '41*, Hal Trosky was up next, needing only a fly ball or a grounder through the infield to score Rosenthal with the tying run. Instead, "He slammed a grounder to Johnny Sturm at first, but a hesitant Rosenthal remained on third. No sense taking a risk. Sturm made the play (to retire Trosky), keeping an eye cocked on Rosenthal.

"Next, Clarence 'Soup' Campbell, hitting for (pitcher Jim) Bagby, bounced a shot back to Murphy that Murphy speared on a hard hop. There was no stopping Rosenthal this time; he was off for the plate. When he realized his folly, it was too late. Murphy had Rosenthal properly pickled between home and third. Campbell sat on first viewing the rundown, though he ought to have lit for second to get into scoring position."

It was the second base-running mistake of the inning, and also turned out to cost the Indians another chance to tie the score, which would have sent the game into extra innings and given DiMaggio another time at-bat.

Because he was still on first base, Campbell was held close by Sturm. And because Sturm was playing close to the bag, he was able to field a shot by Roy Weatherly that would have gone down the right field line for a run-producing hit. Sturm fielded the ball and stepped on first base, retiring Weatherly, ending the inning and the game – and DiMaggio's chance to bat again.

In his very next game, also against the Indians, DiMaggio embarked upon another hitting streak, this one lasting 16 games.

Most of the credit for stopping DiMaggio at 56 is given to Indians third baseman Ken Keltner, who made two outstanding, back-handed plays to rob DiMaggio of hits, shortstop-manager Lou Boudreau, who turned a bad-hop grounder of DiMaggio's into a double play in the eighth inning, and pitchers Jim Bagby Jr. and Al Smith, against whom DiMaggio went 0-for-3 (he walked once).

But it also was Rosenthal, whose mistake earned a share of credit (or blame).

He just 'whammed' the ball over

It would have been - perhaps *should have been* - another classic case of a local boy making good.

It wasn't for a variety of reasons, none of which was the fault of Al Aber, who learned the secret of pitching success early, playing on the dusty fields at Cleveland's Brookside Park in the late-1930s.

Al Aber

"All I do is wham the ball over," Aber was quoted after pitching his team, the Fisher Sports, to the 1937 championship of Cleveland's Class F League for boys under 12.

Aber hurled three no-hitters that year and proceeded through the Cleveland sandlot baseball program, which was then one of the best in the United States.

He was a star southpaw pitcher-hitter-first baseman at West Tech High School and was signed by the Indians after graduation in 1945.

"It was the biggest day of my life," Aber later was quoted in a newspaper story. "It was a dream come true because all I ever wanted to do was play for the Indians."

Aber played well for them, too, always "whamming the ball over," though it took him six long minor league seasons to reach the majors.

Aber went 24-8, with 16 consecutive victories, for Spartanburg of the (Class B) Tri-State League in 1949, and finally got a chance with the Indians in 1950.

Though he didn't stick in spring training, Aber was called up in September and won his only start, beating Washington, 4-2, with a five-hitter.

But 10 days after the season ended, Aber was drafted. He spent the next two years as a military policeman, and pitching for an Army team in Germany instead of the Indians in Cleveland.

Aber rejoined the Tribe upon his discharge in 1953 and pitched six games, mostly in relief, winning one and losing one.

He thought he was on his way. "Nobody was happier, and not just because the money was so good," he said.

The major league minimum salary had just been raised from $5,000 to $6,000.

"I just wanted to pitch for my team, the Indians."

But then came another obstacle preventing the local boy from making good in his hometown. Aber was traded to Detroit on June 15, 1953, in an eight-player deal that, as it turned out, didn't do much for either team.

In addition to Aber, the Indians sent infielder Ray Boone and pitchers Steve Gromek and Dick Weik to the Tigers for pitchers Art Houtteman and Bill Wight, catcher Joe Ginsberg and infielder Owen Friend.

Aber enjoyed limited success in Detroit, going 22-24 the next 3 1/2 seasons, and in 1957 was traded to the Kansas City Athletics.

It was then that a final roadblock got in his way.

Aber developed bursitis and bone chips in his pitching elbow and was forced into retirement at the end of the 1957 season - because he couldn't "wham" the ball anymore.

"**T**hat's for me to know ... and for you to think about," is the way Gaylord Perry usually answered the question he was asked most often, to wit:

Did he throw an illegal pitch, in his case a "grease ball," as batters charged, or was it really a fork ball that looked like an illegal pitch?

Mainly it was a game Perry played, although he admitted in his 1974 autobiography, *Me and the Spitter,* that, yes, sometimes he "loaded" his pitches.

Gaylord Perry

Only once, however, did an umpire catch Perry red-handed, applying a "foreign substance" to the ball.

The fact is, Perry wanted batters to think about the probability that he cheated, and his mind games were a factor in his logging a 314-265 record, and winning Cy Young Awards in the American and National Leagues in 1972 and 1978, respectively.

As he once claimed, "I don't throw illegal pitches ... I just leave a lot of evidence lying around."

One time, to torment Bobby Murcer and plant more doubt in the mind of the Yankee slugger who constantly complained that Perry was "loading" his pitches, Gaylord greased up the palm of a friend and sent him to the New York clubhouse.

The friend was given instructions to shake Murcer's hand and tell him, "Gaylord says hello."

But more than that, Gaylord Perry was one of the fiercest competitors the game has ever known.

When he retired at 45 in 1983, ending a 22-year major league career in which he made 690 starts, Perry said he could remember missing a scheduled assignment only twice, which is amazing.

Perry's acquisition, with shortstop Frank Duffy for Sam McDowell in 1972, was one of the Indians' best-ever deals. Duffy was the Tribe's regular shortstop for six seasons, while McDowell, in the next four years, won only 19 games while losing 25.

Perry made it to the big leagues to stay in 1964 and - whether it was true or just another ploy - he admitted once, "I needed another pitch and I needed to learn it fast. It was the spitter," according to his book.

With the Indians for 3 1/2 seasons, Perry won 70 games and lost 57. After several disagreements with then-Manager Frank Robinson he was traded to Texas, June 13, 1975, for pitchers Jim Bibby, Rick Waits and Jackie Brown, and $100,000.

But Perry proved he was far from finished and continued to pitch well for the Rangers, San Diego (where he won his second Cy Young Award with a 21-6 record in 1978), and five other teams before retiring in 1984.

Perry hurled a no-hitter in 1968, one one-hitter, 13 two-hitters and 53 shutouts, and was one of only four men to win 100 games in both leagues.

He was inducted into the Hall of Fame in 1996.

And, though baseball purists - and batters - might complain that Perry often cheated, his fierce pride, dogged determination and flaming competitive spirit perhaps were the biggest factors in his amazing success.

The 'extraordinary' pitcher

He carried a gun and Dwight Eisenhower hung his 10 most famous quotes on a wall in the White House.

He had a name for each of his pitches – of which he had many - but he had trouble remembering his teammates names.

Satchel Paige

He pitched for teams named the Chattanooga Lookouts, Birmingham Black Barons, New Orleans Pelicans, Baltimore Black Sox, Chicago American Giants, Pittsburgh Crawfords and Kansas City Monarchs.

And when he finally arrived in Cleveland in 1948, he was one of the best known pitchers in the country, even though he'd never pitched in a major league game - because of the color of his skin.

Leroy Robert Paige, better known as "Satchel," was his name.

Bill Veeck, the peg-legged owner of the Indians who challenged baseball's stuffy traditionalists at every turn, was criticized by no less an authority than baseball's "bible," *The Sporting News*, when he signed Paige on July 7, 1948.

J.G. Taylor Spink, editor of *The Sporting News* sarcastically called it "just another stunt by Veeck," and accused him of being a "cheap showman" because Paige was a "washed up old timer."

Age. That was the catch with Paige. But no one, including Satch himself - if the stories are to be believed - knew exactly how old he was.

A former wife said the family bible showed that Satchel was born on July 28, 1905, which would have made him 43 in 1948. But Paige's mother said the bible proved her son was then 44. Paige's draft card also was no help. It listed his birthdate as Sept. 18, 1908. And when he died in 1982, his birthdate was said to be July 7, 1908.

Satchel explained the contradictions simply. "My mother had 11 children and she never could keep track," he said.

But Paige's age didn't really matter in 1948. All that counted were Satch's statistics as he helped the Indians win their first pennant in 28 years - and then the World Series. He went 6-1 with a 2.48 earned run average in 21 games, seven as a starter, striking out 43 batters in 72 2/3 innings while walking only 22, with pitches he called "be-balls," "bloopers," "loopers" and "droppers."

In one two-week period Paige started and won three games, including back-to-back shutouts, and by the and of the season, *The Sporting News* retracted its editorial criticism of Veeck for signing Paige.

The fans couldn't see enough of Paige. On Aug. 13 at Chicago's Comiskey Park, the capacity of which was 44,000, an estimated 10,000 fans were turned away.

Paige said at the time, "I should be working on percentages," as he was when he pitched in the old Negro League.

So, what would he be worth in today's inflated salary market?

Larry Doby, who was Paige's roommate with the Indians in 1948, answered the question several years ago.

"Whoever is the highest paid pitcher today would be No. 2 if Satch was still pitching," Doby said. And Doby probably was right.

To 'recapture the rapture'

Bill Veeck came in like a whirlwind, and things never stopped whirling until he left 3 1/2 years later. Unfortunately for the Indians and Cleveland fans, his departure was entirely too early.

To Veeck, an ex-Marine with half a left leg, the result of a World War II injury, the fan was king. He was baseball's No. 1 entrepreneur in Cleveland from June 21, 1946, until he sold the Indians, November 21, 1949; in St. Louis, as owner of the Browns from 1951-53; and in Chicago, where he resurrected the White Sox from 1959-61, and owned then again from 1975-80.

Bill Veeck

Veeck made the game fun wherever he went, especially if the team was bad, which the Indians were his first two years.

But the customers still came out. Attendance topped a million (1,057,289) for the first time in Cleveland baseball history in 1946, and again (1,521,978) in 1947. The following season, after turning the Tribe into a contender, Veeck no longer needed gimmicks to sell tickets. The Indians set a major league baseball attendance record of 2,620,627 which stood until Los Angeles attracted 2,755,184 fans in 1962.

Though Veeck was the ultimate showman, dreaming up all kinds of unique promotions, including one in which he showered an average fan with gifts, he also was a shrewd operator and judge of baseball talent.

One of his earliest and best acquisitions was infielder Joe Gordon from the New York Yankees, and later, in the winter of 1946, he got pitcher Gene Bearden in another deal with them. Then Veeck pulled a real stunner on July 3, 1947, signing Larry Doby as the American League's first black player, and everything jelled for the Indians in 1948.

Especially player-manager Lou Boudreau. Veeck had wanted to trade Boudreau, but didn't, yielding to pressure by the fans.

Three months into the season Veeck purchased legendary but ancient pitcher Satchel Paige from the Negro National League, in the face of great criticism by his peers. They regarded it as just another stunt by Veeck. It turned out to be another brilliant move; without Paige, the Indians probably wouldn't have won the 1948 pennant.

But the rapture - if not the fun - vanished in 1949. The Tribe fell to third, eight games behind the Yankees, and Veeck, who was having financial problems because of a divorce, sold the team for $3.3-million to a group headed by Ellis Ryan.

Nine years later, with the Indians considering a move to Minneapolis at the urging of then - Vice President Hank Greenberg, Veeck thought about buying the club again. Newspaper accounts said he was ready to pay $4-million.

But on August 23, 1958, the deal was called off. Veeck decided, he said, that it would be impossible for him to "recapture the rapture" the Indians had known a decade earlier.

And, thereafter, nobody else was able to recapture the rapture the Indians and their fans had known during Veeck's regime, until the 1990s when the team, under the ownership of Richard Jacobs, won two American League pennants and five consecutive division championships.

'Too small to be a ball player'

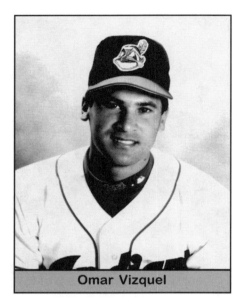

Omar Vizquel

When he was growing up in Venezuela, Omar Vizquel dreamed of being a big league ball player like fellow countryman Luis Aparicio, a Hall of Fame shortstop, and Vic Davalillo, a center fielder for the Indians from 1963-68.

Vizquel was sadly disillusioned, however, though only temporarily when, as a teenager, he attended a tryout camp in Caracas and was told by the director that he should "go to the racetrack and be a jockey," because he was so small.

But Vizquel doggedly stuck to his dream, grew to 5-9 and 170-pounds, became one of the best shortstops in baseball, and in the judgment of a couple of former Indians who should know, is even better than was another Hall of Famer, Lou Boudreau.

It was during a 1998 visit to Cleveland that Al Rosen, a third baseman who was the American League's Most Valuable Player in 1953, and Bob Kennedy, an outfielder who managed two major league teams, were asked their opinion of Vizquel.

"Vizquel is better than Boudreau or Marty Marion or Luis Aparicio or Ozzie Smith or anybody I've ever seen," said Kennedy, who played for the Indians in 1948 when Boudreau was in his prime.

Then Kennedy went even further in his praise of Vizquel, saying, "He might be the best shortstop that ever played the game."

Rosen was equally generous in his assessment of Vizquel: "Boudreau was a better offensive player, especially in 1948, but I've never seen anybody make the plays that Vizquel does. He's remarkable."

Indians Chief John Hart also holds Vizquel in the highest esteem since acquiring the shortstop from Seattle Mariners (in a Dec. 20, 1993 trade for shortstop Felix Fermin and outfielder Reggie Jefferson). It was one of Hart's best-ever deals, and so was the contract extension the general manager negotiated with Vizquel two years later.

Hart signed Vizquel to what was then the longest guaranteed contract ever granted by the Indians – six years through 2001 for $18 million, with a club option for 2002. "With this signing we certainly ensure the stability of the best shortstop in all of major league baseball," said Hart.

Vizquel also was pleased. "Six years feels like a long time to be on a team, but I was really looking for a family and a home. I've never had the chance to sign a long deal and I'm excited about the team and playing in Jacobs Field for a long time," he said.

Three seasons later, in the wake of the continued escalation of player salaries – which was more rapid than Vizquel or his agent anticipated – he had second thoughts.

During the winter of 1998-99 rumblings of discontent surfaced, which would have created serious problems for the Indians had they involved a player of lesser character.

While making it clear that he felt a raise and/or contract extension would be appropriate, Vizquel agreed that a deal is a deal, and went on to have one of his best seasons in 1999. His .333 average tied teammate Manny Ramirez for fifth best in the A.L., he stole 42 bases, only two fewer than the league leader, and scored 112 runs, second most by a Tribe shortstop, to Boudreau's 116 in 1948.

Not bad for a guy who wasn't supposed to be big enough to play in the major leagues.

Hack Wilson drove in 190 runs for the Chicago Cubs in 1930, a record that has withstood the assault of the game's greatest sluggers ever since.

And Cleveland baseball fans also probably thought nobody wearing an Indians uniform would challenge Hal Trosky's club record 162 RBI set in 1936.

But that was before Manny Ramirez, who was the Tribe's first pick (13th overall) in the 1991 amateur draft, arrived in the major leagues late in 1993, and in 1999 made everybody re-think their positions on the records held by Trosky, as well as Wilson.

Ramirez fashioned one of the most dominating offensive seasons seen in baseball in the previous 68 years.

Ramirez broke Trosky's record with 165 RBI in 1999, becoming the first player in 60 years to drive in as many as 160 runs since Jimmie Foxx, with 175 in 1938. Only eight players in baseball's modern era (since 1901) ever drove in 165 runs in one season - although three of them did it more than once – and all are in the Hall of Fame. They are Wilson; Lou Gehrig, New York Yankees (184, 175, 174, 165); Hank Greenberg, Detroit (183, 170); Foxx, Boston Red Sox (175, 169); Babe Ruth, New York Yankees (171); Chuck Klein, Philadelphia Phillies (170); and Joe DiMaggio, New York Yankees (167).

Manny Ramirez

It also was in 1999 that Ramirez's .333 average was tied with teammate Omar Vizquel for fifth best in the American League, his 44 homers were tied for third most, and his 131 runs scored were fourth among the leaders. What's more, Ramirez's 165 RBI, combined with 145 in 1998, gave him the largest total, 310, in two consecutive seasons in franchise history.

All of which prompted Charlie Manuel, then the Tribe's hitting instructor, to speak in awe of the outfielder who was born in the Dominican Republic in 1972, and raised in New York City.

"The more I see him, the more I believe Manny is the best right-handed hitter I've ever seen," said Manuel, who has been a player, coach and manager in professional baseball since 1963, and became manager of the Indians in 2000. "(Ramirez) goes straight through the ball with his swing every single time. That day in Oakland when he hit three home runs, all three pitches were in completely different spots, and Manny hit all three out. Not many hitters can do what he can do."

Those three homers against the Athletics on Aug. 25 were among Ramirez's then career total of 198 in his six-plus seasons in Cleveland, sixth most in franchise history. Ten of Ramirez's homers were grand slams, another club record.

Another who is impressed by Ramirez's ability to hit baseballs often, and far, is Tribe pitcher Dave Burba, who was quoted in *Baseball Weekly*: "As an all-around hitter, Manny is the best I've seen. He can hit for power and for average. He works deep into the count. He won't chase bad pitches. He's very consistent. I can't imagine anyone being a better hitter than Manny is right now."

Ramirez said in that same article that he doesn't give interviews or do endorsements because he doesn't care if, or what people think of him. "I don't worry about that stuff," he said.

Neither do the Indians nor their fans, as long as Ramirez continues to build upon his legacy – and continues to do so while wearing a Cleveland uniform.

The scout who rejected Mantle

You'll not find his name among the stars of the Indians past, and only one line in the *Baseball Encyclopedia* is devoted to Hugh Alexander.

It shows that Alexander, better known as "Uncle Hughie" among his peers, played seven games for the Indians in 1937, and that he made one hit in 11 at-bats.

Hugh Alexander

But there's more, much more to Hugh Alexander than meets the eye of most casual baseball fans. He became known as one of baseball's great talent scouts.

Prior to his scouting career, Alexander had been an 18-year old power hitting outfielder who was signed by C.C. Slapnicka in 1935. Slapnicka was the Indians scout who, that very year, had found Bob Feller.

In his first season in professional baseball, 1936, Alexander hit .348 with 28 homers and drove in 102 runs at Fargo (N.D.) of the Northern League.

The following year, playing for Springfield of the Mid-Atlantic League, Alexander batted .344 and whacked 29 homers, earning a late-season trial with the Tribe.

"That was about the best year anybody could have, and I was on my way, I knew it," Alexander said later.

But first, before he could embark on a major league career, fate dealt Alexander a cruel blow.

"I went home to Oklahoma that winter (of 1937-38) to work in the oil fields, and that's when it happened," he said. Alexander's left hand got caught in the gears of a derrick. "It could have been worse, it didn't cut my hand off, it just mashed it and ground it up."

He was alone when the accident happened and the nearest doctor was 14 miles away – so Alexander drove all the way himself. "I had the thing (his left hand) wrapped up in a pillowcase and there was blood all over the place. I was just about to pass out, but it's amazing what you'll do when you think you're going to die." Obviously, Alexander didn't die.

But he lost his hand and, of course, his promising playing career was ended. It was shortly thereafter that Slapnicka offered his once-prized prospect a job as a scout, launching Alexander's new career. He worked for the Indians for 14 years. One of his first discoveries as a scout was Allie Reynolds, who won 182 big league games, including 51 for the Indians before he was traded to the New York Yankees.

Alexander left the Indians in 1952 and went on to work for the Chicago White Sox, Los Angeles, Philadelphia, and the Chicago Cubs. Prominent among Uncle Hughie's discoveries were Don Sutton, Bill Russell, Frank Howard and Davey Lopes.

But there also were some who got away, and Alexander was big enough to admit it. "The worst mistake of my career," he said, "was listening to a high school principal in Oklahoma when I was working for the Indians in 1948."

Alexander was told that a boy he wanted to see had osteomylitis, a bone disease, in his leg. So Alexander didn't go to see him. "Baseball is tough enough to play when you've got two good legs," he reasoned.

The player Alexander didn't go to see was future Hall of Famer Mickey Mantle.

Frankie Pytlak never gained much fame with the Indians, and another former catcher named Hank Helf was even more obscure.

Pytlak caught for the Tribe from 1932 through 1940, though some old-timers probably remember him better as the guy who said he'd rather be a fireman than a major league ball player.

Helf played seven games for the Indians, six in 1938 and one in 1940, and batted 14 times with one hit for a career average of only .184, though he was considered an excellent receiver.

But both gained a degree of fame on Aug. 20, 1938 when they broke the altitude catching record in front of an estimated 10,000 fans gathered at Cleveland's Public Square.

First Helf, a 25-year old third-string catcher, caught a baseball tossed from the top of the 708 foot high Terminal Tower.

Then Pytlak, 30, duplicated the feat.

Mathematicians estimated the baseballs were travelling 138 miles an hour when they landed in the mitts of Helf and Pytlak.

The two catchers were credited with breaking a record that had been set 30 years earlier, when Gabby Street and Billy Sullivan caught baseballs dropped from the top of the 550 foot high Washington Monument.

Frankie Pytlak

Three other members of the 1938 Indians - regular receiver Rollie Hemsley and coaches Wally Schang and Johnny Bassler, both former catchers - tried but failed to match Helf and Pytlak.

The baseballs were tossed from the top of the Terminal Tower by Tribe third baseman Ken Keltner. The would-be catchers were positioned on the southwest quadrant of the Public Square.

"For a second I didn't know if it was going to hit my head or my glove," Helf was quoted after making his catch.

"It (the ball) stung more than Bob Feller's fast one," commented Pytlak, in a reference to the pitcher who was then in his third season with the Tribe, and whose fast ball had been clocked at over 100 mph.

Pytlak, whose lifetime batting average of .282 in 12 seasons would establish him as a fine hitting catcher by today's standards, was traded to Boston in 1941, but spent the next three years in the service in World War II. His best seasons were 1936-38, when he compiled batting averages of .321, .315 and .308. respectvely, as the Indians regular catcher.

He retired to the Buffalo Fire Department after playing briefly for the Red Sox in 1945 and 1946.

Helf's was a one-handed catch, according to the account in the Cleveland *Press*. "The ball plopped into the pocket of the glove, bounced up, Hank grabbed frantically at it (and) slapped it back into the glove," the newspaper reported.

"Nothin' to it .... I just kept my eye on the ball all the way down," the late Frank Gibbons quoted Helf. "Pytlak got his hands up in front of his face and nabbed it neatly. He looked as he does catching a foul ball at League Park."

The event was held to publicize the Terminal Tower, then the tallest building west of New York, but provided a degree of fame - though not very lasting - for Pytlak and Helf.

The year's greatest comeback

The 1999 season didn't end well for the Indians – they ran away with the American League Central Division championship, but were beaten by Boston and eliminated in the first round of the playoffs – though the season certainly featured several highlights.

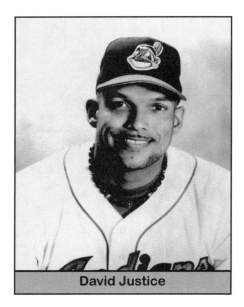

David Justice

One that will be long remembered occurred Aug. 31 at Jacobs Field when the Indians staged one of baseball's great comebacks in a 14-12 victory over the Anaheim Angels, and wound up in a brawl between the two teams.

Trailing 12-4 going into the bottom of the eighth inning, the Indians scored 10 runs, sending 14 batters to the plate, to win.

To make the rally even more impressive, it happened after Anaheim pitcher Mark Petkovsek retired the first two batters.

With the comeback that night the Indians became the first team in major league history to overcome an eight run deficit to win three different times in the same season.

They previously did it on May 7, in beating Tampa Bay, 20-11, at Tropicana Field in St. Petersburg, and on Aug. 7 in another victory over Tampa Bay, this one, 15-10, at Jacobs Field.

But neither was as impressive as the display of power they showed against the Angels in front of 43,284 fans (many of whom had left Jacobs Field when Anaheim went ahead by eight runs in the top of the eighth).

"To score eight runs with two outs, you've got to have a lot of things go right for you," said Manager Mike Hargrove – and a lot of things did go right for the Indians as nine batters went 9-for-12 in that action-packed eighth inning.

As reported in the Lake County *News-Herald*: "How bizarre was it? The Tribe pinch hit for the cleanup spot twice in the same inning. With Anaheim leading, 12-4, the inning began with Hargrove pinch hitting Alex Ramirez for Manny Ramirez, 'which I never would have done if I'd thought we had a chance to comeback,' said Hargrove. When Alex Ramirez's turn came up a second time in the inning, Hargrove used Harold Baines as a pinch hitter." As Hargrove said, "We started the inning with a pinch hitter, then pinch hit for the pinch hitter."

The rally was climaxed by Richie Sexson's three run homer against Angels closer Troy Percival - after which Percival hit the next batter, David Justice, with his first pitch.

Justice charged the mound and threw his helmet at Percival. Both dugouts and bull pens emptied. It was a typical baseball fight - a lot of pushing and shoving, but few punches were thrown.

When order was restored after about 10 minutes, Justice and Percival were ejected and Paul Shuey shut down the Angels in the ninth, saving the victory that was credited to Jim Poole.

Justice was fuming after the game. "The bottom line is we didn't hit their guy (Anaheim third baseman Troy Glaus) after he hit two home runs," Justice said. "We kept playing. I didn't hit the home run and I didn't want to let (Percival) make an example of me. He is as tough as they come, but he's got to take it like a man.

"I'd do it again. I didn't show anybody up. I wish it hadn't happened … and I'll probably get suspended – but that's the only thing I regret."

Those four dreadful days in 1954

It was hard to believe then, and still is, more than four decades later.

The Indians, whose record was the best in baseball in 1954 and whose 111 victories set an American League record were humiliated in the World Series by the New York Giants.

The Giants, managed by Leo Durocher, won the National League pennant with a 97-57 record. They finished five games ahead of Brooklyn as Willie Mays won the N.L. batting championship with a .345 average, and southpaw Johnny Antonelli was their winningest pitcher with 21 victories and seven losses.

But were the Giants good enough to sweep the Indians in the World Series? No way, said Las Vegas, where the Indians were installed as 18-10 favorites.

But the Giants prevailed - and it wasn't even close.

Many believe the Indians' failure to win another pennant, or even to be a serious contender in the American League for 40 years, until they challenged for the Central Division title in 1994, began in that 1954 World Series; some even pinpoint a play that occurred in the eighth inning of the opening game as the one that got it all started.

The score was tied, 2-2, and the Indians were threatening against Don Liddle, working in relief of Sal Maglie. Two runners

Leo Durocher

were aboard with none out when Vic Wertz drilled a drive to deep center field. It would have been a home run almost everywhere - except in the Polo Grounds, where the Series had opened. Mays turned at the crack of the bat and raced to the wall in front of the centerfield bleachers. With his back to the plate, Mays snared the 460 foot drive, retiring Wertz.

Marv Grissom took over for Liddle and walked pinch hitter Dale Mitchell, struck out Dave Pope, and got Jim Hegan on a liner to left field to end the threat, the inning and, as it developed, the Indians.

The Giants won that game, 5-2, in the 10th inning when Bob Lemon walked two with one out, and pinch hitter Dusty Rhodes slapped a homer into the right field stands, 260 feet away.

Rhodes, a part-time player who hit .341 in 82 games that season, became the Giants hero by also delivering key hits in the second and third games.

Early Wynn was a 3-1 loser to Antonelli in Game 2, which started with a home run by the Tribe's Al Smith. It was, however, one of only eight hits Antonelli yielded.

The Indians were held to four hits by Ruben Gomez and Hoyt Wilhelm in the third game as the Giants kayoed Mike Garcia in the third inning and won, 6-2.

Game 4 also was a disaster as the Giants mopped up, winning 7-4, against Lemon and relievers Hal Newhouser, Ray Narleski, Don Mossi and Garcia. Wilhelm and Antonelli came out of the bull pen to save the victory for Liddle.

It was only the second time in baseball history that a National League team swept the World Series, and the first in 40 years, since the 1914 "Miracle" Boston Braves beat Philadelphia four straight.

The Giants' victory shocked fans everywhere - and especially fans in Cleveland, where baseball wasn't the same for more than four decades, after those dreadful four days - Sept. 29-Oct. 2 - in 1954.

A beautiful, but tragic day

It was a beautiful early spring day – March 22, 1993 - in Winter Haven, Fla., and the Indians had a day off from spring training.

Manager Mike Hargrove didn't even schedule a light workout. He told the players to get away from Chain of Lakes Stadium, to do something with their families, to forget about baseball and the season that would be starting in exactly two weeks.

Steve Olin

Tim Crews, a relief pitcher who was an "invitee" to spring training, had a great idea. He owned a home, actually a 48 acre horse ranch, in Clermont, Fla., about 10 miles north of Winter Haven.

Crews also owned an 18-foot, outboard boat that he used on the lake, "Little Lake Nellie," which adjoined his property. He invited several teammates and their families to a cookout. The men would go bass fishing after dinner.

Two pitchers, Steve Olin and Bob Ojeda, were among those who accepted the invitation and, after they ate and as the sun was dipping behind the trees to the west of Little Lake Nellie, the three men packed their fishing gear in Crews' boat. They took off, leaving their wives to clean up after dinner.

Perry Brigmond, identified as Crews' longtime friend who lived in Orlando, accompanied by Indians conditioning coach Fernando Montes, also had planned to go fishing but didn't arrive until shortly after the three pitchers left the dock. It was close to 7:30 when Brigmond flashed the headlights of his truck to let Crews know they were there.

The 150-horsepower engine on Crews' boat roared to life and headed toward Brigmond and Montes, at the south end of the lake. Suddenly the sound of a crash was heard. Then nothing. Total silence. The boat had slammed into a pier. Crews was killed instantly. Olin died shortly after the crash. Ojeda was critically injured, but survived. He suffered massive head injuries and was hospitalized for several months, returning to the Indians in June. He tried to make a comeback, but was unsuccessful and eventually retired. Olin and Crews each left a wife and three children. The Indians were devastated. Not only had the men been close friends, they also were good pitchers.

Olin, 27, who'd been a 16th round selection in the 1987 amateur draft, had come through the Tribe's farm system and, in 1992, led the Indians in saves for the second straight season with 29 in 36 opportunities. In four seasons with the Tribe, Olin appeared in 195 games, all as a reliever, compiling a 16-19 won-lost record, and 3.10 earned run average, with a total of 48 saves. He was being counted upon as the Indians' closer in 1993.

Crews, 31, who'd pitched for Los Angeles since 1987, was signed by the Indians as a free agent the previous winter. In six seasons with the Dodgers, Crews appeared in 281 games, all but four in relief, winning 11 while losing 13, and being credited with 15 saves.

Ojeda, 35, also had been signed as a free agent a few months earlier after pitching for the Dodgers (1991-92), New York Mets (1986-90), and Boston (1980-85).

It was the worst tragedy the Indians had suffered since Aug. 17, 1920, when shortstop Ray Chapman died the day after he was hit in the head by a pitched baseball.

August 16, 1920. The Polo Grounds, New York: the day Indians shortstop Ray Chapman was hit by a pitch and died, the only player in the history of major league baseball to be killed playing the game.

It was baseball's darkest day.

Chapman was felled by a rising fast ball thrown by Carl Mays, the New York Yankees submarine-style right hander.

Mays steadfastly denied to the day he died in 1971 that he intentionally threw at Chapman, though many of the Indians were convinced he did.

Particularly outspoken was Jack Graney, the Indians' left fielder and Chapman's best friend on the team that won the American League pennant and World Series that season.

Graney, who was the radio voice of the Indians from 1932 through 1953, was quoted in a 1962 newspaper account:

"People ask me today if I still feel that Mays threw at Chappie. My answer has always been the same - yes, definitely.

"We had played the Yankees four games in Cleveland before taking off for the return series in New York.

"During the Cleveland games, Mays pitched against us and if Doc Johnston (Indians first baseman) hadn't flipped his elbow up in time to deflect a pitch that was coming at his head, he'd have gotten the same dose Chapman was to get a few days later."

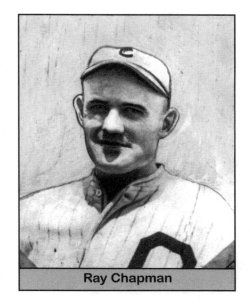
Ray Chapman

Accidental or not, Chapman being hit by Mays' pitch was a tragedy that will be remembered as long as the game is played. And Mays, of course, forever will be remembered as the pitcher who threw the ball that killed Chapman.

The popular little infielder, 29, was leading off the fifth inning with the Indians ahead, 3-0. Mays' pitch was up and in and Chapman tried to duck under it.

The ball struck Chapman on the left temple and bounced back to the mound. Many thought it had hit Chapman's bat because of the resounding crack, until they saw him collapse at the plate.

After Chapman was carried into the clubhouse, he tried to speak, but words wouldn't come. "I knew by the look in his eyes that he wanted desperately to tell me something, so I got some paper and put a pencil in his hand," Graney said. "He made a motion to write, but the pencil dropped to the floor. Paralysis was setting in."

Chapman suffered fractures on both sides of his skull, and a broken neck. He never regained consciousness and died 12 hours later.

Chapman was the Indians' shortstop for nine years; he played 1,051 games with a lifetime batting average of .278.

Mays, who had five 20-victory seasons in his 15-year major league career, retired in 1929 with a 208-126 lifetime record. He was the opposite of Chapman in personality and temperament, according to those who played with and against him.

And just as he steadfastly maintained that he hit Chapman accidentally, so did Mays steadfastly insist that he deserved election to the Hall of Fame, though he was always passed over, possibly because of Chapman's death.

'Go hard or go home'

When the Indians assembled for spring training in Winter Haven, Fla. in 1999, each was issued a tee-shirt upon which was stenciled: "Go hard or go home."

The message was clear. So was Manager Mike Hargrove's avowed goal: to win 100-plus games, and the World Series. As it turned out, the Indians did neither and they went home early. So did Hargrove.

Brian O'Nora/Mike Hargrove

After 8 ½ seasons as the Tribe's 36th manager, Hargrove was fired on Oct. 15, 1999, four days after losing to the wild card Boston Red Sox, 12-8, in the fifth and deciding game of the American League Division Series. It eliminated the Indians from the postseason playoffs after winning their fifth consecutive A.L. Central Division championship under Hargrove.

In announcing his decision to replace Hargrove, General Manager John Hart said simply that it was "time for a change … we feel there is a need for a new energy, a new voice in the club-house," he was quoted by the Cleveland *Plain Dealer*.

Hargrove, the consummate professional and always a gentle-man, was graceful – as ever – in his response.

"There was a part of me that was surprised, and a part of me that was not," he said, then added, "I am proud of what I have done here," as well he should have been.

But Hargrove wasn't unemployed for long. Only 18 days, to be exact, before he was signed to a three year contract to manage the Baltimore Orioles.

Under Hargrove, who replaced John McNamara on July 6, 1991, the Indians' record was a cumulative 721-591, including 97 victories and 65 losses in his final season. Only Lou Boudreau, during his nine years (1942-50) as Tribe manager won more games, 728, with 649 losses.

All told, Hargrove spent 21 seasons in the employ of the Indians, becoming their first baseman on June 14, 1979, upon his acquisition from San Diego in a trade for outfielder Paul Dade, which was one of then-General Manager Phil Seghi's best deals.

Hargrove retired after the 1985 season with a .290 lifetime average in 12 years with Texas, San Diego and Cleveland, and in 1986 launched his coaching/managerial career as the hitting instructor at Batavia (Class A New York-Penn League) in 1986.

He managed Kinston (Class A Carolina League) in 1987, Williamsport (Class AA Eastern League) in 1988, and Colorado Springs (Class AAA Pacific Coast League) in 1989, and was promoted to the Tribe's staff as first base coach under McNamara in 1990.

In Hargrove's first season as Indians manager they lost a franchise record 105 games, though only 53 defeats (with 32 victories) were administered under his tutelage. They improved to 76-86 in each 1992 and 1993, and were within one game, with a 66-47 record, of overtaking Chicago for the A.L. Central title when the season was aborted by a player strike.

Thereafter, Hargrove's teams dominated the division five seasons in a row, though they reached the World Series only twice, losing to Atlanta in six games in 1995, and to Florida in seven games in 1997.

And in 1999, when they collapsed against Boston, after taking a two-games-to-none lead, failing to reach Hargrove's avowed goal, his career with the Indians was abruptly finalized.

The Indians 'Mr. October'

It's been said that Jim Thome is the kind of player his grandfather would have been, to which the Indians first baseman agrees, if not in so many words, then certainly in deeds.

Thome wears his pants high, as players did in his grandfather's and father's days, and – more importantly – exudes the type of personality not often found in a major league clubhouse or, especially, off the field anymore.

That is, unlike so many of his peers, Thome has a miniscule ego, as was evidenced in the wake of the Indians' exit from the 1999 American League Division Series in which he hammered four homers in four games.

They gave Thome 16 home runs in postseason play, third most in major league baseball history, ahead of – are you ready for this? – Mickey Mantle and Reggie "Mr. October" Jackson, who are tied at the top with 18. In fourth place, one homer *behind* Thome is none other than Babe Ruth, a.k.a. "the Sultan of Swat."

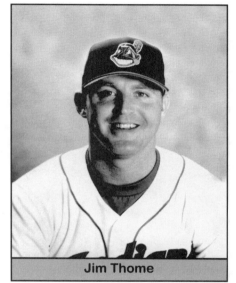
Jim Thome

Equally impressive as Thome's home run total is the number of games he needed to reach that lofty plateau: 50, in 169 at-bats (from 1995-99).

Mantle's 18 homers came in 65 games and 230 at-bats, and Jackson's in 77 games and 281 at-bats. Of the leaders, only Ruth had better numbers: 41 games, 129 at-bats.

Thome also is the only big leaguer to hit two grand slams in postseason play, which he did against Boston's John Wasdin in Game 2 of the 1999 Division Series, and against New York's David Cone in Game 6 of the 1998 A.L. Championship Series.

All of which is irrelevant, according to Thome.

As Thome was quoted in a Cleveland *Plain Dealer* column, "I'm just a guy from Peoria, Illinois. Never, ever growing up as a kid did I think my name would someday be mentioned in the same sentence with guys like Babe Ruth, Mickey Mantle or Reggie Jackson."

But it is – and certainly will be again, often, before Thome hangs up his spikes.

He is living proof that sometimes a team has to dig deep to find otherwise-hidden jewels. Thome was picked by the Indians in the 13th round of the 1989 amateur draft. He was called up to the big leagues for 27 games in 1991, got another brief trial in 40 games in 1992, and made it to stay in 1993 as the Tribe's third baseman.

And if you want further evidence of Thome's unpretentiousness, consider that, when the Indians traded for National League all-star third baseman Matt Williams in 1997, he willingly switched to first base at the request of General Manager John Hart. Thome's comment then: "It wouldn't be my first choice, but if it's for the good of the team, then fine."

Former Tribe star Al Rosen, the A.L.'s Most Valuable Player in 1953, had this to say about Thome during a reunion of the Indians' world championship 1948 team, as reported in *Baseball Weekly*: "Thome would have been one of our leaders. He reminds me of guys like Bob Lemon, Jim Hegan, Larry Doby and Early Wynn.

"There is absolutely no guile about him. He is a ball player and proud of it. He looks like he plays for the love of the game. He plays with a rare enthusiasm you often don't see in today's athlete."

When 'Bad News' used his head

His name was Arvel Odell Hale, and with a handle like that it's no wonder he was nicknamed "Sammy" and "Bad News."

Hale was an infielder, primarily a third baseman for the Indians from 1931-40, then played for the Boston Red Sox and New York Giants in 1941, during which he compiled a .289 lifetime average.

"Bad News" Hale

But of all the plays "Bad News" made in the 1,062 games he played for the Indians, Red Sox and Giants, probably none was stranger than the "three-ply slaying" he started on Sept. 7, 1935, in the ninth inning of the opener of a double header at Fenway Park in Boston.

It has been recorded as the rarest triple play ever made, and Hale is given credit for it because he used his head – *literally* - to start it, enabling the Indians to sweep the Red Sox, 5-3 and 5-4.

Here's how Gordon Cobbledick described it in the Cleveland *Plain Dealer* the next morning.

"(The Indians) won the first game in spectacular fashion by pulling off one of the most unusual triple plays in all the annals of baseball, giving Mel Harder an 18th victory.

"That three-ply slaying came with stunning suddenness in the most dramatic possible situation that distinguished the afternoon from any other baseball day and gave 15,000 fans a memory to cherish.

"It had been a tight ball game most of the way, but Ab Wright had given Harder what looked like a safe lead of 5-1 by hammering a home run over the left field wall in the Indians half of the ninth. But it wasn't as safe as it looked as developments of the next few minutes showed.

"To start that spectacular last half inning (Indians shortstop) Roy Hughes lost Oscar Melillo's pop fly in the sun and it went for a hit. Bing Miller batted for Rube Walberg and singled. Dusty Cooke lined a single to center scoring Melillo, and Bill Werber plunked one to right, filling the bases.

"That finished Harder and brought Oral Hildebrand to the box to be greeted by Mel Almada's single, which drove in Miller and left the bases filled with the tying run on second, the winning run on first, nobody out and three of the best hitters in the Boston ensemble coming up.

"Then it happened. Joe Cronin slashed a whistling liner toward left. Hale leaped in front of it and threw up his hands, but the ball tore through his glove, struck Hale squarely on the forehead and bounced high and to his left.

"The Boston runners, off with the crack of the bat, put on the brakes when they saw Hale grab for the ball, but were off and running again when it ripped through his hands. This set the play up perfectly.

"(Shortstop) Bill Knickerbocker was on the job to grab the ball as it caromed off Hale's head. He whirled and threw to Roy Hughes at second, doubling Werber, and Roy's relay to Hal Trosky easily flagged Almada before he could scramble back to first, ending the inning and the game.

"It was a jubilant gang of Indians that went whooping off the field, and the broadest grin of the lot was the one that split Hale's features as he ruefully rubbed the bump oil his head where the whole thing had started. He told reporters, 'I sure used my head on that play, didn't I?'

"He sure did," said Cobbledick.

They called him "Flip," and nobody played the game harder, nor was more intolerant of losing than Al Rosen.

A third baseman, Rosen was the leader of the Indians in 1954, when they won the franchise's third pennant.

And if you really want to know what kind of a player he was, Rosen played almost all of that season with a broken right index finger.

He did it because that was the only way he knew.

Once, in 1954 as the Indians were winning a then American League record 111 games, Rosen fought a teammate who complained that his leg was too tight to play that night against the New York Yankees.

The teammate played - with a swollen jaw as well as his strained thigh muscle - and so did Rosen, with a broken nose.

And the Indians won the game.

Another example of Rosen's dedication: he willingly switched from third base to first to make room in the lineup in 1954 for Rudy Regalado, a rookie who had a phenomenal spring training.

Al Rosen

It was while he played first base that Rosen suffered the broken finger, but refused to let it stop him.

He hit .300 with 24 homers and 102 RBI in 1954, and was the hero of the American League's 11-9 victory in the All-Star Game that year, hammering back-to-back homers despite being unable to properly grip his bat. It was the fourth time in Rosen's 10 seasons in the big leagues that he was selected on the all-star team.

If he had a regret, other than the Indians' being swept by the New York Giants in the 1954 World Series, it was 1953.

That was the season Rosen was the American League's Most Valuable Player but missed winning the Triple Crown by one percentage point.

Rosen led the league with 43 homers and 145 RBI, but his .336 average (201-for-599) was .001 below Mickey Vernon's .337 (205-for-608).

Their battle went down to the last day. Rosen got three hits in five at-bats in his final game, but Vernon went 2-for-4 to win the batting championship.

After Rosen retired in 1956 with a career .285 average and 192 homers, he joined George Steinbrenner to make a bid to buy the Indians in 1972, reportedly offering then-owner Vernon Stouffer $8.5-million for the franchise.

But Stouffer rejected their offer and sold instead to Nick Mileti for $9.7-million - which was composed of "green stamps and promises," as Gabe Paul later commented.

Rosen got back into baseball a few years later as president of the Yankees in 1978 and 1979, moved on to Houston where he was president from 1981-85, and then served as president and general manager of the San Francisco Giants from 1986 until he retired in 1992.

He operated out of the front office just as he did on the field — all-out, always.

Rosen took over the Giants after they'd lost 100 games, and rebuilt then in a hurry. They won the National League West in 1987, and the pennant in 1989.

The unforgettable southpaw

You won't find a bust of Harry Eisenstat in the Hall of Fame, and his entire major league career is summarized in ten lines of agate type on page 1809 of the Baseball Encyclopedia.

It shows that Eisenstat, a left-handed pitcher for the Brooklyn Dodgers, Detroit and the Indians, won 25 games while losing 27 from 1935 through 1942, when he entered the Army Air Force in World War II.

Harry Eisenstat

But, in his own words, "As long as baseball fans talk about Bob Feller, my name will probably never be forgotten."

He's probably right for several reasons, despite his mediocre won - lost pitching record.

It was Eisenstat, then 23 years old, who pitched against - and beat - Feller on October 2, 1938 when Feller astounded the baseball world by becoming the first pitcher to strike out 18 batters in one game.

One thing people don't remember, though Eisenstat does: "I had a no-hitter going that day until the eighth inning."

The Indians went on to get four hits, but Eisenstat and the Tigers won the game, 4-1.

Not only did Feller establish the single game strikeout record that day, fanning center fielder Chet Laabs five times in a row, the last one to end the game, he also blanked Hall of Famer Hank Greenberg in four at-bats.

Greenberg had 58 homers, going into that final game of 1938, and needed two to tie Babe Ruth's record of 60. But he didn't get them and Ruth's record stood until Roger Maris hit 61 homers 23 years later.

Eisenstat, primarily a relief pitcher in the days when relievers did not get much attention, had another memorable day earlier in that 1938 season.

He won both games of a double header against the Philadelphia Athletics, thanks to three homers by Greenberg. In that double header, Eisenstat relieved the Detroit starter in the fourth inning of the opener, and pitched four more innings in the nightcap to gain credit for that victory, too.

But it's the day he beat Feller - on one of Feller's best days - that Eisenstat is best remembered, and which he remembers so well himself.

It was the highlight of a career that began when Eisenstat was signed in 1935 after being spotted in a high school game in Brooklyn by Al Lopez, then the catcher and captain of the Dodgers, who went on to become the manager of the Indians.

Declared a free agent by then-Commissioner Kenesaw M. Landis at the end of the 1937 season, Eisenstat signed with Detroit in 1938, and was traded on June 14, 1939 to Cleveland for another of the Indians' all-time greats, outfielder Earl Averill, also a member of the Hall of Fame.

Eisenstat went 10-13 for the Indians the next 3 1/2 seasons, before going off to war. When he was discharged in 1945, Eisenstat decided not to return to baseball and entered the hardware business in Cleveland.

And so ended a good but not exceptional playing career - except for that day in 1938, when Harry Eisenstat beat the great Bob Feller in the first great game of Feller's career.

The mere mention of Rocky Colavito invariably brings to mind two dates that were significant in the popular outfielder's career: June 10, 1959, and April 17, 1960.

On June 10, 1959, Colavito, then 25 and playing his fourth season with the Indians, joined one of baseball's most select groups. Rocky blasted four home runs in consecutive times at bat, after walking in the first inning of a game in Baltimore.

Only seven players previously achieved that feat, two of them in consecutive at-bats: Hall off Famer Lou Gehrig in 1932, and old-timer Robert Lowe in 1894. And since Colavito's amazing performance, only Willie Mays in 1961, Mike Schmidt in 1976, Bob Horner in 1986, and Mark Whiten in 1993 have duplicated it, though only Schmidt hit his four homers consecutively.

The other memorable date - April 17, 1960 - in Colavito's career isn't recalled as fondly by Rocky, and certainly not by most Tribe fans. It was the day before the Indians 1960 season opener against Detroit. Colavito was traded to the Tigers for outfielder Harvey Kuenn, who'd won the American League batting championship in 1959 when he hit .353.

Rocky was devastated. So were his adoring fans. Many still are resentful, and also harbor the opinion that the 35-year decline

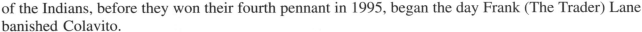
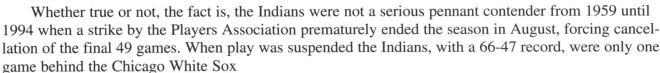

Rocky Colavito/Gabe Paul

of the Indians, before they won their fourth pennant in 1995, began the day Frank (The Trader) Lane banished Colavito.

Whether true or not, the fact is, the Indians were not a serious pennant contender from 1959 until 1994 when a strike by the Players Association prematurely ended the season in August, forcing cancellation of the final 49 games. When play was suspended the Indians, with a 66-47 record, were only one game behind the Chicago White Sox

After Colavito was traded to the Tigers, he went on to hammer 173 homers in the next five years, while Kuenn, sneeringly-referred to as "only a singles hitter" by his critics, played just one season for the Tribe, hitting .308 with nine homers. The following winter Kuenn was traded to the San Francisco Giants for pitcher Johnny Antonelli and outfielder Willie Kirkland, neither of whom distinguished himself in Cleveland.

Gabe Paul, who replaced Lane on April 27, 1961, tried to win back the fans by re-acquiring Colavito in 1965, but it was a costly deal, one that hurt, rather than helped the Indians. To return Colavito to the Wigwam, Paul traded two promising young players, pitcher Tommy John and outfielder Tommie Agee, both of whom became stars, and John Romano, a solid journeyman catcher.

It was a three-team deal with Kansas City and the Chicago White Sox in which the Indians also received young catcher Camilo Carreon, who played only 19 games in a Cleveland uniform.

Though he hit 56 homers the next two seasons, Rocky was unhappy being platooned with Leon Wagner in 1967. And, in the interest of harmony, Colavito was traded away again on July 29, 1967, this time to the White Sox for outfielder-designated hitter Jim King and cash.

Colavito played for Los Angeles and the New York Yankees in 1968, and retired in 1969 with a .266 average and 374 homers - four of which will be remembered as long as baseball records are kept.

The unfairly maligned outfielder

Harvey Kuenn's career in Cleveland was brief and undistinguished, which was both unfair and unfortunate for the outfielder who had been the defending American League batting champion when he was acquired by the Indians on April 17, 1960.

Harvey Kuenn

Kuenn was not popular with Tribe fans and often was booed when he did not hit in the clutch or play well because he'd been obtained from the Detroit Tigers in a deal for Rocky Colavito, one of Cleveland's all-time fan favorites.

The controversial trade, made two days before the season opener by Frank Lane, then general manager of the Indians, did not turn out to be a good one for the Indians.

Not only did Kuenn's average fall 45 points to .308, he also missed the final 28 games of the 1960 season with a broken bone in his left foot. Two months later, on Dec. 3, 1960, Kuenn was dealt to San Francisco for pitcher Johnny Antonelli and outfielder Willie Kirkland, neither of whom made a major contribution to the Tribe.

Then, to re-kindle the anger most fans felt about the loss of Colavito, the situation was further complicated in January 1965 when Gabe Paul, then general manager of the Indians, tried to rectify the "sin" committed by Lane five years earlier.

Paul traded away catcher John Romano and two young prospects who became major league stars, pitcher Tommy John and outfielder Tommie Agee, to re-acquire Colavito. By then Colavito had blasted 139 home runs in four seasons with the Tigers, and 34 for the Kansas City Athletics, to whom he'd been traded in 1964.

Colavito, however, was then near the end of his playing career and was traded again in July 1967. He retired after playing briefly in 1968 with Los Angeles and the New York Yankees – all of which further reminded longtime Tribe fans of the ill-fated deal that brought Kuenn to Cleveland.

Kuenn originally was signed by the Tigers as a shortstop out of the University of Wisconsin. He made it to the major leagues late in 1952, and won the American League "Rookie of the Year" award in 1953 when he batted .308. Switched to the outfield in 1958, Kuenn hit .300 or better in six of his seven full seasons with the Tigers, including .353 to win the batting title in 1959.

A favorite of Lane – who did not have great respect for Colavito, either personally or professionally – Kuenn was the best hitter on the team in 1960.

The Indians that season finished fourth with a 76-78 record, 21 games behind the Yankees, which didn't help Joe Gordon keep his job as manager. He was replaced by Jimmy Dykes on Aug. 3, 1960, in what was the first – and, to date, only – time two managers were traded, Gordon to Detroit and Dykes from the Tigers to Cleveland.

Kuenn played for the Giants from 1961-65, and then the Chicago Cubs and Philadelphia, retiring after the 1966 season with a creditable .303 career average.

He took over as manager of the Milwaukee Brewers during the 1982 season and led them to the A.L. pennant, but was replaced after the team failed to repeat in 1983.

A diabetic, Kuenn lost a leg because of the disease, and died at age 57 on Feb. 28, 1988.

'A fall guy was needed, and I was it'

It happened in mid-August, 1974, as the Indians had begun to skid out of contention in the race in the American League East, after playing well earlier.

Ken Aspromonte, then manager of the Indians, couldn't hide his frustration as he was interviewed in his Dallas hotel room the morning after a 7-3 loss to the Texas Rangers had dropped the record of his then-second place team to 59-56.

Aspromonte had just hung up the telephone after a "heated discussion" with then-General Manager Phil Seghi, and finally admitted he was upset because of what he called "a lack of support" by the front office.

They had argued about several players and, "I told Phil he had to do something," Aspromonte said.

Seghi's response, according to Aspromonte: "I get you the players … it's your job to handle them."

Aspromonte couldn't, and by season's end the Indians lost 29 of 47 games to finish fourth with a 77-85 record, 14 games behind Baltimore, which won the American League East.

Aspromonte was fired and replaced by Frank Robinson, who became major league baseball's first black manager.

Ken Aspromonte

"I was bitter, very bitter. I didn't think it was fair the way things were handled," Aspromonte said several years later.

"But now … well, you could say that all's well that ends well," said Aspromonte, then a successful businessman in Houston as he looked back on his three year career as manager of the Indians. His teams compiled an overall 220-260 won-lost record, and finished fifth and sixth in 1972 and 1973.

"I worked hard for the chance (to manage the Indians)," he said. "I started at the bottom and worked my way up, the way I always thought a manager should."

Following a seven year major league playing career as a second baseman with the Indians and five other teams – Boston, Washington Senators, Los Angeles Angels, Milwaukee Braves and Chicago Cubs - Aspromonte played in Japan from 1964-66. He sat out the 1967 season, and began managing at the lowest rung of the Cleveland farm system.

After starting at Sarasota (Fla.) in the Gulf Coast League for rookies in 1968, he advanced to Reno (Nev.) of the Class A California League in1969, and to Wichita (Kans.) of the Class AAA American Association in 1970 and 1971.

During that late-season slump in 1974, when the Indians fell out of contention, Aspromonte became so stressed out that he began losing his hair in clumps, and had trouble sleeping at night, "the pressure was so overwhelming," he admitted.

The beginning of the end for Aspromonte came on Sept. 12, 1974, when Seghi claimed Robinson on waivers from the California Angels.

"Phil did it on his own," Aspromonte said. "I never knew about it until Robinson showed up in the clubhouse the next day and Seghi told me, 'I got that right-handed hitter you said you needed.'

"I knew then that I was finished. Things were not very good with the Indians in those days. A fall guy was needed for all the bad things that had happened, and I was it."

The big deal for the 'Gray Eagle'

It was, at the time, the biggest deal in the history of baseball.

It also was the first time a sportswriter - Ed Bang of the Cleveland *News* - played a role (acknowledged by all) in a team's acquisition of a major league player, in this case Tris Speaker.

Tris Speaker

It was the winter of 1915-16, Speaker had just hit .322 to lead the Boston Red Sox to the American League pennant and world's championship, and when the postman brought his contract for 1916, the "Gray Eagle" was outraged.

It called for a salary of $9,000, the same money he'd been paid in 1915, and was $6,000 less than Speaker wanted. He sent the contract back, unsigned.

When the Red Sox opened spring training at Hot Springs, Ark., Speaker was still outraged - and still sitting at home.

Speaker and the Red Sox finally struck a compromise in which he agreed to join the team in spring training while they continued to negotiate a new contract.

But Joe Lannin, the president of the Red Sox, was adamant. He absolutely would not pay Speaker the $15,000 the center fielder was demanding. "I'll trade him first," vowed Lannin.

Enter Bang. He read about the impasse between Speaker and the Red Sox, and called Bob McRoy, general manager of the Indians. "I think we can get Speaker and I think you ought to grab him," Bang told McRoy, according to Franklin Lewis' 1949 book entitled, "The Cleveland Indians."

"I know Lannin and I know he'll sell any player for enough money," added Bang.

So, taking Bang's advice, McRoy contacted Speaker and asked him if he'd like to come to Cleveland.

"I wouldn't consider it," answered Speaker "You've got a bad ball club, for one thing. Cleveland isn't a good baseball town, either. I don't want to go to Cleveland and wind up in the second division."

It was then that McRoy told Speaker, "We've made a deal for you. We just bought you." Speaker responded, "I won't go. I'll quit baseball first. Call off the deal."

McRoy said, "It's too late. Just think, Tris, it's the biggest deal in the history of baseball. We've paid the Boston club $55,000 in cash. Think of that. And we're sending two players to boot." They were pitcher Sad Sam Jones and infielder Freddie Thomas.

Finally Speaker relented. "All right, I'll go to Cleveland on one condition," he said. "I want $10,000 of the purchase price." He wanted it from the Red Sox. Lannin objected. But only until Speaker threatened to go home unless he got the money. American League President Ban Johnson ordered Lannin to pay the $10,000, and Speaker agreed to join the Indians.

Speaker played for the Tribe the next 11 seasons, only once hitting under .300 (in 1919) when he averaged .296). He took over as a player - manager of the Indians on July 20, 1919, and led them to their first pennant and World Series championship in 1920.

He compiled a won-lost record of 617-520 through 1926, when he resigned and joined Washington in 1927. Speaker ended his playing career with the then-Philadelphia Athletics at the age of 40 in 1928, finishing with a lifetime .345 average. His 3,514 hits are fifth most in major league history. He was inducted into the Hall of Fame in 1937.

He never swung a bat, threw a pitch or even fielded a grounder for the Indians, but for 28 years Max "Lefty" Weisman was a valuable – and favorite – member of the team.

Weisman was the Tribe's trainer from 1921 until his death at age 54 in 1949, and was as colorful as he was popular.

On Aug. 13, 1946, in observance of Weisman's 25th year with the Indians, then-owner Bill Veeck honored the trainer with a "night" which, in those days, usually was held only on behalf of players.

A throng of 65,765 fans nearly filled the Stadium and Veeck presented Weisman with a wheelbarrow full of an estimated 5,000 silver dollars.

It was one of Veeck's best promotions and, in his 1962 autobiography, *Veeck As in Wreck*, he wrote: "The highlight of the evening came when we wished (Weisman) godspeed and told him to pick up his loot and take it away.

Lefty Weisman

"Lefty grabbed the handles eagerly and shoved. The wheelbarrow shoved right back. Five thousand silver dollars, as we well knew, have about the same tonnage as a light destroyer. A tow truck was under the stands, waiting for the signal to come out and take it away."

Another favorite story about Weisman is how he named one of his sons "Jed" in honor of the Indians' "Million Dollar Outfield" of 1931-33.

Lefty took the first letter of each player's first name – left fielder Joe Vosmik, center fielder Earl Averill, and right fielder Dick Porter. Jed and his brother Fred are prominent lawyers in Cleveland.

Weisman's career as the Indians trainer began almost as a "Horatio Alger" story. He was a newsboy on the streets of Boston when Tris Speaker was playing for the Red Sox from 1907-15 and, after almost every game at Fenway Park, Weisman would wait around to chat with the player, who was nicknamed "Spoke." He became Weisman's idol and when Speaker was sold to the Indians in 1916, Lefty was devastated.

After Speaker became manager of the Indians in 1919, Weisman saved his money and took a trip to Cleveland to visit his favorite player. Speaker arranged for Weisman to help Percy Smallwood, then the Indians trainer, which motivated Lefty to take courses treating athletic injuries.

When Smallwood retired because of poor health in 1921, Speaker got owner James Dunn to give the trainer's job to Weisman. And though Weisman was not highly-trained, he served the Indians well.

"It wasn't at all unusual for Dad to call up from the ballpark at 4:30 and say that Ken Keltner, Joe Gordon and Jim Hegan (all stars on the 1948 world championship team) were coming to the house for dinner," Jed was quoted in a Cleveland *Plain Dealer* story about his dad.

"Then, after dinner we'd all gather around the piano and sing. My dad had a good voice and loved Irish ballads."

Jed also said of his dad, which further established Lefty's value as a member of the organization: "He was a street-trained psychologist. When Bob Feller was a rookie, he complained that his cap was too big. Dad told him, 'Make sure it stays that way.'"

The game Max can't forget

Max Alvis played 1,013 games in his nine year major league career and the one he remembers best is the one he'd like most to forget.

"But I can't," the former Indians third baseman has said. "I was never more embarrassed. I still run into people who remember what happened that day."

Max Alvis

What happened that day, July 8, 1965 at Comiskey Park in Chicago, was that Alvis tripped over third base – yes, he did, he *tripped* over third base! – fell down and missed a pop fly. It fell for a hit that was a key factor in Chicago's 3-2 victory over the Indians.

"The batter (White Sox second baseman Al Weis) popped a ball in the air and, at first, it started to go foul, but then drifted back to the diamond," Alvis remembered painfully.

At the time – the fifth inning – the Indians, behind Jack Kralick, were leading, 1-0, against Tommy John. There was one out when Weis popped Kralick's pitch in the air.

"I broke in quickly, but then I had to back up because the wind took the ball," Alvis explained in a Cleveland *Plain Dealer* article in 1969. "As I was back-peddling the thought crossed my mind that I might be getting close to the base, but I said to myself, 'Oh, no, I've got plenty of room.'

"A moment or two later my head was bouncing off the ground and the ball landed right next to me for a hit. It was crazy … I'll never forget it," he said again.

Which is a shame because there are so many better things for which Alvis should be remembered, beginning in 1963 when he became the first rookie to be voted the Indians "Man of the Year" by Cleveland's baseball writers. That was the season he batted .274 with 22 homers after replacing Bubba Phillips as the Tribe's regular third baseman.

Four years later, in a "Favorite Indians Contest" sponsored by the *Plain Dealer,* Alvis was voted the team's most popular player, beating Rocky Colavito by nearly 3,000 votes from among the more than 53,000 that were cast.

Unfortunately, by then Alvis was prematurely on the down side of his career, the result of an illness – spinal meningitis – that nearly cost him his life. As Alvis recalled, it began on the Indians' flight from Minneapolis-St. Paul to Boston the night of June 25, 1964.

"I'd had a good game against the Twins … hit a couple of dingers (homers), and was busting out of the slump I'd been in. I got a headache on the plane, which wasn't uncommon for me, except this one was unusually intense and kept getting worse. I took a couple of aspirins, but they didn't help and by the time we got to our hotel in Boston it was really bad."

He was taken to Sancta Maria Hospital where the illness was diagnosed. After a long hospital stay Alvis returned to action and played the final month of the season.

"At the time, I didn't think I had any after-effects … I thought I was over it," Alvis said, and he again won the "Man of the Year" award in 1967 when his average was .256 with 21 homers.

But Alvis never played that well again. He was traded to Milwaukee in 1970 (with Russ Snyder for Roy Foster and Frank Coggins), and retired at the end of the season.

It was a decision that broke Bob Feller's heart in 1948, and the memory still pains the Indians' greatest pitcher.

It hurts because Feller failed in his only other chance to accomplish one of the few achievements that eluded him.

"I've always been sorry that I never won a World Series game," said Feller, who set single game and season strikeout records, hurled three no-hitters, 12 one hitters, won 20 games six times and is enshrined in the Hall of Fame.

Feller might have won a game in the 1948 Series had it not been for second base umpire Bill Stewart.

Virtually everybody who saw the game - including the players in it - and those who have viewed movies of Stewart's disputed call, believe as Feller does, that the umpire blew it.

Even Alvin Dark, who later managed the Indians (1969-71) and played on the opposing team, admitted the Boston Braves got a gift from Stewart, which helped them win the game, 1-0.

It was the opener of the World Series in Boston and Feller, whose record was 19-15 that season, drew the assignment against Braves ace Johnny Sain, a 24-game winner.

Bob Feller

Feller allowed only one hit through the first seven innings, but faltered momentarily in the eighth, walking leadoff batter Bill Salkeld.

Phil Masi replaced Salkeld as a pinch runner and took second on a sacrifice bunt by Mike McCormick.

Tribe Manager Lou Boudreau ordered the next batter, Eddie Stanky, intentionally walked, and flashed Feller the signal for their well-rehearsed pickoff play.

Feller went into a stretch, seemingly ignoring the runners, then whirled and threw to second, where Boudreau was sneaking behind Masi.

It was Boudreau's "timing" play that had worked so often - and well - for the Indians all season, but surprised the Braves and Stewart, a National League arbiter.

Masi tried desperately to get back to the base, but didn't in time - though Stewart said he did.

"Masi was out," Dark said without equivocation. "All of us (in the Braves dugout) knew ... that Stewart called the play wrong. Masi knew it, too." But of course, the umpire's call stood.

Feller retired the next batter, Sain, on a routine fly for the second out.

But as fate would cruelly decree, Tommy Holmes, Boston's leading hitter, singled to score Masi and break Feller's heart.

The Indians got the potential tying run to second base with two out in the ninth, but Sain fanned Walt Judnich to end it.

Feller got another chance in Game 5, but couldn't hold a 5-4 lead and was knocked out in the seventh when the Braves erupted for six runs and an 11-5 victory.

And in 1954, Feller, who won 13 and lost three to help the Indians win the pennant, didn't get a start in that Series which the New York Giants swept in four games.

Feller retired in 1956, forever frustrated because of Stewart's controversial call eight years earlier.

Making of a Hall of Fame pitcher

Among the eager rookies hoping to impress Manager Lou Boudreau when the Indians opened spring training in Tucson, Ariz. in 1946 was a returning Navy veteran, a third baseman named Bob Lemon.

A left-handed batter who'd been a very good hitter in the Tribe farm system before serving three years in World War II, Lemon faced stiff competition.

Bob Lemon

The Indians' third baseman was veteran Ken Keltner, so Boudreau was determined to find a place for Lemon to play because of the kid's strong arm and competitiveness.

Boudreau switched Lemon to the outfield and, when the season began, the former sailor was the Tribe's center fielder.

Lemon was great defensively and the season was only a couple of weeks old when he made a sensational, game-saving catch to preserve a 1-0 victory over Chicago for Bob Feller.

But offensively, it was something else. Lemon hit only .180 with one homer in 55 games that year, and by mid-season he was benched, except as a late inning defensive replacement.

Venerable Mel Harder was then a member of the Indians pitching staff and would become a coach in 1947.

Harder also recognized Lemon's strong arm and was made aware that the weak hitting outfielder-third baseman had done some pitching in the Navy.

Harder suggested to Boudreau that Lemon be given a trial as a pitcher; after all, there was little to lose as the Indians, that season, weren't going anywhere. They finished sixth, 68-86, 36 games behind pennant-winning Boston. Boudreau shrugged. Why not?

Hall of Famer Bill Dickey, who also caught Lemon when they played together in the Navy, was another who recommended that Lemon be given a trial as a pitcher.

It turned out to be one of the best decisions in Indians history.

Initially used in relief, Lemon went 4-5 the rest of 1946. He became a regular starter in 1947, winning eleven games while losing five, and burst into stardom in 1948 with a 20-i4 record that included a no-hitter against Detroit on June 30.

It was the beginning of a remarkable pitching career that would continue through the 1958 season.

"Lemon's conversion to pitching was simple," Harder recalled. "When he first started to pitch he had the idea he had to throw as hard as he could ... throw the ball by the batter all the time.

"Lem had one of the best sinkers I've ever seen, but the stronger he was, and the harder he threw, the less the ball would sink. It took him awhile to realize that, but once he did, he became a great pitcher.

"Watching Bob develop from a third baseman-outfielder to a pitcher was a source of much satisfaction to me."

To everybody with the Indians.

Lemon helped pitch them to pennants in 1948 and 1954, and never again played the outfield or third base - or any position but pitcher - after 1946.

He won 20 games seven times, compiled one of the best winning percentages of all-time with a 207-128 (.618) record in 13 seasons, and was elected to the Hall of Fame in 1976. Lemon died January 11, 2000.

When Feller's misfortune helped

Bob Feller will always remember - with anger and frustration - the pickoff play at second base in the opener of the 1948 World Series.

The call was blown by umpire Bill Stewart and led to the game's only run as the Boston Braves beat the Indians, 1-0.

Bob Lemon remembers the play, too, but for a different reason - and with a different emotion.

"I know it hurt Feller, but it might have turned out good for me and the team," Lemon recalled in a recent interview. "If it hadn't happened, I might not have won the next day, and if I hadn't won that game, we might not have won the Series.

"I was on the ropes early in that second game, like in the first inning, and (manager) Lou Boudreau got the bull pen up. The Braves got a run in and had runners on first and second and only one out.

"I knew I was out of the game if I didn't get the next batter, and it was killing me," continued Lemon, who was inducted into the Hall of Fame in 1976 after a 13 year pitching career that produced 207 victories and 128 losses.

"I was really struggling; no pitcher wants to come out of a game in the first inning, especially in the World Series," he said.

Bob Lemon

"I don't remember the next batter, but before I made a pitch to him, we - Boudreau and I - decided to try the pickoff play again. The same one that Stewart blew on Feller the day before.

"This time the umpire at second, Bill Summers from the American League, called the runner out. It was Earl Torgeson and I got out of the inning alive.

"The funny thing, what makes it so ironic, is that Feller's pickoff that wasn't called, helped make mine work. I'm sure of it.

"All the hell that was raised because everybody thought Stewart blew the call for Feller, made the umpires more alert, more aware that we might try it again.

"And because I got Torgeson at second, I got out of the inning - instead of being knocked out of the game - and I stayed out of trouble the rest of the way."

The Indians won it, 4-1, as Lemon, whose record was 20-14 that season, scattered eight hits.

"Something else about that game," continued Lemon. "If my pickoff at second didn't work and the Braves got some runs, they might have won, not only that game, but maybe the whole Series because they would have gone up, two games to zip. Instead, we turned the momentum around and went home with the Series tied at one game apiece."

Unfortunately for Feller, he failed again in the fifth game and this time nobody could blame the umpires as the Braves romped to an 11-5 victory.

But Gene Bearden blanked the Braves, 2-0, in Game 3, Steve Gromek was a 2-1 winner in Game 4, and Lemon came back to win Game 6 with relief help from Bearden, 4-3.

But it was that second game, the one in which he barely survived, that Lemon later called his most memorable performance - thanks, perhaps, to the pickoff play that Stewart blew for Feller in the Series opener.

No longer 'Rollicking Rollie'

One of the beat kept secrets in Cleveland baseball history was the identity of the leader of the Indians' infamous rebellion against Manager Oscar Vitt in 1940.

It has been speculated that first baseman Hal Trosky was the one, and if not him, then pitcher Mel Harder, or outfielder Ben Chapman, or pitcher Johnny Allen, or catcher Rollie Hemsley.

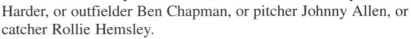

Rollie Hemsley

Only those involved knew, but nobody ever revealed the name of the ring-leader. And those who are alive today, still won't say.

But, on more than one occasion, players seemed to hint that the captain of the insurrection was Hemsley, according to the late Franklin Lewis, then sports editor of the Cleveland *Press.*

Lewis wrote that, at one point during the season, "Hemsley, with Allen, decided that the team wasn't using the hit-and-run enough and a second set of signals, unknown to Vitt, had been agreed upon, and were used."

In another story about the rebellion, the late Howard Preston, a Cleveland *Plain Dealer* columnist, noticed that the Indians seemed to avoid Hemsley in public, apparently for fear of being judged guilty by association.

One night in the diner on the railroad train, Preston wrote, "Hemsley came in and took a seat at a table for four. As the diner filled up, it was apparent not one Indian was going to be seen sitting with a ring-leader such as Hemsley." Preston continued, "One of the most painful sights I ever saw was Hemsley sitting there going through a complete dinner by himself, pretending he hadn't noticed the snub."

But Hemsley was a strong man as well as a fine catcher who'd come to the Indians in a 1938 trade with the St. Louis Browns for pitcher Ed Cole, catcher-infielder Billy Sullivan and infielder Roy Hughes. Hemsley had previously played for Pittsburgh, the Chicago Cubs, and Cincinnati in a career that began in 1928. He was known to be a heavy drinker and, when drunk, a troublemaker, hence his nickname: "Rollicking Rollie."

"But when the 1940 season began," according to Lewis, "Hemsley called the writers together and held a very unusual press conference.

"He told them: 'It's been just a year now since the most wonderful thing in the world happened to me, so I feel safe in telling you boys about it. I didn't have a drink all last season. Alcoholics Anonymous did that for me. I'd like to give credit to this great organization and you'll do me a favor by writing a story about A.A.'"

Lewis commented, "The whisky blush was gone from Rollie's face. His eyes were clear, his speech rational. How different from the Hemsley the boys knew a couple of years earlier, or the talented backstop who drank himself off three teams." Hemsley remained clean and served as Bob Feller's personal catcher until he was sold back to the Reds in December 1941.

He went on to play for the New York Yankees and Philadelphia Phillies before retiring in 1947 with a career .262 average. Hemsley died in 1972 without ever admitting that he was the ring-leader in the Vitt Rebellion, if indeed he was, and nobody else has come forward to name anybody else - or to confirm that it was Hemsley.

There used to be a seat that was painted red in Section 4 of the upper deck in right field at Cleveland's old Municipal Stadium. It marked the spot where the longest home run landed.

The ball was hit by Luscious (his real name) Easter, who was better known as "Luke," before he was murdered March 29, 1979.

Easter hammered his tape-measure homer on June 23, 1950, off a 3-0 pitch from Joe Haynes of the then-Washington Senators. The ball jumped off Easter's bat and landed - by actual measurement - 477 feet from the plate.

Luke Easter

Another time, in 1950, Easter, a 6-5, 240-pound first baseman, came close to walloping a ball into the center field bleachers, which nobody ever did in a game - or even during batting practice - in the 64 year existence of the Stadium, which was opened for baseball in 1932, vacated by the Indians in 1994, and razed after the original Cleveland Browns moved to Baltimore following the 1995 NFL season.

Eyewitnesses claim that Easter's drive would have gone into the bleachers, but didn't because Tribe relief pitcher Dick Weik leaped in front of the wall and caught the ball. In those days the bull pens at the Stadium were behind the left-center and right-center field interior fences.

"The only man I ever saw with more power than Luke was the Babe (Ruth)," said Bob Feller, who joined the Indians in 1936 and later was Easter's teammate. "Luke had as much power as Mickey Mantle, maybe more, and I didn't play with or against anybody else who came close."

Easter's career in Organized Baseball started late because black players were kept out until Jackie Robinson broke the color barrier with the Brooklyn Dodgers in 1947. He was signed by the Indians in 1949 at age 34 - though his birthdate was never really confirmed.

Once Easter was quoted as saying he was born in 1921, another time he said 1911, and later claimed he didn't know. The *Baseball Encyclopedia* lists Aug. 4, 1915 as Easter's birthdate.

Whatever, the Indians brought Easter to Cleveland in August of 1949, after he hit 25 homers in just two months for San Diego of the Class AAA Pacific Coast League.

Easter had three great seasons for the Indians from 1950 through 1952 when he hit 28, 27 and 31 homers, respectively, but suffered physical problems, especially bad knees.

Unfortunately - and unfairly - he was often booed by the fans, probably because they expected so much from the big man. It undoubtedly bothered Luke, though he never let it show.

Because of his bad knees Easter was able to play only 68 games in 1953, and the Indians cut him loose after six games in 1954. But Luke refused to quit.

He played in the minors the next 10 years and was still hitting tape-measure homers and smiling - but not running very well - for Rochester as a player-coach in 1965 when he was at least 44, and perhaps as old as 54.

After returning to Cleveland, Easter took a factory job and soon became a union steward. It was in that capacity that Luke lost his life, murdered by two thieves after he'd gone to a bank to cash $40,000 worth of paychecks for his fellow workers.

The 'Bear' who pitched like a lion

They always said he "walked like a bear and pitched like a lion."

That was Mike Garcia, the "Big Bear" of the Indians from 1949 until he hurt his back in 1958

He was the fourth man on a staff that, in its prime, featured eventual Hall of Famers Bob Feller, Bob Lemon and Early Wynn. But, had Garcia been with any other team, he probably would have been the ace.

Mike Garcia

Fact is, there were some who said that Garcia at times was tougher to hit than Feller, Lemon or Wynn, especially in 1951 and 1952 when he won a total of 42 games.

A back injury in 1958, and an accident in which he lost the tip of his right index finger in 1959, cut short Garcia's career.

But he wound up with a creditable won-lost record of 142-97 and 3.27 earned run average in 14 seasons with the Indians, Chicago White Sox and Washington Senators.

Garcia died of kidney failure in 1986, exactly six weeks after he was honored by the Sports Media Association of Cleveland and Ohio (SMACO).

When he joined the Indians as a rookie in 1949, it was written that he "soaks up advice like a sponge cake soaks up sauce," and that "there isn't the slightest sign of smart aleck newcomer about him."

Garcia never lost that humility, not even in 1954 when his 2.64 ERA was the best in the American League. The only reason he failed to be a 20-game winner was his willingness to be a good team player.

Garcia explained in a 1983 article that, two weeks before the end of that 1954 season, he was called into Manager Al Lopez's office.

"Al said he wanted to go for the record (for most games won in a season) and asked if I'd come out of the starting rotation and pitch relief," related Garcia. "I said, 'I've won 19 and the difference between winning 19 and 20 is like the difference between a Ford and a Cadillac.'

"Al said, 'Don't worry, you'll pick up another one (victory) easy,' so I said "OK."

But he never did.

Finally, in the final game of the season, Lopez started Garcia against Detroit, except, as the Big Bear recalled, "He also put all the scrubbolas in the lineup."

Garcia - as he always did - battled all the way, until the 12th inning. Then, with the score tied, 6-6, the Tigers loaded the bases and Lopez went to the bull pen, ending Garcia's chances for a 20th victory.

Cruel, too, was the way the end of Garcia's career crept up on him. He slipped on a wet mound early in the 1958 season and suffered a slipped disc in his back. Baseball's rules were different then, as teams were allowed only two players on the disabled list at the same time.

When it was determined that Garcia needed an operation, General Manager Frank Lane said he had no choice but to release the Big Bear because, at that time, Vic Wertz and Carroll Hardy both were on the DL. Garcia underwent the surgery and re-signed with the Indians.

But, though he still walked like a bear, Garcia no longer could pitch like a lion.

And two years later, after trials with the White Sox and Washington, he retired.

The Tribe's gruff, tough pitcher

As legend has it, Early Wynn claimed he'd knock his own mother down with a pitch if it meant helping him win a game, though he later said, "Aw, shucks, that was just talk." Perhaps.

Then again, tell it to the batters who faced Wynn in a 23-year major league career in which he won 300 games, 164 of them for the Indians before he retired in 1963.

Never was there a pitcher more intimidating, nor more competitive than Wynn, who was elected to the Hall of Fame in 1971.

Bill Veeck got Wynn - really *stole* him - in a trade with the then-Washington Senators on December 14, 1948. It will forever rank as one of Veeck's best deals, though Frank Lane negated it nine years later.

In addition to Wynn, the Indians acquired first baseman Mickey Vernon for pitchers Joe Haynes and Ed Klieman, and first baseman Eddie Robinson.

Vernon hit .291 and was traded back to the Senators in 1950 for pitcher Dick Weik, who did little for the Indians, though nothing could tarnish the deal for Wynn.

Early Wynn

He became part of the celebrated "Big Four" when the Indians won the pennant in 1954, setting an American League record with 111 victories. Wynn, 23-11, and Bob Lemon, 23-7, were the league's winningest pitchers, while Mike Garcia went 19-8, and Art Houtteman, 15-7, with Bob Feller, 13-3, the fifth starter.

Some considered it the best pitching staff of all-time, especially with relief specialists Don Mossi and Ray Narleski in the bull pen.

Wynn won 20 games four times in his nine years in Cleveland, and was Chicago's ace when the White Sox won the pennant in 1959. He died at the age of 79 in 1999.

It was one of Lane's first and worst deals that sent Wynn to Chicago, with outfielder Al Smith, another hero of the 1954 Indians, after Wynn's record fell to 14-17 in 1957.

Outfielder Minnie Minoso and infielder Freddie Hatfield came to Cleveland for Wynn and Smith, but Minoso didn't have much left, and Hatfield didn't last long.

Wynn once said his "most memorable" game was one he pitched for Washington against the New York Yankees on Sept. 26, 1941 - and that which happened probably set the tenor for his pitching philosophy the rest of his career.

"That little shortstop (Phil Rizzuto) ruined it for me," said Wynn. "There I was, getting out guys like Joe DiMaggio, King Kong Keller, Bill Dickey, Joe Gordon, Red Rolfe and Tommy Henrich, but I lose the game,1-0, because that little pipsqueak Rizzuto hit a home run." It was one of only 38 by Rizzuto in his 13 year major league career.

"From that game on I always thought bad things about anybody who hit a home run off me."

After Wynn was released by Chicago following his 7-15 season in 1962, he needed just one more victory for 300. The Indians' Gabe Paul signed him as a free agent.

Wynn made five starts before he beat Kansas City, 7-4, with relief help from Jerry Walker on July 13, 1963. He was 43 at the time and, yes, to win that game Wynn would have knocked down his own mother with a pitch - as he would've done - in any of the 691 major league games he pitched.

The intellectual 'Bulldog'

Orel Hershiser

Not only was Orel Hershiser one of the smartest pitchers of his era, he also was among the most determined, which was the reason he was nicknamed "Bulldog."

And for those reasons in particular, it's a shame Hershiser didn't join the Indians until 1995 - and it's also a shame they didn't keep him when they had a chance to do so in 1999, instead of letting him go to the New York Mets, for whom he also pitched well at the age of 41.

One of Hershiser's theories that helped him compile a 134-102 record and 3.00 earned run average in his 12 seasons with the Los Angeles Dodgers was the necessity of bearing down against the low average hitters. It was a lesson learned from his manager with the Dodgers, Tommy Lasorda.

"(Lasorda) preached there are only so many guys in the lineup who can beat you," Hershiser was quoted in a story that appeared in *Baseball Digest* in September 1995. "He said, 'You can pitch around the big hitters (but) it's important to get the .220 hitters out. You don't ever want them on base, or creating, or participating in rallies.'"

It was a principle to which Hershiser strictly adhered throughout his career that began as a 17th round selection of the Dodgers in the 1979 amateur draft. After four years in the minors and a late season opportunity with the Dodgers, he made the major league team in 1984.

Hershiser peaked in 1988 when he was the unanimous winner of the National League "Cy Young Award" after going 23-8 with a 2.26 ERA. He set a major league record by pitching 59 consecutive scoreless innings, breaking by one the mark held by a former Dodger right-hander, Hall of Famer Don Drysdale.

He underwent shoulder reconstruction surgery in 1990, putting his career in jeopardy, but, as usual, the Bulldog prevailed. He spent most of 1991 in the minors, and finished the season with the Dodgers, winning "Comeback of the Year" honors by going 7-2.

When Hershiser won only 28 games while losing 35 the next three seasons, the Dodgers gave up on him. He signed with the Indians and launched another comeback. In his three seasons with the Tribe, Hershiser went 45-21, helping them win the American League Central Division championship each year, and the pennant in 1995 and 1997

Expanding on Lasorda's theory, Hershiser said, "Sometimes you don't have enough talent to get the big hitters out. They're going to get their base hits (and) even the best pitchers have moments of failure. It's talent against talent and sometimes the big hitters just flat-out win," though they didn't too often against Hershiser.

In 1997 when the Bulldog was 39, the Indians concluded – incorrectly, as it turned out – that he was only a six inning pitcher and didn't offer him a new contract, and he signed with San Francisco posting an 11-10 record. Hershiser pitched for the New York Mets in 1999, going 13-12.

It was his gutsy performance against Pittsburgh on the last day of the season, in which he allowed only two hits in 5 1/3 innings, that enabled the Mets to beat the Pirates, 2-1. It was a victory they needed to finish in a tie with Cincinnati for the wild card berth in the playoffs, which they clinched the next day, beating the Reds, 5-0.

Baseball historians have called it "the most stupendous pitching duel of all time."

The principals were Adrian "Addie" Joss for the Cleveland team, then nicknamed "Naps" (in honor of player-manager Napoleon Lajoie) and Ed Walsh, the famed spitballer, for the Chicago White Sox.

The game was played at Cleveland's old League Park on October 2, 1908.

Both teams were fighting for the pennant, though they killed off each other in that final series and Detroit won, beating out Cleveland by four percentage points. The White Sox finished third, 1 1/2 games behind.

Joss pitched a perfect game, the first in Cleveland baseball history, while Walsh, who later became an American League umpire, allowed only four hits. Joss's perfecto was the second in modern major league history, and only 12 have been pitched since then, including one in 1981 by another Cleveland hurler, Lennie Barker.

Cleveland won, 1-0, the only run scoring in the third inning on a bloop single by Joe Birmingham, a stolen base, an error and Walsh's wild pitch.

Addie Joss

It was a tough loss for Walsh, but a well-deserved victory for Joss. He hurled another no-hitter in 1910 (though it wasn't a perfect game), and was destined to become one of the game's greatest pitchers. Then tragedy struck.

Prior to the start of the 1911 season, Joss fainted on the bench while the Indians were playing an exhibition game in Chattanooga, Tennessee.

Upon rejoining the team a few days later, Joss apologized to his teammates for having "pulled a baby trick," but soon took sick again.

Joss returned to his home in Toledo. His illness was diagnosed as tubercular meningitis and, within a week, on April 14, he died at age 31.

It devastated the Indians as Joss seemed to be in the prime of his life and career.

A big right-hander, Joss had an overwhelming fast ball that batters complained "came out of his hip pocket."

Cleveland purchased his contract for $500 from Toledo of the Inter-State League, and Joss hurled a one-hitter against St. Louis in his major league debut in 1902. He went on to post a 17-13 record that season, and his one-hitter was the first of six Joss would pitch among his 160 victories and 97 losses.

Beginning in 1905, Joss won 20 or more games in four consecutive seasons, including 27 in 1907.

Forty-five of Joss's victories were shutouts. His 1.89 earned run average was second best on the all-time list to the 1.82 registered by none other than Walsh, Joss's opponent in that "most stupendous pitching duel" of 1908.

Joss was initially denied admission to the Hall of Fame because the rules stipulated that candidates had to play in the major leagues 10 seasons, and he had played in only nine before his untimely death.

But special dispensation was granted and, in 1978, Joss was enshrined - where he belonged - joining Ed Walsh, who had been elected to the Hall of Fame 32 years earlier.

Alva Bradley's pitch for Gehrig

The course of baseball history in Cleveland, as well as New York, would have been drastically different if Alva Bradley had been successful in prying away a player who became one of the greatest in the game.

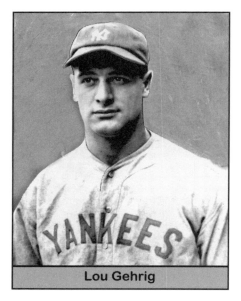

Lou Gehrig

Lou Gehrig.

Shortly after Bradley and two partners bought the Indians on November 17, 1927 for the then "outrageous" sum of $1-million, he wrote the following letter to Ed Barrow, owner of the Yankees.

"Dear Mr. Barrow: From time to time during the last week, there have been articles in the Cleveland newspapers referring to your inability to sign Lou Gehrig.

"'The thought has occurred to me that if you are having real trouble with him, you might want to sell him. I am authorized to make an offer (for Gehrig) of $150,000."

It was rejected, but Bradley, an affable though somewhat introverted man who admittedly knew little about baseball or the business of the game, was persistent.

He made another offer, this one $175,000 plus first baseman George Burns. In those days $175,000 - even $150,000 - was a tremendous amount, and Burns was no slouch; he'd hit .319 in 1927 and .358 the year before that.

Rebuffed again, Bradley tried $250,000, but still Barrow said no, and finally signed Gehrig.

With the deal definitely off, Bradley wrote another letter to Barrow under the date, January 11, 1928. "I was selfish to hope you would have more trouble (signing Gehrig)," Bradley said to Barrow. "My effort is to build up an organization that will put Cleveland back on the baseball map."

The acquisition of Gehrig by the Indians undoubtedly would have done that. The famed "Iron Horse," who'd completed his third season with the Yankees - and hit.373 with 47 homers - when Bradley tried to get him for Cleveland, played in a record 2,130 consecutive games from June 1, 1925 to April 30, 1939. It was a major league mark that wasn't broken until 1998, when Cal Ripken Jr. of the Baltimore Orioles played 2,632 in a row.

Gehrig retired in 1939 and was elected to the Hall of Fame the same year, when the five-year waiting rule was waived because Gehrig was suffering a terminal illness. He died June 2, 1941, one day after the 16th anniversary of the start of his iron man streak.

Without Gehrig - or any player close to his caliber - the Indians challenged for the pennant only once during Bradley's 19-year tenure as owner. That was in 1940, when the Tribe finished second, one game behind Detroit, after Bradley had to quell a player rebellion against then-Manager Oscar Vitt. Six years later, on June 21, 1946, Bradley and his partners sold the franchise to Bill Veeck for $2,2 million.

Still, under Bradley in 1932 the Indians moved into a new park, the Cleveland Municipal Stadium, at least on a part-time basis; in 1936 signed Bob Feller, one of the greatest pitchers of all-time; and in 1941 named 24-year old shortstop Lou Boudreau player-manager.

But it would have been so much different - and so *very much better* — for the Indians if Bradley's big pitch for Lou Gehrig had been a strike.

Boudreau's strange request

It was March 1942 and the Indians had just assembled in Ft. Myers, Fla. for spring training under their new manager, Lou Boudreau.

Then a 24-year old shortstop who'd played only two full seasons in the major leagues, Boudreau had been hired four months earlier, earning the title, "Boy Manager."

In one of his first moves, Boudreau called a meeting of the reporters covering the Indians and made an unusual request.

"I'd like to suggest that, in the future, you gentlemen show me your stories before they go into the papers," Boudreau said.

The writers were speechless.

Finally Gordon Cobbledick of the *Plain Dealer* spoke up. "Look, Lou," he told Boudreau, according to a report published at the time, "you run the ball club, we'll write the stories. And while we're on the subject," added Cobbledick, "we wish you would quit referring to us as your newspapermen. We work for our papers, not the Indians."

The episode was a perfect example of Boudreau's inexperience as a manager, though the fact is, he learned in a hurry - and he learned well. Cleveland at the time was sarcastically referred to as "the graveyard of managers," based on an oft-repeated remark

Lou Boudreau

by then-owner Alva Bradley, to wit: "I hire the manager, but the fans fire him."

Roger Peckinpaugh managed the Tribe in 1941, but was fired - either by the fans or Bradley - after that one season. It was Peckinpaugh's second time around as he also held the job from 1928 until he was replaced in mid-1933 by Walter Johnson, who didn't last long either.

The Indians' stars of Boudreau's days were first baseman Les Fleming, third baseman Ken Keltner, outfielders Roy Weatherly and Jeff Heath, and pitchers Jim Bagby Jr. and Mel Harder - and, of course, Boudreau the shortstop.

Fleming, who temporarily "retired" in 1943 to work in a war plant to avoid being drafted, hit .292 with 14 homers and 82 RBI.

Bagby, whose father helped pitch the Indians to the American League pennant and world's championship in 1920, won 17 and lost nine games with a 2.96 earned run average, and Harder was 13-14.

Boudreau, apparently unaffected by the rigors of managing, hit .283 and drove in 58 runs, while continuing to develop into one of the game's premier shortstops.

The highpoint of the season came early, as the Indians won 13 straight from April 18 through May 2. It was the longest winning streak in the franchise's history (tied by the 1951 team).

But they faded after the All-Star Game, which was played in front of 62,094 fans at the Stadium between a team of American Leaguers and a group of major league players – including Bob Feller - who were in the service. The A.L. won, 5-0.

The Tribe finished fourth, the same as in 1941, and with an identical 75-79 record.

Boudreau kept his job for nine years, longer than any of the 14 Indians managers who preceded him, as well as all the managers who have followed him, and his teams also won the most games, 728, in franchise history.

The remarkable 'Boy Manager'

It was the winter of 1947-48 and Indians owner Bill Veeck was a man with a mission.

He was determined to trade Lou Boudreau.

It wasn't that Veeck, who'd purchased the Indians in 1946, didn't consider Boudreau to be a good player. Veeck's rationale was that he didn't want Boudreau to continue as manager of the Indians, but the only way he could replace him, was to trade Boudreau the shortstop.

Bill Veeck/Lou Boudreau

A deal - Boudreau for Vern Stephens, then a power-hitting shortstop for the St. Louis Browns - was in the negotiating stage when the Cleveland media learned of it.

A poll of fans was launched and they voted overwhelmingly, by a five-to-one majority, to keep Boudreau the shortstop, which meant keeping Boudreau the manager.

Veeck, who was no dummy, reconsidered and rejected the trade for Stephens, which turned out to be the best deal that was never made.

Boudreau, baseball's "boy manager" when he was hired in 1942 at the age of 24 by the team's previous owner, Alva Bradley, proceeded in 1948 to lead the Indians to what probably was their most exciting season in the history of the franchise.

They wound up in a tie with the Boston Red Sox, each with 96-58 records, and won the pennant in a one-game playoff, 8-3, as Boudreau - the unwanted shortstop-manager - hit two homers and went 4-for-4. Then Boudreau led the Tribe to a four-games-to-two victory over the Boston Braves in the World Series.

Naturally, Boudreau was acclaimed a managerial genius, but the unvarnished truth is, he was a great manager primarily because he was such a great player that season.

Hall of Famer Ted Williams, who won the American League batting championship with a .369 average as a member of the Red Sox in 1948, said of Boudreau: "He came the closest to being the most complete player of anyone I've ever seen in the game.

"Boudreau was a great hitter, a great shortstop and a great manager."

Indeed, Boudreau hit .355 - second to Williams - with 18 homers and 106 RBI in 1948, and won the A.L. Most Valuable Player award practically by acclamation.

But Boudreau never had another season like it - as a player and/or manager - and neither did the Indians until they won the pennant in 1954. By then Veeck and Boudreau both were gone.

Veeck sold the club in November 1949, and a year later Boudreau was released (at his own request, it was announced) after the Indians failed twice to repeat as A.L. champion.

Boudreau went on to manage the Red Sox in 1952 through 1954, Kansas City 1955-57, and the Chicago Cubs in 1960, but never finished higher than fourth - probably because he no longer had Boudreau, the great shortstop, in the lineup.

Boudreau, who was established as a star in 1940, his first full season in Cleveland, compiled a .295 lifetime average in 15 seasons. He was elected to the Hall of Fame in 1970.

And, as long as the game is played, Boudreau will be remembered as a great manager - partly because he was such a great player in 1948.

A most memorable moment

It has been indelibly etched in the memory banks of those who saw it, and were thrilled by the remarkable courage of Lou Boudreau on a sultry, hot day in the Stadium, Aug. 8, 1948.

The Indians swept a double header from the New York Yankees in front of 73,484 fans, and it proved to be the turning point in their relentless pursuit of the pennant that season.

Here's how Franklin Lewis, in his 1949 history of the Indians, described one of the most unforgettable events in the history of baseball anywhere, not just in Cleveland.

"Only two percentage points separated the Indians, (Philadelphia) Athletics, and Yankees, the top three teams (in the American League). The (Boston) Red Sox were in fourth place, a mere game-and-a-half behind the three leaders.

"With Boudreau hurt and aching, the Indians were fireless.

"In the seventh inning of the first game, the Yankees led, 6-4. But the Indians filled the bases and in came Joe Page, the big Yankee left-hander, to stem the rally. Thurman Tucker, a left-handed batter, was kneeling in the ring near home plate. He turned his head toward the dugout. There, pawing over the bats in the rack, was Boudreau. Tucker walked to the bench as every voice in the place cut loose with a cheer, a gasp, or possibly an epithet.

Lou Boudreau

"Boudreau, taped like a mummy, walked slowly to the plate. His right thumb, injured earlier, was so tender it could not be pressed against the bat handle. Lou was limping, and he favored his right side when walking. The announcement of 'Boudreau batting for Tucker' was lost in the ovation to the young manager.

"There were other right-handed pinch hitters on the bench. Why had Boudreau put himself squarely on the hottest spot imaginable, the startled spectators asked their neighbors.

"The answer was in Boudreau, in Lou's almost fanatical desire to win the pennant and, in the process, to show up (Bill) Veeck just a little.

"Whatever the motive, Lou rose to the situation. He lashed a solid, line single to center. Two runners raced across the plate and the score was tied, 6-6. The Indians scored again in the eighth and won, 8-6. They also won the nightcap, 2-1.

"If Boudreau could do it, so could his men, it seemed."

And they did. The Indians went on to win 39 of their final 58 games, including the historic, one-game playoff against the Red Sox that gave the franchise its first pennant in 28 years.

Boudreau was superb all that season. He hit .355 and drove in 106 runs - and won the A.L.'s Most Valuable Player award practically by acclamation.

He also proved Veeck wrong. The previous winter the owner wanted to trade Boudreau to the St. Louis Browns for shortstop Vernon Stephens.

But a newspaper campaign, and the subsequent outpouring of fan support convinced Veeck to keep Boudreau, whose courage as a manager, and skill as a player provided one of baseball's most memorable moments.

'Slap some color in his face'

This was during the bad old days of 1990, when John McNamara was the manager of the Indians and they were in dire need of a pitcher to start a game against the California Angels at the old Stadium on June 29.

Charles Nagy

A desperate, hurry-up call was made to the Tribe's Canton-Akron team in the Class AA Eastern League for a pitcher, and a 23-year old right-hander who'd been a first round draft choice two years earlier was summoned.

The players were all on the field taking batting practice when the kid arrived at the Indians locker room about 90 minutes before game-time, and McNamara was in his office chatting with broadcaster Herb Score and a Cleveland *Plain Dealer* sportswriter.

McNamara excused himself and went into the clubhouse to greet the rookie. When he returned, a smiling McNamara said to Score, "Herbie, go out there and slap some color in that kid's face … he looks like he's scared to death." The kid was Charles Nagy.

Score didn't "slap some color in that kid's face," although it might have helped. Nagy, that night, lasted only 4 1/3 innings. Pitching against Jim Abbott, he gave up four runs on seven hits, and the Indians lost to the Angels, 7-2.

Thereafter, however, Nagy obviously hasn't needed to be slapped, and developed into one of the Indians' most dependable pitchers. For the sixth straight season, from 1994-99, Nagy never missed a start. In fact, through 1999, when he went 17-11, Nagy became the 12th winningest pitcher in franchise history with 121 victories (and 86 losses), one less than Jim Bagby Sr. (1916-22) and Sam McDowell (1961-71).

Those 17 victories in 1999, the fifth highest total in the American League, tying his career best, allowed Nagy to join Atlanta's Greg Maddux as the only pitchers in baseball to win 15 or more games in five consecutive seasons, from 1995-99.

The last Tribesman to win 15 or more five years in a row were Hall of Famers Bob Lemon, who did it nine straight seasons (1948-56), and Early Wynn seven (1950-56).

Further testimony as to the esteem in which Nagy is held since his major league debut and McNamara thought he was scared to death, is the fact that he was honored twice by the Indians, first in 1993, and again in 1994.

Nagy was the last pitcher to start a game in the old Stadium, on Oct. 3, 1993, and the first to take the mound to open Jacobs Field on April 2, 1994, in an exhibition game against Pittsburgh.

In a convoluted sort of way, it could be said that the Indians have their one-time center fielder, Brett Butler, and the San Francisco Giants to thank for the presence of Nagy. Because the Giants signed Butler as a free agent during the winter of 1987-88, they forfeited their first pick in the draft to the Indians, who made Nagy their second choice in the first round, behind shortstop Mark Lewis.

Nagy was an American League all-star three times, in 1992, 1996 and 1999 – and is the answer to a great trivia question, to wit: Who was the first pitcher in 30 years to get a hit in an All-Star Game, since Ken McBride of the Los Angeles Angels in 1962?

The answer: Nagy, who in 1992 no longer needed to have some color slapped in his face.

The once perfect pitcher

It's impossible to improve upon perfection, which might have been Lenny Barker's problem.

He pitched major league baseball's eighth perfect game (including Don Larsen's in the 1956 World Series) - and second in Indians history - on May 15, 1981, to beat Toronto, 3-0.

But not much went right for Barker thereafter.

Oh, he rebounded from an 8-7 record to go 15-11 in 1982.

But it turned out to be the start of the downside of Barker's career. He never came close to recapturing the rapture of that glorious game against the Blue Jays.

Barker made 103 pitches in his perfect performance, 74 of them strikes, 41 fast balls, 60 curves and two change-ups, and struck out 11 batters, all of them swinging.

Two batted balls were close to being hits, but second baseman Duane Kuiper fielded both, one by Rick Bosetti in the sixth, the other by Alfredo Griffin in the seventh.

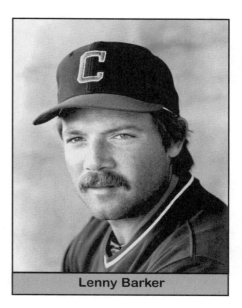

Lenny Barker

Kuiper back-handed Bosetti's shot on one hop, and raced four strides to his left to reach Griffin's grounder. Each Blue Jay was thrown out by half-a-step.

Third baseman Toby Harrah also made a spectacular catch of a foul to retire Willie Upshaw in the fifth, and Rick Manning ran a long way to haul down Damaso Garcia's liner in the second.

Dave Garcia, then manager of the Indians who had been in professional baseball since 1939, spared no accolades for Barker. "I've never seen a better pitched game," Garcia said after Manning caught Ernie Whitt's routine fly to end the masterpiece.

Few had.

Barker was speechless - almost.

"I don't know what to say," he said. "All the plays behind me were outstanding. I started taking (the perfect game) seriously around the eighth inning.

"I guess the big thing was I felt good and I was able to get my curve ball over."

The perfect game was Barker's third victory in four decisions, but he struggled the last two months of the season.

Barker developed arm trouble which later was diagnosed as a spur in his elbow, and he was in and out of the rotation most of 1983.

In August, after he'd won eight and lost 13 - and because he could become a free agent at the and of the season - the Tribe traded Barker to Atlanta.

It proved to be a great deal for Barker and the Indians (who got outfielder Brett Butler, third baseman Brook Jacoby and pitcher Rick Behenna) - but definitely not for Atlanta.

The Braves promptly signed Barker to a five-year $5-million contract but, as it turned out, they were badly short-changed in the deal.

Barker, won only 10 games while losing 20 for the Braves the next two-plus years, through 1985, and spent most of the last two seasons of his contract in the minors.

Finally, after a late-1987 chance with Milwaukee in which he won two games and lost one, Barker - the once perfect pitcher - was finished in baseball with a mediocre 74-76 lifetime record.

An unforgettable wild pitch

It's possible that the best thing that ever happened to Jack Graney was that he "beaned" Napoleon Lajoie, then the manager of the Cleveland club during spring training in 1908.

Otherwise, Graney, then a rookie pitcher, might never have made it to the big leagues. And if he hadn't, a generation of fans would not have had the chance to enjoy Graney's staccato accounts of Indians games on the radio from 1932 through 1953.

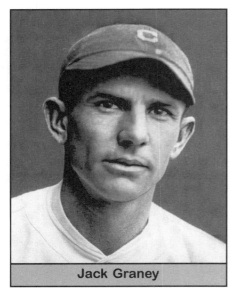
Jack Graney

As Graney, who died in 1978 at age 91, told the story: "I'd had a pretty good (pitching) record the year before (1907) in the New York State League, and I was determined to make an impression in batting practice.

"I did, but it wasn't the kind of impression I wanted, or the kind of impression that Lajoie appreciated. I wasn't content to just lob the ball up ... I wanted to put something on it, show the boys what I had.

"The result was that each hitter was up there about 15 minutes before he got four or five (pitches) he could have reached with a fishing rod, I was that wild. The fourth batter was the manager, Lajoie, who also played second base. I knew all about him ... every kid in America did.

"I was pretty cocky and had a crazy idea I could strike Lajoie out. So I wound up, reared back and cut loose with a fast ball that was supposed to go past him before he ever saw it. But it didn't. Though Larry (Lajoie's nickname) tried to duck, the ball hit him above the left ear and he went down like a load of bricks.

"Instead of striking him out, I knocked him out. And that evening I was told Lajoie wanted to see me. I went to his room and found him with an ice bag to his head. I started to tell him I was sorry, but he stopped me.

"He said, 'They tell me the place for wild men is out west. So, you're going west, kid, so far that if you went any farther your hat would float. Here's your railroad ticket.'"

Graney went to Portland of the Pacific Coast League where, because of his lack of control, he was switched to the outfield – "for humanity's sake," as one newspaper reported at the time.

By 1910, a year after Lajoie had stepped down as manager, Graney got another trial with Cleveland, this time as a good hitting outfielder. Graney took over as the team's left fielder and developed into one of the best in baseball the next 13 seasons. Graney also had the distinction of being the first batter to face Babe Ruth, then a rookie pitcher for Boston, in 1914.

And, in 1919, as the leadoff batter for the team then called the "Indians," Graney also was the first major leaguer to appear at the plate with a number on the back of his uniform.

Nine years after Graney retired in 1923 with a lifetime average of .250, he became the radio voice of the Indians.

"Billy Evans, then the Indians general manager, asked me if I wanted to try announcing," Graney said. "He took me into the radio booth at League Park, introduced me on the air, and then I was on the air."

Graney stayed on the air for 22 years - but it probably would not have happened if he hadn't tried to strike out his manager in 1908, and "beaned" him instead.

'Not for sale at any price'

Herb Score says he doesn't look back, that he doesn't think about what might have been.

But if he doesn't, many others do.

One of them was Bob Feller. "If Herb hadn't gotten hurt, he would have been as good as Sandy Koufax," Feller said of the misfortune that struck Score - and the Indians - in 1957.

The date was May 7.

Score, then the best young pitcher in baseball, fired his fast ball at Gil McDougald, the second batter in a game against the New York Yankees at the Stadium.

McDougald's bat flashed and the ball flew back at Score like a rocket.

Herb Score

It smashed with a sickening thud against Score's right eye. He went down as though he'd been shot. Blood spurted out of his eye, nose, mouth. He was hospitalized three weeks.

Score was fortunate in that the force of the blow didn't destroy his vision. Or even kill him. He recovered, but didn't pitch again that year. He did in 1958, but not as well as before.

And never as well again.

The rookie of the year in 1955 when he won 16 and lost 10, Score struck out a record 245 batters, and went 20-9 with 263 strikeouts in 1956. He was 2-1 when he was injured.

The next two seasons Score won 11 and lost 14. He was traded to Chicago on April 18, 1960 and his record was only 6-12 the next three seasons.

He retired in 1962 to the broadcasting booth - instead of going into the Hall of Fame as expected - with a lifetime record of 55-46. Score broadcasted Indians games until his retirement in 1997. He survived a severe truck-automobile accident in 1998.

Score wouldn't blame his pitching problems on the eye injury.

"I came back as good as ever," he says. "People forget that I tore a tendon in my elbow the next year (1958). 1 kept throwing with an arm that hurt and it just never came back.

"I could throw hard, but the ball didn't move as it had before. I guess because of the earlier pain I changed my motion and the ball straightened out."

The eye injury - or the torn tendon - made a prophet of Tris Speaker, then a member of the Indians front office.

"If nothing happens to Score, the kid has got to be the greatest," Speaker was quoted by Gordon Cobbledick in the Cleveland *Plain Dealer* only a week before the pitcher was hit in the eye.

Something else that happened in spring training that year serves as another footnote to the loss of the star pitcher.

On March 19, 1957, Boston General Manager Joe Cronin called his counterpart with the Indians, Hank Greenberg, and offered to buy Score's contract for $1-million.

Greenberg, who was part of the group that only three weeks earlier had bought the franchise for $3.9-million, told Cronin:

"We wouldn't sell Score for two million dollars. He's not for sale at any price."

The ever patient Senor

The irony of Al Lopez's resignation as manager of the Indians in 1956 came into sharper focus every year the team failed to contend for the pennant.

Lopez quit after six seasons, during which he compiled the best winning percentage of any manager in the history of the franchise, for a reason that was often hard to comprehend.

Al Lopez

Simply, the Indians were too successful during Lopez's tenure, though they won only one pennant under him, in 1954, when they set an American League record with 111 victories.

Fans complained that the Indians almost always finished second, that they couldn't beat New York.

Which was true. They were second five times - in 1951, 1952 and 1953, and again in 1955 and 1956 - on each occasion behind the hated Yankees.

"I could tell the fans were tired of it ... I decided maybe they needed a change," Lopez said a few years ago.

Lopez's Indians won 570 games and lost 354 for a .617 winning percentage. Only Oscar Vitt with a .570 percentage (262-198) from 1938-40 came close to being as successful, though Vitt wasn't in command for nearly as long.

Any doubt about Lopez's ability was dispelled after he left Cleveland and piloted the Chicago White Sox from 1957-65, and 1968-69. They also won one pennant and finished second five times.

When Lopez retired in 1969 his record as a manager in 17 years was 1,410-1,004, .584, 10th best of all-time.

That record and Lopez's nature belie the contention of Leo Durocher when he managed the Brooklyn Dodgers in the 1940s that "nice guys finish last."

Lopez, known as "the patient Senor," was one of the all-time favorites of club executives, players, the media and fans.

Twice Lopez reportedly rejected offers to manage the Yankees because he didn't want to replace his friend, Casey Stengel.

Elected to the Hall of Fame in 1977, Lopez also was one of the best and most durable catchers to ever strap on a chest protector.

Until Bob Boone topped him in 1987, Lopez held the major league record for catching most games, 1,918, in a playing career that began in 1928 in Brooklyn, and continued through 1947 in Cleveland.

Bill Veeck traded Gene Woodling to Pittsburgh on December 7, 1946 to get Lopez as a possible manager of the Indians the following year.

Those plans were aborted, however, when Cleveland fans voted overwhelmingly in a newspaper poll against Veeck's intention to trade shortstop-manager Lou Boudreau.

In 61 games in 1947, Lopez hit .262, one point over his 19-year career average, and then began his apprenticeship as a manager at the Tribe's Class AAA farm club at Indianapolis.

Three years later Lopez replaced Boudreau - and only Mike Hargrove came close to being as successful a manager of the Indians since then.

He was called "one of the most unusual ball players in the history of the game" in a Cleveland *Press* story, Dec. 15, 1954, and the description was accurate.

Ralph Kiner also was one of the greatest home run hitters of all-time.

It's a shame Kiner didn't play for the Indians before he did in 1955, the last season of his very productive, 10 year major league career.

Imagine what Kiner's 54 homers would have meant for the Indians in 1949, or the 114 homers Kiner hit from 1951 through 1953, when the Tribe finished second to New York each year.

Ralph Kiner

Instead, the former National League slugger, who was elected to the Baseball Hall of Fame in 1975, didn't make it to Cleveland until the end of his career, when his legs were gone and his back was stiff and sore.

The reason Kiner was called "unusual" had to do with his integrity and humility. When Kiner was acquired from the Chicago Cubs for two minor league players and $60,000, he immediately entered into salary negotiations with Hank Greenberg, then general manager of the Indians. He insisted upon a contract that called for a 40% salary cut amounting to $26,000 less than the $65,000 he made with the Cubs in 1954.

It was so unusual because, at that time, baseball's rules did not permit a major league club to cut a player more than 25 % from one season to the next. (The maximum cut has since been changed to 20%.)

But Kiner, who acknowledged, "Maybe I should go to a psychiatrist," said he was only trying to be fair. He hit .285 with 22 homers and 73 RBI for the Cubs in 1954. "This is not a grandstand play," he was quoted as saying. "I simply want to begin a career with a new team in a new league on a fresh basis. I want my performance with the Indians to determine my future salary."

Kiner's contract "demand" was so unusual, Greenberg needed permission from American League President William Harridge, who said the 40% cut would be OK if it was OK with the player. Which it was, of course, and Kiner played for $39,000 in 1955.

By today's standards, Kiner would be considered crazy, not merely unusual.

As it turned out, Kiner wasn't worth much more than he got - at least not then. He hit .243 with 18 homers and 54 RBI as the Indians failed to repeat as the A.L. champion, falling back into second place.

But if Kiner, the only player to lead a league in homers seven consecutive seasons, were in today's free agent market. with his 1954 career statistics - a nine-year total of 351 homers and batting average of .281 – the bidding for his services surely would begin around $5 million or $6 million a year, perhaps even more.

By late-August 1955, Kiner was discouraged and announced his intention to retire. "The time has come," he said then. "You can see it and I can see it, and I don't feel like prolonging it."

Fifteen years later Kiner looked back at 1955 and said he'd always remember his year in Cleveland. "It was the closest I came to being on a pennant winner and it was my biggest disappointment that we didn't win."

He truly was a very unusual player.

'Fat Pat,' everybody's favorite

Baseball fans called him "Fat Pat," but they did so with affection, not derision, because everybody loved James Patrick Seerey, despite his penchant for striking out.

Pat Seerey

Seerey fanned an average of once every 3.7 at-bats during his seven year major league career.

But he also was one of the strongest hitters in the game from 1943, when he came up with the Indians, through 1949.

When Seerey was traded to the Chicago White Sox on June 2, 1948, along with pitcher Al Gettel for outfielder Bob Kennedy, Ed McAuley wrote in the Cleveland *News*: "Seerey was at once the most frustrating and most fascinating character ever to wear the Cleveland uniform.

"He numbered his friends by the thousands and his critics by the tens of thousands. But even among the latter there was no real malice. They just couldn't stay mad at the guy.

"Pat's matchless color was recognized in every other city of the league as quickly as it was in Cleveland. The public address system never had to introduce him. His bulging biceps and the short sleeves twisted up around them; his long jaw and the wad of tobacco distending his cheek; his massive stomach - all these were his trademarks.

"But that big bat was the real secret of his appeal to the customers. Americans think in superlatives, and Pat could hit a baseball with more sheer line-drive force than anyone else in the history of the game. The late Harold Irelan, the Indians scout who discovered both Seerey and Lou Boudreau, predicted, 'Pat won't be a good hitter. He'll be one of the greatest hitters of all time.'"

It didn't turn out that way, of course. But the genial Irishman who was built like a fireplug - 5-9, 220 pounds - had his moments before he retired with a .224 lifetime average. Incredibly, more than one-fifth of his 406 hits were homers, 86 in all, including 26 in 1946.

As a "wartime" player his first three seasons (1943-45) with the Indians, Seerey never hit for a higher average than the .237 he posted in 1945, and it fell to .171 in 82 games in 1947, the year before the Indians finally - reluctantly - gave up on him.

Born on St. Patrick's Day in 1923, Seerey reached the pinnacle of his career six weeks after he was traded. It was, however, a very brief stay.

On July 18, 1948, Seerey hammered four homers in one game, an achievement duplicated by only four players previously, and only seven since.

Bill Veeck, then the owner of the Indians, tried virtually everything to make Seerey a more consistent hitter, without sacrificing his home run power.

One year Veeck hired Hall of Famer Rogers Hornsby as a personal tutor for Seerey, but to no avail.

Another time Veeck even separated Seerey from his roommate and best friend on the team, Jim Hegan, on the theory that the two players with hitting problems were mutually discouraging.

But that didn't work either and the Indians finally, reluctantly, gave up on Fat Pat.

"I hated to quit on him," Veeck was quoted then. "I have known only about five players with his color and possibilities." It could be added to Veeck's quote: "And few have come along since."

It was, and always will remain one of the great tragedies in baseball, though it could have been much worse.

When Ted Williams first saw Tony Horton hit a baseball in spring training in 1963, his only advice was no advice. "The kid is a natural," Williams said of Horton. "He has everything. Leave him alone. Don't fool with a swing like that."

Tony Horton

Williams was right. Horton did have everything, including, perhaps especially, a fierce determination to excel.

It might have been that fierce determination to excel that proved to be Horton's undoing.

On Aug. 28, 1970, the handsome, 25-year old first baseman who had everything, attempted suicide by slashing his wrists. Horton survived, but never played another game of baseball.

It was one of the saddest episodes in Indians history for many reasons, not the least of which was the fact that Horton failed because he wanted so badly to succeed. "I don't think I ever knew a more intense player than Tony Horton," said Gabe Paul, president of the Indians at the time.

When it happened, when Horton suffered the breakdown, he was hitting .269 with 17 homers and 59 RBI in 115 games, far below the standard he'd set for himself.

Details of Horton's attempted suicide were never revealed and the Indians simply announced that he was ill, leaving the impression that his status was the usual "day-to-day."

But Horton never came back. In the three decades since his breakdown, Horton literally dropped out of sight - and memory - after returning to his home in California where it all began for him as a high school all-sports phenom in the early-1960s.

Tony was offered dozens of college scholarships and finally chose the University of Southern California. But before his college classes began, Horton played sandlot baseball and was scouted by the Boston Red Sox, who offered him $125,000 to sign.

He accepted and two years later Horton made his major league debut, though he wouldn't be there to stay until 1967 when he was traded to the Indians on June 4, with Don Demeter for Gary Bell.

Horton blossomed in 1969, hitting .278 with 27 homers and 93 RBI. The following winter he held out for $65,000, which was $19,000 more than was offered by manager Alvin Dark, who then negotiated Tribe contracts.

Dark wouldn't yield, citing the availability of Ken Harrelson to play first base if Horton continued to hold out. On March 18, 1970, Horton finally, reluctantly, capitulated. He had no choice. In those days management was all-powerful. And then fate struck Horton and the Indians a cruel blow.

Harrelson broke his leg the very next day. His injury absence would have provided all the leverage Horton would have needed to win his holdout. It might have been what pushed Horton over the edge.

Nobody tried harder, or worked more diligently than Horton.

And nobody put more pressure on himself than Tony Horton, who wanted to bat 1.000, and refused to accept that nobody could.

Only a footnote in history

Baseball fans - especially Cleveland baseball fans - little noted nor long remembered Jerry Kenney.

He was a utility player of marginal ability who came to the Indians in a November 1972 trade with the Now York Yankees that featured five others, all of greater renown.

Jerry Kenney

In that deal, third baseman Graig Nettles and catcher Gerry Moses were sent to the Yankees for Kenney, outfielders Charlie Spikes and Rusty Torres, and catcher John Ellis.

Kenney didn't do much for the Indians and didn't last long with them.

But he would have been one of baseball's most famous - or infamous – people in the game if he had heeded the advice of Marvin Miller, then executive director of the Players Association.

Instead, the notoriety Kenney would have received went to Andy Messersmith and Dave McNally.

Messersmith and McNally are credited (though blamed by the owners) for breaking, in 1975, a key portion of baseball's long standing reserve system that bound a player to a team as long as it wanted his services.

Messersmith's and McNally's victory resulted in the players gaining the right to become free agents after six seasons in the major leagues.

It also led to the escalation of salaries from an average of about $45,000 in 1975, to more than $1.2 million and climbing.

Kenney, at Miller's urging, had the opportunity in the spring of 1973 to do what Messersmith and McNally did two years later, though he backed out at the last moment.

It involved the interpretation of the "renewal clause" in baseball's standard player contract which gives a team the right to renew an unsigned player's contract without his approval for one year.

Prior to the Messersmith-McNally test case it had been assumed - because management said it was so - that clubs could invoke the renewal clause year after year after year, even if the player never re-signed a new contract. It was Miller's contention, subsequently upheld by arbitrator Peter Seitz, that the renewal clause was valid for only one year.

After Seitz's ruling, a revision in the reserve clause was forced upon the owners.

The reason Kenney could have done what Messersmith and McNally did is because he refused to sign the 1973 contract General Manager Phil Seghl offered.

Miller urged him to challenge the system and, initially, Kenney agreed to do so.

However, shortly before the March 10 deadline, Kenney capitulated.

Thus, Miller had to wait two years to find somebody else unhappy enough - and more determined than Kenney - to challenge the system.

Messersmith and McNally were, and prevailed.

As for Kenney, whose lifetime statistics show that he batted .237 in 465 major league games over parts of six seasons, his career with the Indians didn't last long.

He was released less than a month into the 1973 season, becoming only a footnote in baseball history, instead of the notorious rebel who broke the system.

Sometimes the grass isn't greener

More than anything, it was a matter of economics that led to the trading of Kenny Lofton to the Atlanta Braves on March 25, 1997.

And, also more than anything, it was a matter of competitiveness, and the willingness to pay the price to win, that brought Lofton back to the Indians on Dec. 8, 1997, less than nine months after he all but forced the deal that sent him to the Braves.

Early in 1997, after five splendid seasons with the Indians, during which he batted a cumulative .316 in 680 games, Lofton made it clear to General Manager John Hart that he expected to be well compensated – actually, *better* compensated – than the Indians were willing to pay.

Lofton was to receive $4.75 million in 1997, the last season of a four year contract, and rejected the Indians' five-year, $45 million offer because he wanted $11 million a season.

That dialogue transpired shortly after Albert Belle also had priced himself off the Indians roster and signed a five-year, $55 million contract with the Chicago White Sox, making him the highest paid player in the history of baseball at that time.

And so, Hart, preaching fiscal responsibility, pulled the blockbuster trade that sent Lofton and young relief pitcher Alan Embree to the Braves, in exchange for outfielders Marquis Grissom and David Justice.

Kenny Lofton

It was a deal that shocked everybody, including – perhaps most of all – Lofton.

"I've done everything they've asked me to do in Cleveland, and I thought I would be rewarded," he said in *USA Today*. "I guess they rewarded me by trading me."

Maybe so. But, significantly, not only did the deal shock Lofton, apparently it also awakened him.

He played out the final year of his contract with the Braves in 1997, batting .333 in 122 games, during which, according to published reports, he had fallen into disfavor with Manager Bobby Cox as well as some of his teammates.

When the season ended, Lofton jumped at the opportunity to return to Cleveland. Apparently so eager was he to rejoin the Tribe, Lofton signed for $24 million over three years, with a club option for 2001 worth $8 million - considerably less than his asking price a year earlier.

"You've got to look at it as being happy," Lofton was quoted in the Cleveland *Plain Dealer.* "To me, it's like I never left. It's like I was a ghost for a year. A lot of times you think the grass is greener on the other side of the mountain. But then you get there and it's not.

"All I can say is that Atlanta was different. I can be myself here (in Cleveland). In Atlanta, I didn't say much. I knew a couple of guys on the team, but I never said much."

To make room on the roster and in the budget for Lofton, the Indians traded Grissom and his $4.85 million salary to Milwaukee (along with pitcher Jeff Juden, for pitchers Ben McDonald, Mike Fetters and Ron Villone, all of whom subsequently also were dealt away).

And so, it was a matter of economics, as well as ability that sent Lofton packing – and in the end, brought him back.

Such is baseball in the era of free agency and mega-buck contracts.

The 'hot-dog' first baseman

He was an unabashed "hot-dog," a "show-boat," in the vernacular of baseball.

But Vic Power also was a very good baseball player for the Indians from 1958-61, during his 12 year major league career that began with the Philadelphia Athletics in 1954.

Vic Power

Power came to Cleveland (with outfielder Woodie Held) for outfielder Roger Maris, who was then a young prospect, pitcher Dick Tomanek and first baseman Preston Ward. The deal was made a few hours before the trading deadline on June 15, 1958, and Power later played for Minnesota, the then-Los Angeles Angels, Philadelphia Phillies and again with the California Angels, until his retirement after the 1965 season.

His antics on the field infuriated baseball purists, including then-Chicago White Sox manager Al Lopez, who once had to be restrained from going after Power during a game at the old Stadium in 1959. On another occasion Power tried to go into the stands at the Stadium to fight a heckling fan, who turned out to be Woody Hayes, then-Ohio State's football coach. He also had an on-field altercation with then-Boston center fielder Jim Piersall, among others who resented his flamboyant style.

Needless to say, Power's career – during which he batted .284 with 126 home runs, made the all-star team four times, and won seven Gold Glove awards - was seldom tranquil. His best year was 1955 when he batted .319 for the Athletics, then in Kansas City.

The highlight of Power's 3 ½ seasons with the Indians occurred on Aug. 14, 1958, against Detroit at the Stadium, when he did something that hadn't been accomplished in the major leagues since 1927. Power stole home twice in the same game, in the eighth and tenth innings, the latter giving the Tribe a 10-9 victory.

As the Cleveland *Plain Dealer* reported the next day, Power's two thefts of the plate made it one of the most thrilling games ever played. His first steal of the plate came after he'd singled to drive in a run that broke a 7-7 tie, advanced to third on a subsequent hit, and raced home as Detroit pitcher Bill Fischer took a full windup. "It was easy," Power was quoted. "I got a good jump."

After the Tigers tied the score, Power lashed his third hit as the game went into extra innings, again advanced to third with two out, and dashed home with Rocky Colavito at the plate with a 2-and-1 count against Frank Lary.

Of his penchant for making one-handed catches – for which he was ridiculed by critics – Power once said, "If God wanted players to catch with two hands, he would have put gloves on both hands."

He was proud of his versatility, having played every position except pitcher and catcher in the major leagues, after being traded by the Indians (with pitcher Dick Stigman) on Aug. 2, 1962 to the Twins in a deal for pitcher Pedro Ramos. Power also took credit for the single season home run record Maris set with 61 in 1961, breaking the mark that had been held by Babe Ruth in 1927.

"If it wasn't for me," Power said in a recent article in the *Plain Dealer*, "Maris wouldn't have beaten Ruth. He would have played in Cleveland where it was hard to hit homers. When Kansas City traded him to New York, he had that short right field in Yankee Stadium."

The snowball that ended a career

It happened in the winter of 1962-63, when Wynn Hawkins returned to his home in New Waterford, Ohio from the Army It was a year after Hawkins had established himself as an outstanding pitching prospect for the Indians and the future looked bright for the right-hander.

He'd been an outstanding high school athlete, and a basketball star at Baldwin-Wallace College where he set a career scoring record of 1,175 points in just three seasons, from 1954-57. Hawkins was ruled ineligible for his senior year because he'd been playing minor league baseball for the Indians, who gave him a $4,000 bonus to sign in 1955.

In those days a professional in one sport was considered by the NCAA to be a professional in all sports.

Hawkins progressed through the Indians farm system and, after going 14-9 at Mobile (Ala.) of the Class AA Southern Association, made it to the varsity in 1960.

Wynn Hawkins

He won seven games as a spot starter in 1961, but then the Army beckoned and Hawkins was called to active duty during what was then the "Berlin Crisis." After a year in the service, Hawkins returned to civilian life and, with the tantalizing forkball he'd developed, figured prominently in the Indians' plans for 1963 under new manager Birdie Tebbetts.

Hawkins was shoveling snow in his driveway in New Waterford, that day in December 1962, when a couple of neighborhood kids threw snowballs at him.

"I fired one back and felt something pop in my shoulder," Hawkins recalled in a newspaper article several years ago. "I didn't think much of it at the time, and even though I had some pain the next day, it wasn't bad. I thought it would go away."

But it didn't. The pain persisted when spring training started in March.

The Indians doctors told Hawkins he'd torn a tendon in his shoulder. "They said an operation might be successful, but there was no assurance, no guaranty," he said. So, Hawkins decided against surgery.

"I thought I could pitch through the pain," he said. But he couldn't. Rest didn't help either.

Hawkins tried a comeback in the Class AAA Pacific Coast League in 1964, but it was no use. "I could hardly pick up a cup of coffee without my shoulder hurting, and by then it was too late to consider surgery," he said.

And so, Hawkins' once-promising pitching career was finished, reduced to less than three full seasons and a 12-13 record.

The Indians kept Hawkins on the payroll as a farm system administrator and scout, and he always hoped his shoulder would get better. But it never did. In 1969, when popular traveling secretary Charlie Morris died suddenly in spring training, Hawkins took over that job and did it well for two years.

Then, in a budget crunch in 1971, with the Indians struggling on the field and at the box office, Hawkins was let go. His duties as traveling secretary were taken over by coach Bobby Hofman and trainer Jim Warfield.

And with that, Hawkins, once a brilliant pitching prospect, was finished in baseball - primarily because of a snowball he'd thrown 10 years earlier.

Rudy, the 'red hot rapper'

It was the kind of spring training that players only dream about. Especially rookies trying to make a big league team.

It also was the kind of spring training that almost nobody ever has. Especially rookies. But Rudy

Rudy Regalado

Regalado did, in 1954, the year the Indians won the pennant and set an American League record with 111 victories.

"It was amazing ... I couldn't do anything wrong, at least until the season started," Regalado once recalled. "I don't know what happened, why everything I did was so good. If I knew, I would have kept doing it."

Regalado wasn't even on the Indians roster that spring. It was only Rudy's second season of professional baseball and he was ticketed for a return to the minors, probably to Reading, Pa. of the Class A Eastern League, or possibly Indianapolis, Ind. of the Class AAA American Association.

Regalado, whose home was in San Diego, was in Tucson, Ariz. because he'd asked General Manager Hank Greenberg if it'd be OK to stop by to pick up some tips from the big leaguers on his way to the Tribe's minor league camp in Daytona Beach, Fla.

As fate would have it, when it came time for the Indians to play their first intrasquad game, they needed a second baseman because Bobby Avila was late reporting for spring training from his home in Mexico.

So, even though Regalado was a third baseman, Manager Al Lopez played him at second and, in Rudy's words, "I hit the ball well." Oh, did he ever.

And Regalado never stopped hitting the ball "well" that spring, which is what he meant when he said it was "amazing," that he "couldn't do anything wrong."

For a whole month he couldn't do anything wrong. And in that month, Regalado became a living legend, earning the nickname, "Rudy, the red-hot rapper."

Regalado hit .447 with 11 homers that spring and, when it came time to break camp and open the 1954 American League season, he was signed to a major league contract. To get Regalado's hot bat in the lineup, Lopez switched All-Star third baseman Al Rosen to first.

But reality soon set in and, unfortunately, Regalado turned out to have been only a mirage in the Arizona desert.

Just as Regalado didn't know what caused him to hit so well in spring training, nobody - especially Regalado - could figure out what caused him to revert to normalcy when the season began.

By midseason Regalado, struggling with a .250 average and two homers in 65 games, was on the bench, Rosen was on third and newly-acquired Vic Wertz at first bass.

Regalado returned to Tucson the following spring, hoping to rediscover the success he'd found the year before and regain a regular position. But then - as mysteriously as he'd burst into stardom in 1954 - his batting eye failed in 1955.

Soon Rudy, no longer the red-hot rapper, was back in the minors. He got another trial with the Indians in 1956, but again the magic was missing, and four years later he was out of baseball.

It was - and always will be - one of the great mysteries in Indians history.

"**I**'ve made that play hundreds of times. It's an easy play. You take a couple of steps to your right, pick up the ball and just sort of flip it side-arm to first base.

"But that time it sailed … it sailed right over Tom McCraw's head."

The quotes belong to Dick Bosman and "that time" was the play that deprived him what would have been the eighth perfect game in the major leagues since 1901.

The date was July 19, 1974, and the Indians were playing Oakland in the old Cleveland Stadium.

"Sure, a perfect game would have been great, but it was still a no-hitter," said Bosman, who retired after a 4-2 won-lost season with the Athletics in 1976, and became a pitching coach, first with Baltimore and then with Texas.

The ball Bosman threw over McCraw's head was hit by Sal Bando, who went to second on the error, and was the only Oakland batter to reach base in the game.

"I'm sorry I made the error, but, hey, it was only the fourth inning and nobody was thinking about a no-hitter, let alone a perfect game at that point. I certainly wasn't."

An inning earlier the Indians had scored twice against Dave Hamilton, and added two more runs in the bottom of the fourth that

Dick Bosman

Bosman protected for a 4-0 victory. It kept the Indians in third place, only three games out of first.

"We were still in the race and it was exciting," said Bosman, whose record at the time was 2-0. It was only his fifth start after having been banished to the bull pen for ineffectiveness.

"My back was against the wall. I hadn't been pitching well and I had to turn it around," said Bosman, who came to the Indians from Texas (nee Washington Senators) on May 10, 1973 (with out-fielder Ted Ford in a trade for pitcher Steve Dunning).

Bosman's no-hitter, the 13th of 15 by Tribe pitchers in 99 seasons, was the highlight of his 11 year major league career, which began in 1966 with the Senators.

He was traded by the Indians (with pitcher Jim Perry) to Oakland for pitcher John "Blue Moon" Odom and cash on May 20, 1975.

It was another of the deals in that era that did not turn out well for the Indians.

In his no-hitter, Bosman made only 79 pitches, including 60 for strikes, and the Athletics had only two hard hit balls. In the fifth, Joe Rudi smashed a grounder toward the hole on the left side of the infield that was backhanded by shortstop Frank Duffy, whose throw to first was in time. And in the eighth, Pat Borque blasted a long drive to right that Charlie Spikes caught on the warning track.

When Bosman took the mound for the last of the ninth, he was given a standing ovation by the 24,302 fans in the Stadium. He responded by retiring Dick Green on a grounder to third baseman Buddy Bell, and Jesus Alou, batting for Larry Haney, on a grounder to second baseman Jack Brohamer.

Then he finished with a flourish, striking out Billy North to cap the game, undoubtedly the best of the 82 victories (with 85 losses) in Bosman's 11 year major league career – although it would have been even better with a more accurate throw on that "easy" play he'd made "hundreds of times" on other occasions, before and after.

The $250 temper tantrum

If he were playing today, Johnny Allen most definitely would be considered one of baseball's premier pitchers.

He also would be paid much - make that *very much* - more than his top salary of $20,000, which made him the second highest paid pitcher in baseball in 1938.

Johnny Allen

That was the season after Allen, a right-hander with a flaming fast ball and temper to match, went 15-1, setting an American League record that since has been tied but not broken.

Allen won 17 consecutive games, including his final two in 1936 and 15 straight in 1937, before losing - with only two days' rest - a 1-0 heart-breaker to Detroit on the final day of the season.

Unfortunately for Allen, who died in 1959 at age 55, he is better remembered by longtime Indians fans for something other than his commendable major league career record of 142 victories and 75 defeats over 13 seasons.

Allen began with the New York Yankees in 1932, was traded to the Indians four years later, and also pitched for the St. Louis Browns, Brooklyn Dodgers and New York Giants from 1941 until he retired in 1945.

It was in 1938, his third of five seasons with the Indians - for whom his record was 67-34 - that Allen gained lasting notoriety, primarily because of his torrid temper. During a game at Boston's Fenway Park on June 7, Red Sox batters complained they were being distracted because the right sleeve of Allen's undershirt was torn and tattered, and flapped everytime he made a pitch. They asked umpire Bill McGowan to order Allen to change his undershirt.

McGowan did, but Allen wouldn't.

McGowan was adamant; but so was Allen.

Finally the pitcher stalked off the mound and into the dugout runway to the clubhouse - but never returned to the field. Manager Oscar Vitt promptly fined Allen $250 for his walkout, and Allen retaliated by vowing that he'd never pitch for the Indians again.

It required the intervention of Indians owner Alva Bradley - and the Higbee Co., then Cleveland's largest department store - to get Allen back on the team.

Bradley, who owned the Indians from 1928 until he sold to Bill Veeck on June 21, 1946, made a deal with Higbees.

Higbees agreed to buy Allen's undershirt with the torn and tattered right sleeve for $250 - which, coincidentally, of course, was the exact amount that Allen was fined.

And so, Allen relented, but not until he got the money in hand. Higbees then dressed a mannequin in Allen's uniform - and undershirt - and displayed it in the store's window on Public Square. Presumably, Higbees recouped the money because so many people flocked to the store to see the display.

And Allen, of course, was happy, too, because he'd defied the establishment and prevailed.

Unfortunately, the "undershirt controversy" has become Allen's more lasting epitaph than his 20 victories for the Indians in 1936, his 15-1 mark in 1937 - or even his record 17 consecutive victories over two seasons – notwithstanding.

It was Joe Vosmik's blond hair and classic good looks that got him a contract with the Indians in 1929, and it was his bat and style of play - as well as his handsomeness - that enabled him to become one of the team's best and most popular players.

Vosmik hit .300 six times in his 13 year major league career, and came within .0006 percentage points of winning the American League batting championship in 1935.

A native Clevelander, Vosmik went 1-for-4 in the final game of that 1935 season, but Buddy Myer, a second baseman for the Washington Senators, went 4-for-5 that day, to win the title.

Myer finished with a .349025 average, while Vosmik's was .348387 with a league-leading 216 hits in 620 at-bats.

The Indians' decision to sign Vosmik off the local sandlots was interesting, as reported in the Cleveland *News* in 1937.

Joe Vosmik

"Billy Evans, then general manager of the Indians, had promised officials of Cleveland's amateur baseball program that he would farm out several of the city's best-looking prospects. He agreed to make his selections from an all-star (amateur) game at League Park."

According to the account in the *News*, "Evans watched the performances from the grandstand, in attendance with his wife. On the spur of the moment, he turned to Mrs. Evans and asked, 'Which of those players do you like?' She answered, 'That good looking blond Viking over there.'"

It was Vosmik, then a member of the Rotbart Jewelers amateur team.

The next day he was signed to a 1929 contract to play for Frederick, Md. of the (Class D) Blue Ridge League, and Vosmik's career was under way - thanks to Mrs. Evans.

Vosmik hit .381 in 112 games at Frederick, and .397 the next season at Terre Haute, Ind. of the Class D Three-I League. He was promoted to Cleveland where he played with distinction the next six years, earning the adulation of Tribe fans. Vosmik was the left fielder, with Earl Averill in center and Dick Porter in right, forming what many consider to have been the Indians' all-time best outfield.

As an interesting aside to the Vosmik-Averill-Porter triumvirate, Lefty Weisman, then the Indians trainer, named one of his sons "Jed" as a tribute to the outfielders. The boy's name was a combination of the first initials of the first names - Joe, Earl and Dick - of Vosmik, Averill and Porter.

Cleveland fans were outraged when the Indians traded Vosmik to the St. Louis Browns on Jan. 17, 1937 (with pitcher Oral Hildebrand and infielder Billy Knickerbocker for pitcher Ivy Paul Andrews, infielder Lyn Lary and outfielder Julius Solters).

Some were so angry, in fact, they threatened to boycott Indians games that season.

Vosmik played well for the Browns, hitting .325 in 1937, but was traded to the Boston Red Sox in 1938 and again led the AL in hits with 201. He slumped to .276 in 1939 and was dealt to Brooklyn the following season.

Then, obviously, Vosmik's good looks weren't enough to prolong his career. He was released after 25 games in 1941 and got one more chance with Washington in 1944. He remained with the Senators for just 14 games and retired with a .307 lifetime average. Vosmik died in 1962 at the age of 51.

The rebellious rookie outfielder

It didn't create the controversy that resulted when Rocky Colavito was traded to Detroit in 1960, but an earlier deal - also with the Tigers - was resented almost as much.

The Indians sent Earl Averill to Detroit on June 14, 1939, and the customers were outraged.

Earl Averill

"Averill was as popular with the fans as he was unpopular with the front office," the Cleveland *Press* reported that day.

Averill had come to the Indians in 1929 in what was then a very big deal; he was purchased for $40,000 and two players from the Pacific Coast League San Francisco Seals.

When he joined the Tribe, Averill immediately demanded - and received - a $5,000 bonus. "If I'm worth $40,000 in cash, I'm worth $5,000 for myself," he argued.

And when Alva Bradley, then the Indians owner, saw Averill, he asked General Manager Billy Evans, "You mean we paid all that money for a midget!"

Averill, in his very first at-bat, homered and went on to hit .332 that season. He also was a great center fielder, probably second best (to only Tris Speaker) in Tribe history.

But Averill really fell from favor with Bradley when he held out after the 1936 season, when he almost won the American League batting championship with a .378 average and led the league with 15 triples.

Averill wanted a $2,000 raise over the $14,000 he'd been paid, and Bradley was outraged.

Finally Averill agreed on a contract that would pay him $15,000, plus a $2,000 bonus if he had a good year.

"It will be a $1,000 gamble on my part either way," Averill was quoted in a Cleveland *Plain Dealer* story on March 13, 1937. "If I accept the straight $16,000 (salary) offer it may ultimately turn out that I lost a thousand dollars. On the other hand if I accept the bonus contract and fail to collect at the end of the season, I will lose the same amount."

Which he did, because of the standards of the day.

Averill hit 21 homers in 1937, but his average fell to .299 and the rift between him and the front office worsened.

As Bradley said after Averill was dealt to Detroit: "Earl was dissatisfied ... he went on record early in the season to the effect that he would like to be traded."

The Indians got pitcher Harry Eisenstat in exchange, and Averill's career declined in Detroit. He retired in 1941.

But Averill is still the Indians franchise leader in five offensive categories: runs batted in, 1,084; runs scored, 1,154; triples, 121; total bases, 3,200, and extra base hits, 724. His former team record of 226 home runs was wiped out in 1996 by Albert Belle, who holds the record with 242.

Averill was elected to the Hall of Fame in 1975, and his uniform No. 3 is one of six retired by the Indians (the others being Lou Boudreau's No. 5, Larry Doby's No. 14, Mel Harder's No. 18, Bob Feller's No. 19, and Bob Lemon's No. 21).

Not bad for a guy who was considered a rebellious malcontent.

The slogan could not have been more appropriate: "Win plenty with Sam Dente."

And win plenty the Indians did with Dente, their jack-of-all-trades infielder in1954, when they set an American League record with 111 victories, and won the franchise's third pennant.

Dente was no superstar. Far from it. But he played everywhere in the infield, anywhere the Indians needed him. And he hit, too.

In 68 games in1954, Dente batted .266 as a sometimes replacement for third baseman Al Rosen, shortstop George Strickland and second baseman Bobby Avila.

Sam Dente

The only positions Dente was unwilling – or unable – to play were pitcher and catcher, though he was ready to get behind the plate once. "I was saved when we didn't need a pinch hitter," he was quoted in a newspaper article at the time.

"It takes a player with remarkable temperament and ability to do what Sam did for us (in 1954)," Manager Al Lopez praised the unheralded utility infielder. "And Dente was remarkable."

Remarkable, too, in retrospect, was the Indians ability to acquire Dente.

He was purchased from the Chicago White Sox for the waiver price in May 1953, and assigned to the Indians' top farm club at the time, Indianapolis of the Class AAA American Association.

Given a chance with the Indians the following spring, Dente not only won a place on the roster, he soon became a key man in the Tribe's pennant drive.

"I guess I have Cooch (Indians coach, Tony Cuccinello) to thank," Dente said of the opportunity he got in Cleveland.

Cuccinello remembered Dente when he was with the White Sox in 1951 and he was a key man as Chicago swept a series from the Indians.

"For 10 days Dente can be as tough at bat as anybody, and his glove always is as good as anybody's," Cuccinello said in his endorsement of the utility infielder.

Actually, baseball wasn't even Dente's best game. Soccer was.

From the time he was 16 in 1938, until Dente was 21 and concentrated on baseball, he played halfback for the Scots-Americans of Kearney, N.J., which won the national championship each year.

With the exception of the World Series, when the Indians were swept by the New York Giants, that 1954 season always will be the high point of Dente's otherwise unspectacular career.

He broke in with the Boston Red Sox in 1947, was part of a five player deal that sent him to the St. Louis Browns in 1948,was traded to Washington in l949 and played every game for the Senators for two years, hitting .273 in 1949 and .239 in 1950, and went to the White Sox in 1952, before the Indians purchased his contract a year later.

Dente played in 745 games in his nine year major league career. After hitting .257 in 73 games in 1955, Dente retired with a lifetime batting average of .252.

They're not Hall of Fame credentials, to be sure.

But in 1954, when the Indians needed to win plenty to win the pennant, they probably could not have done so without Sam Dente.

Hell knows no fury ...

It's been said that "hell knows no fury like a woman scorned." It's also true that hell knows no fury like an Indians fan scorned, at least not in the case of Albert Belle.

Belle was a Tribe favorite from the time he burst into stardom in Cleveland in 1991 and led the team into the postseason playoffs for the first time in 41 years in 1995, until he left as a free agent in 1997 for what was then the largest contract in baseball history.

Albert Belle

When Belle returned to Jacobs Field wearing a Chicago White Sox uniform, not only was he booed, the fans also threw coins at him to show their displeasure. It got so bad that Belle, as a member of the American League team for the 1997 All-Star Game held in Cleveland, refused to play.

All of which was unfortunate as Belle, before his defection, came through the ranks of the Indians since his selection in the second round of the 1987 draft, and was treated well despite numerous transgressions by the temperamental outfielder.

On one occasion in 1991, in a fit of anger, Belle threw a baseball at a heckling fan in the stands, hitting the man in the chest. Another time he struck a photographer in the hand with a thrown baseball in 1996 because he objected to his picture being taken. It led to a lawsuit that eventually was settled for an unannounced, but reportedly "hefty" sum. Belle also wound up in court and was sued for $850,000 by the guardian of a boy he chased with a car and allegedly injured in 1995, after a Halloween prank.

The Indians benched Belle several times for disciplinary reasons, and also suspended him for "lack of effort" and other similar offenses, but always forgave him.

He was ordered to undergo anger counseling by American League president Dr. Gene Budig after colliding with, and intentionally injuring Milwaukee Brewers second baseman Fernando Vina in 1995.

And, during a game in Chicago in 1994, Belle was caught using an illegal, corked bat and was handed a 10 game suspension (later reduced to seven games).

Originally known as "Joey" his first four seasons in the minor leagues, Belle announced in 1990, while playing for Canton-Akron of the Class AA Eastern League, that he was changing his name to Albert after undergoing treatment for alcoholism at the Cleveland Clinic.

But, despite his personality problems, there was no doubting Belle's ability as one of the game's all-time greatest hitters. After brief trials with the Tribe in 1989 and 1990, he smashed 28 homers and drove in 95 runs in 123 games with the Indians in 1991. In his five ensuing seasons in Cleveland, from 1992-96, Belle hammered 34, 38, 36, 50 (most in the A.L.) and 48 homers, for a total of 242, a club record. His 751 RBI are eighth most in franchise history.

When Belle's contract with the Indians expired after the 1996 season, he eventually signed a five year, $55 million pact with the White Sox. The contract also gave Belle the right to become a free agent if he did not continue to be among the top three highest paid players in the game.

When he no longer commanded the largest salary with the White Sox (after hitting .274 and .328 in 1997 and 1998), Belle became a free agent again and signed with Baltimore for $60 million over five years in 1999. He batted .297 with 37 homers and 117 RBI.

Much was made of the fact that Jim Thome set a new Indians record - albeit a *negative* one - when he struck out 171 times in 494 official at-bats in 1999.

It came close to the American League record of 186 held by Milwaukee's Rob Deer in 1987, which was only three fewer than the major league record of 189 set by Bobby Bonds of San Francisco in 1970.

Nothing much was mentioned then, however - and seldom is - about the record for the *fewest* strikeouts in a season, which is much more significant.

Joe Sewell, the diminutive shortstop who joined the Indians after the tragic death of Ray Chapman in 1920, is baseball's all-time leader with statistics that are truly amazing.

Sewell played 14 years in the big leagues, 10 of them with the Indians after the final 22 games in 1920, and it's doubtful his records will ever be matched.

A left-handed hitter, Sewell struck out just four times in 608 at-bats in 1925, an average of once every 152 trips to the plate, and only 114 times in 7,132 total official appearences in his entire career!

For comparative purposes, consider that Thome, in his six full and two partial seasons with the Indians (through 1999) made 3,077 official plate appearances and struck out 882 times, an average of once every 3.49 at-bats.

Joe Sewell

More on Sewell: recent research has discovered that one of his strikeouts in 1923 should have been charged to third baseman Rube Lutzke. It reduces Sewell's career total to 113.

Amazing, too, is that Sewell, while not a free swinger, wasn't a slap hitter either.

Sewell hit 49 homers in his career, including 11 for the New York Yankees in 1932, a year after he was released by the Indians. His lifetime average was a very good .312.

Without Sewell, the Tribe probably would not have won the 1920 pennant after Chapman was killed.

Until Chapman was killed, a utility infielder named Harry Lunte was his immediate successor, and then outfielder Doc Evans was tried at shortstop.

But the team slumped and owner Jim Dunn recommended the promotion of Sewell from New Orleans, then a Tribe farm club. Manager Tris Speaker initially resisted Dunn's advice, according to Franklin Lewis' book, *The Cleveland Indians*, published in 1949.

Finally Speaker relented. But only after long consideration.

"Let's gamble on anything now ... we've got to have some help to win this race, and anyone is better than no shortstop at all," Speaker was quoted as saying.

It was a very costly deal because, based on the rules in effect then, the Indians had to pay the New Orleans club $6,000 cash, and give up rights of option on all of the minor league team's players. But it also proved to be a valuable deal for the Indians as Sewell became the catalyst, the unsung hero of 1920.

Sewell hit .329 the rest of the season, and his fielding was near-flawless as the Indians won their first pennant with a 98-56 record, beating Chicago by two games, and then winning the World Series against Brooklyn.

A testament of courage

Al Rosen once called Paul O'Dea "the greatest natural hitter I ever saw."

Which is quite a compliment, coming from the likes of Rosen, who was a great hitter himself.

Unfortunately for the Indians, Paul O'Dea was never able to prove to others what Rosen had seen in him.

Paul O'Dea

In one terribly cruel instant in spring training, on March 21, 1940, Paul O'Dea's promising baseball career was all but ended, shattered by a batting practice accident that had never occurred previously and hasn't happened since.

As O'Dea stood near the edge of the batting cage in the Indians training camp at Ft. Myers, Fla., awaiting his turn to hit, he leaned around the protective screen to pick up a ball that had been fouled off.

In that moment the batter, a fellow rookie named Lou Kahn, swung at a pitch and lined it squarely into O'Dea's face.

Squarely in O'Dea's right eye, to be precise.

The force of the blow destroyed O'Dea's vision in the eye and, for a man of lesser character, would have ended any hope for a baseball career.

But not Paul O'Dea, who had grown up on Cleveland's west side, starred in baseball, basketball and football at West Technical High School, and signed a Tribe minor league contract at the age of 17 in 1937.

Two years later O'Dea got the trial with the Indians that turned into disaster. But he refused to quit, though it took time and several operations before he could play again.

Being a left-handed batter, O'Dea had to adjust his hitting style to utilize his good left eye, and launched a comeback on the Cleveland sandlots in 1942.

He was back in the minors in 1943, and rejoined the Indiana in 1944, becoming their regular right fielder, though he was not the same hitter as before the accident when he saw the ball with two good eyes instead of only one.

Still, O'Dea impressed everybody who saw him perform. "It's simply remarkable the way that boy hits the ball," the legendary Connie Mack was quoted as saying after seeing O'Dea play a game against the Philadelphia Athletics.

And Lou Boudreau, then the manager of the Indians, said, "The kid is a marvel," when O'Dea returned to the team in 1944. That was the season O'Dea hit .318, an eloquent testament to O'Dea's courage, determination and perseverance.

Imagine what the future might have held for O'Dea - and the Indians - but for that terribly cruel instant in spring training 1940 when he leaned around the corner of the batting cage and was struck in the eye with a batted ball.

Unfortunately, despite O'Dea's courageous attempt to do with one eye what most men can't do with two, he struggled with a .235 average in 87 games in 1945.

And when the stars returned from World War II in 1946, O'Dea's playing career ended. He took a front office job with the Indians and, until his death in 1978, was one of their best scouts - always trying to find another Paul O'Dea.

Dennis Eckersley came to the Indians in 1975 as a free-spirited, brash young pitcher the "experts" figured wouldn't last long, that his arm would blow out eventually because of what they perceived to be an unorthodox delivery.

But it wasn't until 24 years later that Eckersley finally hung up his spikes at age 44, after pitching the most games in major league history, 1,071, for five different teams, Boston, the Chicago Cubs, Oakland and St. Louis, in addition to Cleveland.

Dennis Eckersley

Actually, Eckersley had two careers in the big leagues, 13 years as a starter for the Indians, Red Sox and Cubs, and then, after winning a battle with alcohol, 11 years as one of the most dominating relievers the game has seen. "It's hard to walk away," Eckersley said on Dec. 10, 1998, as he announced his retirement. "Baseball has been a major part of my life since I was eight years old."

He was a No. 3 pick of the Indians in the 1972 amateur draft, and made it to Cleveland by way of Reno of the Class A California League, where his two year record was 17-13, and San Antonio of the Class AA Texas League, 14-3 in 1974.

The high point of Eckersley's three seasons with the Indians, when he won 40 games and lost 32, was on May 30, 1977, in a 1-0, no-hit victory against California.

But the Indians, then bereft of talent and desperately in need of help, traded Eckersley (with catcher Fred Kendall) on March 30, 1978 to the Red Sox (for pitchers Rick Wise and Mike Paxton, catcher Bo Diaz and third baseman Ted Cox). It was a deal the Tribe lived to regret.

After several good years in Boston, Eckersley was traded to the Cubs in 1984. Then followed 2 ½ so-so seasons in Chicago, during which it seemed his baseball career was nearly over, and he was dealt to Oakland on April 3, 1987. No sooner did he join the Athletics than then-manager Tony LaRussa, acting on the advice of his pitching coach, Dave Duncan, assigned Eckersley to the bull pen.

As Duncan testified in a story that appeared in *Baseball Digest*: "It was not a stroke of genius on anybody's part. When we got Dennis, the only reason we got him was that he wasn't throwing well. He didn't fit into the Cubs' plans, and we were looking for someone who would bolster our starting pitching.

"We wanted Dennis to be a starter whenever the need arose. In the meantime, we had to get him in shape, so we pitched him in middle relief. He did so well that we started moving him down to more significant roles. Then all of a sudden, (reliever) Jay Howell gets hurt, and Eckersley is the logical guy to be the closer. The rest is history."

Indeed it is. Eckersley became the best relief pitcher in baseball. He went to the Cardinals with LaRussa and Duncan in 1996 and, three years later retired with Hall of Fame credentials. In addition to his 197-171 record, 20 shutouts and 100 complete games as a starter, Eckersley's 390 saves are third best all-time.

Eckersley won the A.L. Cy Young and Most Valuable Player awards in 1992, when he was credited with 51 saves and had an ERA of 1.91, and was a six time all-star.

Not bad for a one-time free-spirited, brash young pitcher who wasn't expected to last long in the major leagues - but fooled everybody, especially the Indians.

When 'Operation Reclamation' failed

It was June 2, 1966, but Dick Radatz said it felt like "Christmas Eve" after he'd been traded to the Indians.

But Christmas never came for the once unhittable relief pitcher the fans in Boston called "The Monster."

Dick Radatz

It had been an appropriate nickname for the 6-6, 260-pound right-hander, and not just because of his physical dimensions. Radatz was a monster when it came to stomping out enemy rallies - until, mysteriously, he lost his touch.

It got so bad that Radatz couldn't even throw a baseball close to the plate if a batter were standing there, and he was out of the game almost as quickly as he'd come to dominate it from 1962-65. In those four seasons for the Red Sox, Radatz was credited with 49 victories and 100 saves, and struck out 608 batters in 538 1/3 innings. He won the "Fireman of the Year" award in 1962 and 1964.

But Radatz wasn't his old self in his first six appearances for Boston in 1966. He walked 11 batters in 19 innings and, though he saved four victories, he failed to protect leads on two other occasions in late-May, and the Red Sox moved swiftly. They traded him to the Indians for pitchers Lee Stange and Don McMahon, and "Operation Reclamation" - as Manager Birdie Tebbetts called it - got underway.

"We think he just needs to regain his confidence," Tebbetts said of the deal. Radatz agreed. "If I pitch the way I can, the Indians will win the pennant," he said.

But it was false hope. And false promise.

Radatz was credited with 10 saves the rest of 1966 - but also was charged with three losses and a 4.61 ERA in 39 games. The trouble, he surmised, began in Boston when he decided he needed another pitch to go with his 98 mph fast ball.

"I made up my mind to come up with a sinker and, unfortunately, I developed one, and you saw what happened," he said before spring training opened in 1967.

"Now I know what I should have known. I'm a fast ball pitcher and when I'm going good, I throw fast balls 90% of the time. "I'm going to do that next season, and the confidence thing will take care of itself."

But it didn't, and when spring training began, Radatz couldn't find the plate.

Radatz threw well enough on the side, but once he took the mound and a batter stepped in against him, Radatz was pathetic. There's no better way to say it.

"It defies all reason, all logic," the onetime Monster admitted. "It's like someone turned off a switch up here in my head. I honestly can't figure it out. I feel fine physically. I really do. I throw fine on the sideline. But when I get on the mound I can't do it, and I don't know why."

Finally, the Indians admitted they didn't know either. A week into the 1967 season they traded Radatz to the Chicago Cubs, ending "Operation Reclamation" in Cleveland. Radatz pitched briefly for the Cubs, Detroit, and then Montreal after leaving the Indians.

But whatever Radatz had lost was still missing, and by mid-1969, he was out of baseball, his once-brilliant career finished.

Gabe and the 'Sleeping Giant'

The Indians never won a pennant during Gabe Paul's reign as Chief - indeed, they didn't even come close - but it is to his credit that the franchise remained in Cleveland through some very difficult times.

On several occasions in the 1960s the Indians nearly moved because of the strapped financial condition of ownership.

Seattle, Oakland, Dallas and New Orleans tried to induce Vernon Stouffer and the Tribe's board of directors to relocate, but Paul staunchly defended Cleveland as a good baseball city. "Cleveland is a sleeping giant," he often said, meaning that, given a winning team, the fans would flock to the Stadium again as they did in the Golden Years, 1947 through 1955.

Unfortunately - for Gabe and Cleveland - the closest the Indians came to being a pennant contender was in 1968 when they finished third with an 86-75 record, 16 1/2 games behind the pennant-winning Baltimore Orioles.

During the 19 seasons Gabe called the shots in Cleveland, he made some good deals, especially when he got Gaylord Perry for Sam McDowell in 1972, and some bad ones, as when he traded Tommy John, Tommie Agee and John Romano in 1965 to reacquire an almost-finished Rocky Colavito.

Gabe Paul

And because of the organization's poor financial condition, Paul also on occasion was forced to trade or sell players to meet the payroll, as when he sent Mudcat Grant to Minnesota and Pedro Ramos to the Yankees in 1964, Don McMahon to Boston in 1966, and Max Alvis and Russ Snyder to Milwaukee in 1970.

Prior to joining the Indians in 1961 under then-owner William R. Daley, Paul helped build the Cincinnati Reds into a National League pennant contender, though he left them in 1960 to put together the expansionist Houston Astros (then known as the Houston Colt 45s).

Paul became president of the New York Yankees in January 1973 after they were purchased by George Steinbrenner. And with Steinbrenner's money in plentiful supply, the Yankees flourished under Paul's leadership, winning the pennant in 1976 and 1977.

Paul rejoined the Indians in 1978 at the urging of his longtime friend, F.J. "Steve" O'Neill, who purchased controlling interest in the franchise. But neither Paul's expertise, nor O'Neill's willingness to pay the price could get the Indians out of sixth place, and the giant continued to slumber. O'Neill died in 1983, and Paul retired in 1985, ending a 56 year career in baseball. He died in 1997.

Paul's career in baseball began in 1928 when, as a budding sportswriter at the age of 18, he got a job doing publicity and managing ticket sales for Rochester, then a minor league affiliate of the Cincinnati Reds of the Class AA International League. Paul became publicity director of the Reds in 1937 and traveling secretary in 1938.

After returning from the Army in World War II, Paul was promoted to assistant to Cincinnati president Warren Giles. And when Giles was elected president of the National League in 1951, Paul replaced him as president of the Reds.

All of which proves that, in some cases even a sportswriter can make it all the way up the ladder in professional baseball.

The 'unforgettable' catch

If it had happened during a World Series, or even in one of the media centers, fans would still be talking about what Al Luplow did in Boston on June 27, 1963.

It was called "one of the all-time great catches in baseball history" in the Cleveland *Plain Dealer*

Al Luplow

the next day, and enabled the Indians to win, 6-4, though Red Sox manager Johnny Pesky subsequently protested the victory, in vain.

It was one of the few bright spots in an otherwise mediocre, seven year major league career for Luplow. He joined the Tribe in 1961 with impressive credentials following an outstanding collegiate career as a star halfback at Michigan State.

Luplow never played up to expectations with the Indians, however, and after five seasons as a part-timer, he was sold to the New York Mets at the end in 1965.

Luplow went to Pittsburgh in 1967, which was his last year in the major leagues, and he wound up with a very forgettable .235 career batting average in 481 games.

But anyone who saw Luplow steal what would have been a three-run, game-winning homer by Dick Williams - or even read about it - will remember the catch as one of the best ever made in baseball.

Here's how it was described in the *Plain Dealer* the next day:

"Williams swung at a pitch thrown by Ted Abernathy and sent it rocketing to deep right center.

"Luplow flashed toward the fence. Going full speed, he leaped high, so high that his knees cracked the top of the five-foot barrier (in front of the bull pen).

"The spring carried Luplow over the fence and as he flew through the air he stuck up his glove and the ball went in it.

"The force of Luplow's momentum continued him over the fence. He landed on his shoulder in the bull pen.

"At first nobody was sure Luplow had hung on to the ball. But in the next instant he popped up from behind the fence and held the ball aloft. The crowd of 6,497 went crazy."

Pesky and his players also went crazy when the umpire ruled it a legal catch.

"He (Luplow) can't catch the ball outside the field," raved Pesky. "That should have been a bleeping homer."

His protest, of course, fell upon deaf ears. Joe Cronin, then-president of the American League, refused to overturn the umpire's decision and the Indians' victory stood - and so did Luplow's sensational play.

And despite his complaint, Pesky did not mince words when asked to comment on the catch. "It was the greatest I ever saw," he said.

Unfortunately for Luplow, he was soon forgotten, even if his catch was not.

As with so many outstanding minor league batters, Luplow had trouble hitting curve balls thrown by big league pitchers and his baseball career was soon ended.

But memories of his catch live on, even if only 6,497 fans in Fenway Park actually saw it.

As Pesky admitted during a visit to Cleveland when he was a coach for the Red Sox, "It still was the greatest catch I ever saw."

It was an unbelievable deal.

Imagine! A contract paying two million, three hundred thousand dollars over 10 years to a pitcher who'd had one good season! Unbelievable - *then*.

That was 1976 and Wayne Garland was holding all the trump cards. It was the first year of free agency in baseball and Garland, who had refused to sign a 1976 contract with the Baltimore Orioles, was coming off a 20-7 season.

What's more, General Manager Phil Seghi was looking for an opportunity to prove to the fans that the Indians would go to any extent to build a winner.

Wayne Garland

"Bidding for free agents is always a crap-shoot," Seghi reflected on the deal. "No one is worth $2-million. We simply tried to gauge what Garland's value to the club might be. We could spend that much in our farm system and not produce a 20-game winner. Besides, we had no idea what other teams were offering. We didn't know what it would take to get Garland."

Nor did Garland, who'd won only seven games and lost 11 prior to his 20 victory season with the Orioles in 1975.

"I wasn't worth the money," Garland acknowledged after his career was prematurely ended in 1981, five seasons short of fulfilling his guaranteed contract. "No one is worth that much. But if the Indians were willing to pay it, I was willing to take it. Who wouldn't?"

Indeed, who wouldn't?

But three decades later the controversy drips with irony.

Garland's average salary of $230,000 a year - which was so "unbelievable" to so many in 1976 - is less than half the average salary of all major league players today.

And, in 2000 the major league *minimum* salary was $200,000!

Only three years after Garland signed with the Indians, Nolan Ryan became baseball's first $1-million-a-year player. Less than three years after that, in February 1982, George Foster broke the $2-million-a-year salary barrier; and in 1991, Kirby Puckett was paid $3-million annually for three years.

Unfortunately, Garland hurt his arm while going 13-19 in his first season in Cleveland, probably from trying too hard to justify the deal that so many fans criticized each time he lost a game.

The following spring, when Garland's record was 2-3 and the pain in his shoulder persisted, he got the bad news.

He had suffered a torn rotator cuff.

Garland underwent surgery and tried to make a comeback, but to no avail. He won only four games while losing 10 in 1979, his record was 6-9 in 1980, 3-7 in 1981, and then it was over.

Oh, Garland didn't take the money and run; he attempted to resurrect his career in the minors, but couldn't. The fast ball was gone, and his curve ball, which had been one of the best in baseball in 1976, lost its snap.

And just like that the Indians $2.3-Million Man - as the media called Garland - was reduced to a memory and a few lines in the record book.

'Beer Night' wasn't the only forfeit

Most longtime Indians fans are well aware of the ugly incident that transpired at the Stadium on June 4, 1974, during the ill-fated managerial career of Ken Aspromonte.

It was the infamous "Beer Night" riot that caused the Indians to forfeit a game they were rallying to win against the Texas Rangers.

Alva "Ted" Bonda

Spectators from among the crowd of 25,135 - most of whom had too much to drink - swarmed onto the field in the ninth inning, preventing the Indians and Rangers from completing the game. Umpire Nestor Chylak tried in vain to restore order, but couldn't and finally forfeited the game to Texas.

It was a sorry spectacle, but it was neither the first nor last time a major league game was forfeited; 38 have ended that way, most recently on Aug. 10, 1995.

The Indians have been involved in six of those forfeits, winning over Washington on July 23, 1901; Philadelphia on July 20, 1918; and Chicago on April 26, 1925; and losing to Detroit on Aug. 8, 1903; and Chicago on Sept. 9, 1917; in addition to the Rangers in 1974.

The strangest of those six forfeits involving the Indians occurred in 1903 and 1917.

In the 1903 loss to Detroit, umpire Tom Connolly declared the game forfeited in the bottom of the 11th inning with the Indians trying to overcome a 6-5 deficit.

Napoleon Lajoie, who would become the Indians player-manager in 1904, was angered by Connolly's unwillingness to put a new ball in play. When Lajoie took the dirty ball and flung it over the grandstand at League Park, Connolly immediately declared the game forfeited.

It was a similar incident that caused the Indians to lose to Chicago in 1917.

In this one, trouble between the Indians and umpire Brick Owens began in the top of the 10th inning, when the Indians were trying to break a 3-3 tie. Jack Graney, who would become the radio voice of the Indians in 1932, was called out in a close play at third base leading off the inning. It set off a violent argument that delayed the game for 10 minutes.

According to a newspaper account, the Cleveland players "demonstrated their unhappiness by throwing their gloves in the air, and a couple of them rolled around on the ground."

Order finally was restored, but trouble began again in the bottom of the 10th. After Chicago pitcher Dave Danforth struck out, Tribe catcher Steve O'Neill, another who would become manager of the team, "heaved the ball to the center fielder, and Owens quickly forfeited the game to the White Sox."

"Beer Night" was an ill-conceived promotion dreamed up by then-Tribe owner Ted Bonda. Unlimited amounts of draft beer were sold for 10 cents apiece and, by late in the game, many fans in attendance were drunk and unruly.

The game was declared forfeited as the Indians were rallying for two runs in the ninth to fashion a 5-5 tie. They had loaded the bases with two out when the frenzied fans invaded the field.

When order could not be restored after more than 15 minutes, Chylak ended the game, awarding the victory to Texas.

"It was like a jungle out there," Chylak said upon leaving the field after ending the game.

Gabe Paul's biggest mistake

It was late in 1966, a season that had started wonderfully well for the Indians with 10 consecutive victories, but had swiftly and surely deteriorated into near-total disarray.

Birdie Tebbetts was fired on Aug. 19 and replaced by George Strickland, but the change in managers only seemed to make matters worse. Under Strickland the Indians won just 15 games and lost 24, finishing with an 81-81 record, and General Manager Gabe Paul went shopping for a new manager.

An early applicant was Bob Lemon, the former Tribe pitcher who had begun his managerial career that year with Seattle, then a Pacific Coast League farm club of the California Angels.

But Paul was convinced the Indians, who had been so undisciplined under Tebbetts and then Strickland, needed a stronger leader, "Somebody with an iron fist," he said then.

And so, Paul hired Joe Adcock, who did indeed have an iron fist - an iron fist that was seldom sheathed in a glove.

A big (6-4, 235-pounds) first baseman who physically resembled actor John Wayne, Adcock began his pro career in 1947 with Columbia (S.C.) of the Class A Carolina League, a Cincinnati farm club when Paul was then the Reds' general manager.

Joe Adcock

Adcock made it to the major leagues in 1950 and stayed for 17 years, hitting .277 with 336 homers in 1,959 games with the Reds, Milwaukee Braves, Indians and Angels.

The highlight of Adcock's career came on July 31, 1954, against Brooklyn, when he became one of only 12 players in the history of baseball to hit four homers in one game.

Paul, who always admired Adcock, had acquired him for the Indians in 1963, along with pitcher Jack Curtis, from the Braves for pitcher Frank Funk and outfielders Don Dillard and Ty Cline.

And, though Adcock was traded a year later to the Angels with pitcher Barry Latman for outfielder Leon Wagner, he remained one of Paul's favorites.

It was Adcock's great self-discipline and fierce desire to win that had always impressed Paul. Which is why, after a brief interview, Paul offered Adcock the job of revitalizing the Indians, and restoring discipline. "After listening to Joe for just half an hour, I knew he was the man I wanted," Paul said then.

Adcock vowed to "run a tight ship," saying, "lf I don't succeed, it won't be because somebody else caused me to fail."

He also promised, "From the first day things are going to be different around here. You've never seen a spring training like the one I'm going to run. There'll be no hanky-panky, and if I see things I don't like, well, the players are going to think that hell was turned loose backwards."

Unfortunately for the Indians, Adcock's good intentions soon failed.

The season became a disaster and the day it ended, with the Indians dragging a 75-87 record behind them, Adcock was fired.

And a few years later Gabe Paul would concede that the biggest mistake he'd made in more than a half-century as a baseball executive was not hiring Bob Lemon to manage the Indians in 1967.

When McCarthy chose Galehouse

He's probably best known as the Boston Red Sox pitcher who lost to Gene Bearden and the Indians in the historic one game playoff for the American League pennant on Oct. 4, 1948.

But Denny Galehouse also should be remembered as one of the Tribe's most promising young pitchers of the 1930s, though he never fully lived up to the bright future predicted for him.

Denny Galehouse

Galehouse pitched for the Indians from 1934 (when he appeared in one game) through 1938, and went on to enjoy a 15-year major league career that included two starts - and a victory - for the St. Louis Browns in the 1944 World Series.

In the torrid, four-team AL pennant race of 1948, Galehouse won eight games while losing eight for Boston.

In choosing him to start the playoff game instead of well-rested Joe Dobson (16-10) or Mel Parnell (15-8), Red Sox manager Joe McCarthy obviously had in mind a performance Galehouse had given in Cleveland two months earlier, on July 30.

Then, taking over in relief in the first inning, Galehouse choked off an uprising and held the Indians to two hits the remaining 8 2/3 innings as the Red Sox rallied for a victory.

Ah, but in the playoff game, the Tribe got to Galehouse in a hurry.

Lou Boudreau solo homered in the Tribe's first at-bat and, though the Red Sox tied the score in their half of the inning, Galehouse was knocked out in the fourth.

The Indians took a 4-1 lead when Ken Keltner homered after singles by Boudreau and Joe Gordon, sending Galehouse to the showers in favor of reliever Ellis Kinder.

The Red Sox never recovered and the Indians won, 8-3.

Galehouse, born and raised in Doylestown, O., was signed by the Indians in 1931 after he'd been scouted playing semi-pro baseball in the Akron area. In a 1932 story in the Cleveland *News*, Galehouse was called "one of those pitchers ordered for future delivery."

When Galehouse made it to the big leagues in 1934, the *News* described him as "a right-hander who has tremendous speed and a powerful body to keep producing it."

But Galehouse was only 25-29 as a starter and reliever the next four seasons and, on Dec. 15, 1938, was traded with shortstop Tommy Irwin to Boston for outfielder Ben Chapman.

Galehouse didn't stay in Boston long either, though he was destined to finish his career there. The Red Sox dealt Galehouse to St. Louis in 1941, and it was with the old Browns that he enjoyed his greatest success.

Galehouse pitched and won a key game against Detroit in the final week of the 1944 season as the Browns finished one game ahead of Detroit for the AL pennant.

Boston re-acquired Galehouse in 1947 and he went 11-7 to help the Red Sox stay in pennant contention most of that season. He retired in 1949, after 15 years in the big leagues, with a 109-118 record. He died in 1998.

And while he's best known for losing the 1948 playoff game to the Indians, there was much more about Denny Galehouse's career worth remembering.

One of baseball's favorite cliches - usually cited to placate fans - is that often the best trades are those that weren't made. Sometimes it's true. But not always.

Certainly not in the case of a deal that could have been made, but wasn't in the early days of the Indians, then called the "Naps" when their manager was Napoleon Lajoie.

If owner Charles W. Somers had said "yes" to the Detroit Tigers, it would have reshaped the destiny of the Cleveland franchise for many years. Instead, Somers rejected a chance to get Ty Cobb, who went on to become baseball's all-time hits leader (until Pete Rose broke the record in 1985).

Elmer Flick

It happened during spring training in 1908, after Cobb had won the batting championship with a .350 average in his first full season. Somers received a phone call from the Tigers. It was Hughie Jennings, then manager of the Tigers, who said he was authorized by Detroit owner Frank J. Navin to make the call.

After exchanging pleasantries, Jennings got to the point. "Mr. Somers," he said, "I'd like to make a deal ... I'll give you Ty Cobb for Elmer Flick, even up."

Somers was "baffled" because Cobb was regarded as a "sure comer," according to an account published then. But Somers liked Flick. So did the fans. A fleet outfielder, Flick was born and raised in the Cleveland suburb of Bedford and had played for the Naps the previous five seasons.

Somers pondered the proposal, then asked Jennings, "Why are you so anxious to trade Cobb? Anything wrong with him physically?"

Jennings replied that Cobb was in perfect health ... then gave the reason the Tigers wanted to trade Cobb. "He cannot get along with our players and we want to get him away. He's had two fights already this spring. We want harmony on this team, not scrapping."

Obviously - unfortunately - Somers wanted harmony, too. He said no to Jennings' offer, in effect choosing Flick over Cobb.

It was an unfortunate decision because, though Flick was good enough to be elected to the Hall of Fame in 1963, he got sick in that season of 1908 and played only nine games, while Cobb was hitting .324 in 150 games. What's more, Cobb played 20 more seasons for a total of 24, never batting less than .300, and twice hitting over .400.

Flick retired after playing only 90 games in 1909 and 1910, when he hit .255 and .265. His lifetime average was a creditable .313 for 13 years.

Perhaps worst of all, Cleveland finished a half-game behind Detroit in the 1908 pennant race; the Tigers had a 90-63 record - in those days teams weren't required to make up postponed games once the season ended - and the Naps were 90-64.

Detroit prevailed again in 1909, while Cleveland waited until 1920 to win its first American League championship.

And Cobb, despite his inability to get along with teammates, was a star for the Tigers and Philadelphia Athletics through 1928, winding up with a .367 lifetime average.

The Tribe's fearless catcher

Baseball fans, especially those who follow the Indians, can't possibly mention Ray Fosse's name, or even read it without immediately thinking of another player - Pete Rose.

The two are linked forever in baseball lore.

Ray Fosse

Oh, not by statistics. Fosse was a hard-working catcher, who *would* have been great, while Rose, baseball's all-time hit leader, *was* great.

The violence of baseball is the thing that joined them.

On July 14, 1970, in the 12th inning of the All-Star Game at Riverfront Stadium in Cincinnati, Rose launched himself into Fosse on a play at home plate. It scored the winning run in the National League's 5-4 victory.

But it was the collision, not the result of the game, that people still vividly remember.

Fosse, who knew the throw was going to be late, moved a step up the third base line and tried to block the plate. His only chance was to stall Rose, catch the ball and make the tag.

Rose, who'd been on second base, was running on Jim Hickman's hit to center.

The collision could have been avoided. Fosse could have given Rose a piece of the plate, and/or Rose could have slid, or even let up. It was, after all, the All-Star Game. An exhibition.

But letting up was not a part of either man's nature.

Rose, in typical style, threw himself into Fosse with a head first dive. The catcher absorbed the impact and went down. The run scored and the game ended. Television showed the replay of the collision again and again. It still does, especially when the All-Star Game is near.

In Cleveland, Fosse was called "Fearless Fosse," because of his courage in standing up to Rose. But that which happened in the aftermath of the collision is what's so important. Especially to Fosse.

Rose missed a few days with a variety of bruises, but went on to hit .316 that year, one of 10 times he'd bat .300 following his jarring meeting with Fosse.

Fosse, whose shoulder was injured in the collision, also was back in the Indians' lineup a few days after the most famous play of his career. He ended the season hitting .307 with 18 homers and 61 RBI.

But he'd never have another season like it.

In the eight years following the collision, Fosse managed to hit .300 only one more time. He never again reached 18 homers, and topped 61 RBI just once.

The fact is, Fosse was never the same after injuring his shoulder, and the statistics substantiate that contention.

The Indians traded Fosse to Oakland in 1973, which proved to be a great break for him. Fosse was the Athletics catcher as they won the American League pennant, and the World Series in each of the next three seasons.

But despite those three World Series rings, Fosse always will be remembered as the man who came out second best in an All-Star Game collision with Pete Rose - and whose once promising career suffered because of it.

First it was Jimmie Foxx, "the Philadelphia slugger with the blacksmith build."

Then it was Al Rosen, who wasn't even going to play because of a broken finger.

Willie Mays followed and took center stage all by himself.

An "ecstatic" Gary Carter was next.

And finally it was Sandy Alomar Jr. who did himself – and his fans – proud.

Sandy Alomar Jr.

Those five players – Foxx of the Athletics, Rosen of the Indians, Mays of the Giants, Carter of the Expos, and Alomar also of the Indians – were heroes of the five All-Star Games played in Cleveland in 1935, 1954, 1963, 1981 and 1997.

No other city hosted the "Mid-Summer Classic" as often as Cleveland, and the Indians also own the distinction of attracting the three largest crowds ever to see the game. Attendance in 1981 was 72,086, it was 69,831 in 1935, and 68,751 in 1954.

All of those games, as well as the one in 1963, were played at the old Municipal Stadium, which was replaced by Jacobs Field as the Indians' home in 1994, the capacity of which is 43,368.

The first one at the Stadium was billed as a "dream game" and, as described in the *Plain Dealer*: "Foxx, the Philadelphia slugger with the blacksmith build, took the All-Star Game into his huge hands and wrapped it up for the American League (4-1).

"With one smashing blow in the first inning, a 340 foot home run into the left field stands, Foxx hurled back the forces of the National League to give the A.L. its third straight victory."

While Rosen was the hitting star of the 1954 game, giving the A.L. a 13-8 lead in the series after winning, 11-9, it was the oddest victory ever credited to a pitcher in All-Star competition.

Dean Stone, then a rookie for the Washington Senators, was the winner even though he made only three pitches and didn't retire a batter.

Stone took over in the eighth inning with two out and the score tied, 9-9. After Stone's first two pitches to Duke Snider, the runner on third, Red Schoendienst, tried to steal home. Stone quickly delivered his third pitch in time for catcher Yogi Berra to tag Schoendienst for the third out. The A.L. scored twice in the bottom of the eighth and Virgil Trucks preserved the lead in the ninth.

Mays was the star in 1963, driving in two runs and stealing two bases as the N.L. prevailed, 5-3.

Carter said he was "ecstatic" with happiness after hitting two homers as the N.L. won the 1981 game, 5-4, for its 10th straight victory and 18th in 19 years.

And then it was Alomar's turn to wear the hero's crown in 1997. He smashed a two-out, two-run homer off Shawn Estes in the seventh inning, breaking a 1-1 tie, and became the first player in major league history to be named the Most Valuable Player in the game played in his home park.

Alomar's homer provided the A.L. with its 27th victory in 68 games (one of which ended in a tie in 1961), in the series that began in 1933. The All-Star Game wasn't played in 1945 because of wartime travel restrictions, and two were played each year from 1959-62. The A.L. also won the last two games, 13-8 in 1998, and 4-1 in 1999.

The once 'Immortal Cuban'

They called him "The Immortal Cuban," and for awhile the nickname was entirely appropriate.

Joe Azcue, it seemed, could do nothing wrong after being obtained as a "throw-in" by the Indians on May 25, 1963.

Joe Azcue

Neither, it also seemed, could the Indians do anything wrong after Azcue was pressed into daily duty behind the plate when regular catcher John Romano broke a couple of bones in his hand and was sidelined for more than two months that season.

Eventually, of course, Azcue proved to be only human.

Ah, but in those early days with the Tribe, he really was something special.

OK, even *immortal* - if only temporarily.

The day Joe joined the Tribe in the deal that revolved around the acquisition of shortstop Dick Howser from the then-Kansas City Athletics for catcher Doc Edwards, Azcue fell asleep in the bull pen.

It was during that game that Romano was hurt and Indians manager Birdie Tebbetts called for Azcue, who awakened, went behind the plate and, subsequently, delivered a key hit.

He delivered many more key hits that season, hence the nickname, and wound up with a .281 average, 14 homers and 46 RBI in 96 games. The catcher who came as a "throw-in" looked like a steal.

A year later Romano was traded and Azcue became the regular catcher, a job he held until 1969 when he, too, was dealt away. The Indians sent Azcue to Boston in a trade that brought Ken "The Hawk" Harrelson to Cleveland.

But it was with the Indians that Azcue gained his fame and did his best work, not only as a solid contributor on the field, but also as a steadying influence in the clubhouse.

Until he came to Cleveland, Azcue was buried in the A's farm system and claimed - then proved - all he needed was a chance to play in the big leagues.

"My trouble with (owner) Charlie Finley in Kansas City," he said, "was because I had worms." How's that?

"Yeah," said the once Immortal Cuban, explaining why he failed to stick with the A's in 1962. "I was getting a chance in Kansas City and hitting pretty good, about .250. Then one day in Washington, I came back to the dugout and fell down. I was so sick they put me in the hospital for a month. They found out I had worms.

"I lost weight. A lot of weight. I went from 230 (pounds) to 170. I was weak, but I tried to play anyway. But I couldn't play good. So Charlie sent me to Portland (of the Pacific Coast League). All because I had worms. I was mad, but now I am glad," Azcue said after his first season with the Tribe.

He went from the Red Sox to California in 1969, and finished his career with Milwaukee in 1972.

As it turned out, there was nothing immortal about Azcue's lifetime statistics: in 11 seasons and 909 games in the big leagues he hit .252 with 50 homers and 304 RBI.

But those first couple of years in Cleveland - especially 1963 after Azcue woke up in the bull pen - really were special.

Born much too soon

If ever a ballplayer was born too soon, it was Joe Heving, one of the first premier relief pitchers in baseball history.

Heving, a 13 year major league veteran, was the Indians' ace fireman in 1937 and 1938, and again from 1941-44.

"In those days," as Heving said in a newspaper article in 1970, a few months before his death at age 70, "relievers were guys who weren't good enough to start.

"Nobody liked being a reliever, but I did. I just wish the times would've been different, and I would have been appreciated more."

Who could blame Heving? He didn't get to the major leagues until 1930, when he was 30, with the New York Giants.

Heving was a minor league outfielder for two years, and didn't start pitching until 1926 when his team was short of pitchers and threw him into the second game of a double header. Heving hurled a three-hitter and was a pitcher thereafter.

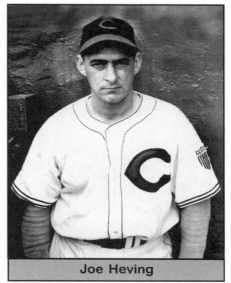
Joe Heving

Though he appeared in 430 games, including a then-American League record 63 in 1944, Heving never made big money. What's more, he always seemed to be on the brink of being released, which Heving also lamented in that newspaper story.

"That's the way it was in my day," said Heving, who was demoted by the Indians in May 1938 after a clubhouse altercation with a teammate.

The trouble was, Heving's altercation was with Earl Averill, then one of the Indians' best players.

According to a published account at the time, "Heving grumbled something about 'high-salaried stars who take third strikes with their bats on their shoulders.'

"Averill's reply was a well-placed right hand punch to Heving's mouth."

The next day then-manager Oscar Vitt, never a great admirer of Heving, sent the relief pitcher to the minors. But Heving did not stay there long.

He was soon picked up by the Boston Red Sox, who put Heving in their rotation. It was the only time he was a regular starter. and Heving responded by winning eight games, losing only one.

The next year he was back in the bull pen. The Indians rectified their mistake in 1941, getting Heving back in a cash deal after Roger Peckinpaugh had replaced Vitt.

Heving, who was out of baseball in 1935 because he wouldn't play for the money he was then offered, retired for good after the 1945 season at age 45.

Though he often was credited for being a "smart" pitcher, and being able to recognize a hitter's weakness, Heving - never one to mince words - scoffed at the praise.

"That's poppycock," he said. "I always had control and I just kept throwing that sinker of mine in the same spot.

"When it's breaking right, it just can't be hit hard, even by a batter supposedly at his best against low-ball pitching." Most of the time Heving's sinker was breaking right.

There was no such thing as a "save" statistic in those days. But there's no doubt Heving was one of baseball's premier relievers - long before recognition came to premier relievers.

The terrible-tempered pitcher

Talk about your temperamental players ... few are, or ever have been worse than Wes Ferrell, a star pitcher for the Indians and five other teams in the late-1920s and 1930s.

Ferrell, a chronic complainer, staged long contract holdouts three times in his 15 year major league career, once for six weeks into the 1931 season, and was frustrated and embittered when he retired in 1941 at the relatively-young age of 33.

Wes Ferrell

But there never was any doubt about Ferrell's ability to pitch.

He hurled a no-hitter against St. Louis in 1931, and won 193 games while losing 128, including a 102-62 record for the Indians. On May 25, 1934, Ferrell was traded - during one of his holdouts - to Boston (with outfielder Dick Porter for pitcher Bob Weiland, outfielder Bob Seeds and $25,000).

In his first four seasons with the Indians, Ferrell won 21, 25, 22 and 23 games and, believe it or not, one of his idiosyncrasies was a firm belief that getting stung on his arm by bees made him a better pitcher.

Ferrell told the story in 1941, after he'd gone from the Red Sox to Washington, and on to the New York Yankees, Brooklyn Dodgers and Boston Braves, who were then also called the "Bees".

"Ferrell augmented doctor's treatments with ideas of his own. He got the idea that the sting of a bee somehow would put new life into his ailing flipper," a Boston paper reported. "Ferrell would go around golf courses with bees on his mind, or bees in his bonnet, as they say, and everytime he'd see one, he'd bare his arm and invite the bee to sit down.

"The arm must have looked like a tire tread after a particularly profitable round. Whether it did any good or not is a question, but at any rate, he's still with the Bees (the Boston Bees, that is!)."

Ferrell also was renowned for his battles with managers.

He was suspended twice, first by Cleveland's Roger Peckinpaugh in 1932 for refusing to leave the mound when replaced by a reliever, and then by Joe Cronin of Boston in 1936 for walking off the mound without being replaced by a reliever.

After his dispute with Peckinpaugh, Ferrell was suspended for 10 days and fined $1,500 for insubordination, and Stuart Bell, then the sports editor of the Cleveland *Press,* wrote:

"The suspension of Wesley Ferrell is seen as the first step of the Indians' management to clip the wings of a young pitcher who gained fame and riches so fast it changed his perspective from that of an ambitious kid pitcher trying to make good to that of a mound monarch who could do no wrong."

And when he was fined $1,000 by the Red Sox, Ferrell swore he would "punch Cronin in the jaw as soon as I can find him."

He didn't, of course, and went on to win 20 while losing 15 for Boston, but often alienated the fans by thumbing his nose at them.

After the Boston Braves released Ferrell at the end of the 1941 season, he tried to get a job as a pitching coach, but nobody would have him.

"For what I've done for baseball, baseball has done nothing for me," Ferrell lamented, and when he died in 1976, he was as frustrated and embittered as ever.

The Indians were wracked with dissension in 1935, which cost them a chance to catch the Detroit Tigers, who won the pennant.

It also cost them the loss of two players, and resulted in the firing of Manager Walter Johnson, who'd been one of the greatest pitchers in baseball.

Willie Kamm, the team's popular third baseman, and Glenn Myatt, a veteran backup catcher, allegedly were the trouble makers on the team and both were dismissed by Johnson. Myatt was cut loose on May 23, and Kamm on June 1. It set off a chain reaction of events that contributed to the Indians' third place finish with an 82-71 record, 12 games behind the Tigers.

Willie Kamm

The dissension became public on May 23, when the Indians were in Philadelphia for a three game series against the Athletics.

Johnson announced that Kamm was being sent back to Cleveland under suspension, and that Myatt was being released. Both actions were taken, Johnson said, "for the good of the team" because he had discovered an "anti-Johnson" bloc headed by the two players.

Both players, supported by most of their teammates, proclaimed their innocence, but to no avail, and neither played another game for the Indians.

Kamm demanded and received a hearing before then-Commissioner Kenesaw Mountain Landis in a futile effort to clear his name. Myatt signed with the New York Giants and finished the 1935 season with them, and retired after playing briefly for Detroit in 1936.

And to complete the sorry story, Johnson, a great pitcher but incompetent and troubled as a manager, was fired 2 ½ months later, on Aug. 4, after the Indians fell into fifth place with a 46-48 record. He was replaced by Steve O'Neill and never managed again.

The loss of Kamm was especially costly as he was an excellent fielder and consistent hitter whose career batting average was .281 in 13 seasons. He started in the major leagues with the Chicago White Sox in 1923, and was acquired by the Indians on May 17, 1931 (in a trade for infielder Lew Fonseca).

Kamm had played for San Francisco in the Class AA Pacific Coast League when his contract was purchased by the White Sox in 1922 for $100,000, then the highest price ever paid for a minor leaguer.

It was after Kamm's unsuccessful attempt for reinstatement with the Indians in a meeting with team owner Alva Bradley that he appealed to Landis. Bradley wanted Kamm back, but was compelled to support his manager. But the commissioner ruled that he could do nothing about what he called "a personality clash" between Kamm and Johnson.

Kamm never played again, though he returned to the minor leagues and managed San Francisco in 1936 and 1937. He died at age 88 in 1988.

Myatt, who played for the Athletics in 1920 and 1921, was demoted in 1922 to Milwaukee of the Class AA American Association where he batted .370 to lead the league and was purchased by the Indians. Myatt was their starting catcher in 1924 and 1925, when he hit .342 and .271, respectively, but lost his regular job in 1926 and served in a backup role the rest of his career, compiling a .270 batting average in 16 major league seasons. He died at age 72 in 1969.

The 'crooked-arm' southpaw

Don Mossi had a left arm that he couldn't straighten and a nickname that he couldn't shake.

But his timing was great.

When Mossi reported to spring training in 1954 as a 25 year old rookie, then-Tribe manager Al Lopez barely knew his name.

Don Mossi

In fact, Lopez didn't even know Mossi was in the Indians organization until he was added to the big league roster at the end of the 1953 season.

It was obvious the Tribe expected the relief pitcher with a crooked left arm to spend 1954 in the minors.

But Mossi, nicknamed "The Sphinx" for his dim view of the spoken word, quickly became the talk of spring training.

However, unlike so many other past and present players who bloom in the desert but fade like a mirage when the game-playing turns serious, Mossi continued to blossom.

"Mossi is the only pitcher in camp I haven't had to repeat something to," then-pitching coach Mal Harder was quoted. "I tell him once and he goes to work."

Al Rosen couldn't stop talking about Mossi's curveball.

"It never stops breaking," Rosen said then. "When he comes in for a relief job, all of us in the field feel completely confident. We've been up against him in batting practice and we know how hard he is to hit."

When spring training ended, Mossi was on the team.

And he proceeded to form the left side of the most famous bull pen tandem in Indians history. Ray Narleski took care of the right side.

"They were the best lefty-righty combination I've ever seen," said one-time teammate Herb Score, who was an Indians broadcaster for 34 years after retiring as a pitcher.

Mossi went 6-1 with a 1.94 earned run average and seven saves in 1954 as the Indians won the American League pennant with a then-record 111 victories.

He did it with a left arm that was so crooked it kept him out of the service. "I went all through my physical for the draft," Mossi explained during the spring of 1954. "When the doctor asked it anything bothered me, I told him my elbow did once in awhile, that sometimes it locked. They took some x-rays and I was rejected.

"I don't even know how it happened. The doctors said I must have hurt my arm somehow, some-time, but I don't remember it. First time I ever noticed that I couldn't straighten my arm was in high school. It bothered me some then, but not enough to stop me from pitching."

Mossi, whose other prominent physical characteristic was a pair of large, protruding ears, had a simple remedy when his elbow ached.

"The more it hurts, the harder I throw," said Mossi, a pleasant man, but a tough interview.

He gave mostly "yes" and "no" answers to reporters' questions, and justified it by saying, "I came here to pitch not talk."

And pitch Mossi did, very well, for the Indians through 1958, and then for Detroit, the Chicago White Sox and Kansas City until he retired in 1966.

Imagine the comfort a manager would feel knowing that baseball's best left and right handed stoppers are only a phone call away, waiting in the bull pen.

With that in mind, consider the luxury enjoyed by then-Indians manager Al Lopez in 1954, which was, not coincidentally, the season the Tribe set an American League record (since broken) with 111 victories.

Lopez, who piloted the Tribe from 1951 through 1956, had at his disposal what might have been the best righty-lefty relief tandem in baseball history.

Their names were Ray Narleski and Don Mossi.

Neither made it to the Hall of Fame, nor commanded salaries equivalent to the money they probably would be making today.

But no team had a more effective bull pen than the Indians, thanks primarily to Narleski and Mossi.

Narleski was right-handed, Mossi a southpaw. Both made their major league debuts in 1954, the season - again, not coincidentally - the Indians won the franchise's third pennant.

Mossi, the quiet one, relied on a sweeping curveball and excellent control. He went 6-1 in 1954, and was credited with seven saves (though the qualifications for earning a save have been liberalized considerably since then).

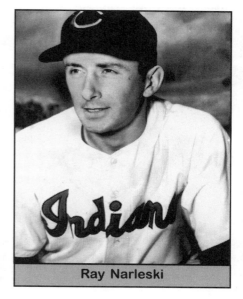
Ray Narleski

Narleski threw harder and spoke more. He went 3-3 with 13 saves in 1954, and through 1958 was the Indians' all-time saves leader with 53. It stood as a team record until Doug Jones broke it in 1989.

After Narleski led the league in 1955 with 60 appearances, going 9-1 with 19 saves, he was granted what was considered a very generous raise by then-General Manager Hank Greenberg.

It boosted Narleski's salary all the way up to $15,000!

Narleski always said he owed his success to his fastball and his father, who insisted he throw hard every day. "My dad was a pretty good ball player and he worked out all the time with us kids," Narleski was quoted at the time. "He made me throw hard every day. I suppose that's how I developed into a reliever."

Something else the older Narleski taught his son - and also which young Ray never forgot - was: "Never give in to a hitter. Fight him all the way." Which Narleski did. Every hitter. All the time.

Narleski, like Mossi, could start when necessary, though their primary value was as closers. In fact, when Narleski made the All-Star team in 1958, he was picked on the strength of his starting ability. That was the season Narleski went 13-10 in 44 appearances, 24 of them starting assignments.

It proved to be Narleski's final season in a Tribe uniform.

It also was Mossi's swan-song in Cleveland as - appropriately - the two relievers who'd pitched as a tandem, were traded as a tandem, to Detroit on Nov. 20, 1958. The deal brought pitcher Al Cicotte and second baseman Billy Martin, neither of whom made much of a contribution to the Tribe.

Mossi, employed as both a starter and reliever by the Tigers, had five good seasons (through 1963) in Detroit, and pitched for the Chicago White Sox in 1964 and Kansas City Athletics in 1965, after which he retired with a 101-80 record. Narleski, also used a a starter and reliever by the Tigers, went 4-12 in 1959 and retired with a career record of 43-33.

'Another Koufax' he wasn't

He was called "another Sandy Koufax" when the Los Angeles Dodgers signed Mike Kekich in 1964.

Not only was he left-handed, Kekich also launched baseballs with nearly the same velocity as Koufax, and was every bit as wild as the pitcher who went on to hurl four no-hitters and is enshrined in the Hall of Fame as one of the game's greatest players.

Mike Kekich

But Kekich's resemblance to Koufax ended early, even before his career was devastated by the most unique trade in baseball history.

In 1973, after Kekich was dealt to the New York Yankees, he and fellow southpaw Fritz Peterson announced in spring training that they would trade wives, children and houses. It sounded like a soap opera – though it wasn't. This was real, and the entire country watched as the drama unfolded.

Peterson and Susanne Kekich married and eventually found religion. Kekich and Marilyn Peterson found nothing but pain.

The Yankees were determined to break up the two pitchers. Kekich was more expendable because he had not been as successful as Peterson, and was traded to the Indians on June 12, 1973.

When Kekich arrived in Cleveland, he couldn't concentrate on the mound. He could throw strikes in the bull pen, but couldn't do so in a game. Fans booed Kekich everywhere he went. He began getting anxiety attacks and by late August was seeing a psychiatrist.

"I was desperately depressed," Kekich was quoted later. "The last good thing I could do in my life was throw a baseball, and it, too, was leaving me. I had lost everything; my friends, my Yankee team, my family and then my physical talent."

Once, after a game in Milwaukee, Kekich said he had walked to the mound and couldn't breathe. "I literally forgot how," he said. "I was afraid I was going to choke to death. I knew I wasn't ready to pitch. How could I control the flight of a baseball when I couldn't control myself?"

Kekich never said what went wrong between Marilyn and himself. She returned to New Jersey and taught school.

But Kekich did say after the break-up, "I'm not sorry for anything. Nor is Marilyn. Our side of the story never has been told, and it never will be. I've been offered $100,000 by a publisher, but children on both sides have been hurt enough."

Certainly, so was Kekich. He went 2-5 in 1973 and the Indians released him a week before the start of the 1974 season. From there Kekich's career drifted aimlessly.

Over $20,000 in debt because of his divorce, Kekich pitched in Japan in 1974. He returned and got a chance with Texas, but suffered a broken left elbow while - of all things - driving his motorcycle to spring training in 1976.

Kekich went home to Artesia, Calif. and waited for the telephone to ring. Finally, Seattle called and offered him a job in the Mexican League. Kekich jumped at the opportunity and made it back to the big leagues with the Mariners in 1977, when he won five and lost four games.

But that was it for the star-crossed southpaw, whose career ended with a very un-Koufax-like 39-51 record.

Prior to the rebirth of the Indians as a pennant contender in 1994, the last generation of Cleveland baseball fans to see the team win a championship still mention his name in awe: Jim Hegan.

Indeed, Hegan was the Indians' catcher for the ages.

Tall, handsome, almost regal in bearing, Hegan was behind the plate for the Indians most of the time from 1941 through 1957, though he missed three seasons while serving in the Coast Guard during World War II, from 1943 through 1945.

Those who were fortunate enough to watch him play saw a man develop the art of catching to a new level.

And when those fans of the 1940s and 1950s talk about Hegan, they invariably bring up his ability to catch foul balls.

"Hegan didn't even have to watch the ball going up," they'd say. "He could tell by the sound of the ball off the bat where it was going to land. He'd just run to the spot and catch it."

Baseball men felt the same way about Hegan's ability.

"As far as I'm concerned, you start and end any discussion of catchers with Jim Hegan," it was said by Birdie Tebbetts, a former Tribe manager and a long-time scout - and a very good major league catcher himself from 1936 through 1952.

Jim Hegan

"Add all the things a catcher has to do – catch, throw, call a game - and Jim Hegan was the best I ever saw."

He was the best that many ever saw.

Though only a .228 lifetime hitter, Hegan made his reputation catching some of the best pitchers in Indians history: Early Wynn, Bob Feller, Mike Garcia, Bob Lemon, Herb Score, Mel Harder, Satchel Paige, Art Houtteman, Ray Narleski, Hal Newhouser and Don Mossi.

But Hegan always minimized his contributions to their success.

"They threw the ball, all I did was catch it," he often said.

As testament to his popularity, the Indians, in 1953, held a "Jim Hegan Night" that was one of the best attended games of that season.

Hegan claimed his greatest satisfaction was catching the Indians' 1954 pitching staff, which helped the team set an American League record (since broken) of 111 victories in one season.

"Everytime you put your fingers down to give a signal you worry if it's going to be the right pitch," Hegan talked about his position, and especially how it related to the three no-hitters he caught - by Don Black (1946), Lemon (1948) and Feller (1951).

"It's really the pitcher's game. If he doesn't feel good about a pitch you call, chances are he won't throw it well."

But not many pitchers questioned Hegan's decisions on or off the field, as Score reminisced recently. "In a tight spot you always went with Jim's call," said the former broadcaster, who knew Hegan as well as anybody.

On June 17, 1984, Hegan died suddenly of a heart attack at age 64.

He was giving an interview at the time and, as he was wont to do, Hegan was talking about his teammates when he was stricken.

Thirteen years too late

For five days in 1938, Johnny Vander Meer was the greatest pitcher in baseball. Unfortunately, the Indians didn't get him until 13 years later and by then the magic was gone.

Now he is remembered in Tribe records only with a line of agate type that reads, "Vander Meer, John ('51)."

Johnny Vander Meer

As Frank Gibbons reported in the Cleveland *Press* on April 7, 1951: "It has been no secret for a long time that the Indians need relief in relation to their relief pitching.

"Today it was indicated more firmly than ever when the ghost of Johnny Vander Meer was summoned to our side for an effort to prove he has more than ectoplasm on the ball."

There certainly was more than ectoplasm - which Webster defines as "the supposed emanation from the body of a medium" - on Vander Meer's pitches when he became the only man in baseball history to hurl back-to-back no-hitters in 1938.

Then, pitching for the Cincinnati Reds, Vander Meer fired a no-hitter against the Boston Bees, beating them, 3-0, on June 11. In his next start, five days later, Vander Meer held the Brooklyn Dodgers hitless in a 6-0 victory.

And to top it off, on June 19, the then-23-year old southpaw went on to hurl three more hitless innings - for a total of 21 in a row - before Boston outfielder Debs Garms singled with two out in the fourth to break the spell.

"I truly believe that's the greatest defensive record in baseball," Vander Meer was quoted in a 1974 story.

Former Tribe manager Lou Boudreau at that time predicted that Vander Meer's consecutive no-hitters would be "one of two records that will never be matched ... the other being Joe DiMaggio's 56-game hitting streak."

Gibbons certainly was accurate in that 1951 story when he referred to the "ghost" of Vander Meer joining the Indians.

Vander Meer appeared in only one game for the Indians, against the Washington Senators on May 7. He was knocked out in the fourth inning, after giving up five consecutive singles.

It proved to be Vander Meer's final major league performance, and left him with a 119-121 lifetime record for 13 seasons.

The Indians released him June 28, 1951.

Later, reflecting on his career, Vander Meer wondered if those back-to-back no-hitters might have done him more harm than good. "They came too fast," he conceded. "I was just a kid who had done a freakish thing. I was more confused than thrilled. All the publicity, the attention, the interviews, the photographs, were too much for me.

"As I look back at it now, those days are the haziest period of my life, sort of like a dream."

Perhaps so. But there's no doubt Vander Meer was an excellent pitcher in most of his 11 seasons in Cincinnati.

And neither can there be any doubt that he - instead of his "ghost" - would have looked very good in a Cleveland uniform at the beginning, instead of the end of his career.

A victim of too much coaching

They called him the "Case Ace" when Ray Mack was a rampaging fullback for Case Institute of Technology in the mid-1930s, and that college was a football power in Northern Ohio.

At the time, Case was a member of the rugged "Big Four," along with John Carroll, Western Reserve, and Baldwin-Wallace College, and in 1962, Mack was honored by being named the recipient of the *Sports Illustrated* Silver Anniversary All-American Award.

A second baseman, Mack grew up on Cleveland's east side - his family name was Mlckovsky - and played at all levels on the local sandlots. It would have been a perfect story plot if he had become a big home town hero with the Indians.

Ray Mack

Back then Mack also was called a very good hitter – even better than Lou Boudreau, who also was coming up through the minor leagues – and batted .378 at Fargo-Moorhead (N.D.) of the Class D Northern League in 1938.

The following season Mack and Boudreau, a shortstop, played together at Buffalo of the Class AA International League and formed one of the best double play combinations in baseball, earning them a promotion in tandem to the Indians on Aug. 7, 1939.

However, while Boudreau got off to a good start in the final six weeks of their first season in Cleveland, Mack struggled, batting only .152 in 36 games.

Mack improved to hit .283 with 12 homers and 69 RBI in 1940, and on Opening Day made a spectacular play to preserve Bob Feller's no-hitter in Chicago. It happened with two outs in the ninth on a ball hit by Taft Wright. Mack ranged far to his left, almost behind first base, made a diving stop of the grounder and, while on the ground, threw to Hal Trosky at first base to retire Wright, ending the game.

"That was the greatest thrill I ever had in sports," Mack was quoted at the time. "Had I missed the play, I probably never would've forgiven myself."

Mack's average fell to .228 in 1941, and then to .225 in 1942, and .220 in 1943, after which he lost his job as the Indians regular second baseman. As a part-timer in 1944, Mack batted .232 in 83 games, then spent 1945 in the Army during World War II. He returned to play 61 games in 1946, but hit for only a .205 average.

That winter, in one of then-new owner Bill Veeck's many deals to re-structure the team, Mack was dealt to the New York Yankees (along with minor league catcher Sherman Lollar) for pitchers Gene Bearden and Al Gettel, and outfielder Hal Peck.

It didn't help Mack's career as he played only one game for the Yankees in 1947, and was demoted to Newark (N.J.) of the Class AAA International League. Later that season Mack's contract was sold for the waiver price to the Chicago Cubs, for whom he batted .218 in 21 games. It was his final year in the big leagues.

By his own admission, Mack, who died at age 52 in 1969, was a victim of too much coaching. After his retirement, Mack said, "I always believed I could hit, but the way it worked out, I let too many people try to tell me what to do, and I tried too many different things. I would have been better off if I'd gone on my own."

'Too small and too slow'

It took the Indians 11 years to admit their mistake, but they finally did in 1970.

Unfortunately, by then it was too late.

"They told me I wasn't big enough, that I was too slow, wore glasses and couldn't hit a curve ball," Rich Rollins remembered in 1962 when he became an overnight sensation with the Minnesota Twins.

Rich Rollins

Obviously, the Twins didn't think Rollins was too small, too slow and couldn't hit a curve ball, and neither did they mind that the red-haired kid who grew up in Parma, O. wore glasses.

"I'd always wanted to play for the Indians, but they weren't interested when I got out of (Kent State University)," he said.

One of the best players to come out of the Cleveland sandlots, Rollins played three years for the Rosenblum team in the Cleveland *Plain Dealer* Class A League and was signed in 1960 by the Washington Senators (who became the Minnesota Twins in 1961), receiving what was then a generous $9,000 bonus.

In his professional debut at Class B Wilson (N.C.), Rollins had the dubious distinction of singling into a triple play.

As Rich told it, there were runners on first and second when he lined a hit to left. The runner on second was thrown out the plate, the runner on first rounded second and was trapped off the base, and when Rollins tried for an extra base during the ensuing rundown, he was thrown out, too.

Less than two seasons later Rollins was promoted to Minnesota, and in his first game delivered a bases-loaded single off Ryne Duren, one of the hardest throwing relief pitchers in baseball.

Because he spent more than 45 days with the Twins in 1961, Rollins wasn't eligible for the Rookie of the Year Award in 1962, but would have won in a landslide.

That was the season he caught the attention of all of baseball by hitting in the high-.300s most of the year, and being selected - by the players, who did the voting then - as the American League's third baseman in the All-Star Game.

Rollins finished with a .298 average that included 16 homers and 96 RBI.

Then, he was voted "Sophomore Player of the Year," winning over outfielders Floyd Robinson, Chuck Hinton and a future Hall of Famer named Carl Yastrzemski.

Rollins played for the Twins through l968, when he was selected by the then-Seattle Pilots in the expansion draft. After 14 games in 1970 with Milwaukee, which inherited the Pilots, Rollins was released.

That's when the Indians signed Rollins, trying to correct the mistake they'd made 11 years earlier.

By then, however, Rollins, 32, was on the down side of his career, a career that would have meant so much had all of it been spent in Cleveland.

Rollins appeared in only 42 games for the Indians, hitting.233 with two homers.

It capped a 10 year major league career in which Rollins compiled a lifetime average of .269 with 77 homers and 399 RBI.

When Rollins wasn't offered a contract in 1971, he retired as an active player, and worked briefly in the front office of the Indians.

How different the story of "Eight Men Out" - the Black Sox Scandal of 1919 - might have been if "Shoeless Joe" Jackson had stayed in Cleveland.

Probably the best of the eight players barred from baseball by then-Commissioner Kenesaw Mountain Landis, Jackson most certainly would be among the Indians who are now enshrined in the Hall of Fame.

Jackson, who hit .408 in 1911 for the Cleveland club, then called the "Naps," was traded to Chicago in 1915 for long forgotten pitcher Ed Klepfer and outfielders Bobby (Braggo) Roth and Larry Chappell, and a reported $25,000.

It was during his time with the White Sox that Jackson and seven teammates allegedly conspired to throw the 1919 World Series.

The others: pitchers Eddie Cicotte and Claude Williams, third baseman Buck Weaver, shortstop Swede Risberg, outfielder Happy Felsch, first baseman Chick Gandil (who played for the Indians in 1916 but was sold to Chicago the following year) and utility infielder Fred McMullin.

It's interesting to wonder if Jackson might have stayed straight had he not been traded to Chicago - and it also is fascinating to contemplate how much better the Indians might have fared over the years if they'd kept him.

"Shoeless Joe" Jackson

After his .408 season in 1911, Jackson batted .395, .373 and .338 from 1912-14. He was hitting .327 in 83 games when Charles W. Somers, then owner of the Cleveland club, traded Shoeless Joe to the White Sox.

With the White Sox, Jackson hit .341, 301, .354, .351 and .382 from 1916 through all but the final week of the 1920 season - which leads to even more compelling speculation.

The eight Chicago players under investigation were indicted by a Grand Jury on September 28, six days before the season would end.

They were immediately suspended by White Sox owner Charles Comiskey. On that day Cleveland and Chicago were running one-two in the pennant race; the Naps leading by a half-game. After Jackson and the others were barred, the White Sox floundered and the Indians finished first by two games.

It was their first-ever pennant; they wouldn't win another for 28 years, and only four in the next 78 years.

The eight accused players were not convicted when they went to trial in the winter of 1920-21, but Landis suspended them for life to "preserve the integrity of baseball."

As it turned out, the acquisition of Roth for Jackson proved to be a good deal for the Indians - though not because he played so well in Cleveland.

It was because of the players the Indians obtained in a subsequent deal for Roth.

A fair hitter for three seasons, Roth was traded to Philadelphia for three players, two of whom became regulars, Larry Gardner and Charley Jamieson.

Klepfer won 21 and lost 16 in 3 1/2 seasons with the Indians and retired in 1919, and Chappell played three games and was sold to the Boston Braves.

Twenty-eight years after the fact

Rod Carew broke it in 1969, but until then a long-forgotten Indians outfielder named Bobby (Braggo) Roth held the American League record for stealing home six times in one season.

And to add some spice to Braggo's record, it was achieved 28 years after he died – sort of.

Bobby "Braggo" Roth

That is, Roth wasn't credited for the record he set in 1917 until 1964, when a Tribe farmhand named Paul Comstock ran across an old baseball book published in 1918.

In it Roth's six steals of home in 1917 were listed: April 15 vs. St. Louis; May 19 vs. Philadelphia; June 1 vs. Boston (with Babe Ruth pitching); July 1 vs. Chicago; July 12 and Aug. 27, both vs. Washington.

Until then another former Indian, Ben Chapman, was credited as being the only player to steal home six times in one season, 1931 for New York.

And then Carew stole home seven times in 1969 for the Minnesota Twins.

Oddly enough, Roth was not recognized as a great base-stealing threat. In his eight year major league career (with the Chicago White Sox, Indians, Philadelphia Athletics, Boston Red Sox, Washington Senators and New York Yankees) Roth swiped an average of only 23 a season, making his six thefts of home in 1917 even more impressive. In those eight seasons he played in the major leagues, Roth batted .284 in 811 games, with 30 homers.

Roth's primary claim to fame had to do with something other than stealing home. His career began in 1914 with the White Sox when he hit .294 in 34 games.

On Aug. 21, 1915, Braggo was a key man in what would be a memorable trade for both the White Sox and Indians. Roth was packaged, along with Larry Chappell, Ed Klepfer and $31,500 (a grand sum in those days!) in a deal that sent Joe Jackson from Cleveland to the White Sox.

Yes, the same "Shoeless Joe" Jackson who would, four years later, become one of eight White Sox players to be banned from baseball for life by then-Commissioner Kennesaw Mountain Landis for fixing the 1919 World Series against Cincinnati.

Fans can't help but wonder how different baseball history might have been if Jackson had not been traded in that deal that brought Braggo Roth to Cleveland.

It's possible that, without Jackson, the White Sox would not have won the American League pennant in 1919; he hit .351 with 96 RBI, and the Indians finished second, only 3 1/2 games behind Chicago.

It also is probable that, had Jackson remained with the Indians and not been allegedly involved in fixing the 1919 World Series, he'd be in the Hall of Fame today, with his .356 lifetime average over 17 seasons.

Roth was involved in another significant trade, one that brought Charlie Jamieson and two others to the Indians in 1919. The same Charlie Jamieson who is regarded by many as the best player - other than Shoeless Joe Jackson - not in the Hall of Fame.

But the legacy of Braggo Roth is that he's the man who finally was credited with stealing home six times in one season - 28 years after his death.

A good deal, then a bad one

Mickey Vernon was a key figure in one of the Indians' best-ever trades – and also was involved in one of the worst.

Fortunately, Vernon was a member of the team in 1949, when he batted .291 – but unfortunately was playing with the then-Washington Senators in 1953 when he won his second American League batting championship with a .337 average.

First, Vernon came to Cleveland, along with pitcher Early Wynn, from the Senators on Dec. 14, 1948, in exchange for pitchers Joe Haynes and Eddie Klieman, and first baseman Eddie Robinson. It was speculated that the deal was made because Haynes was then the son-in-law of Senators owner Clark Griffith.

Then, after he appeared in 28 games with a .189 average in 1950, Vernon was returned to Washington for reliever Dick Weik, who lasted only 11 games in Cleveland.

The Indians re-acquired Vernon, a left-handed hitting first baseman, in a 1958 cash deal with the Boston Red Sox. By then he was near the end of what would be a 20 year major league playing career, but still hit .293 in 119 games that season.

When the 1958 season ended the Indians traded Vernon again, this time to the Milwaukee Braves for minor league pitcher

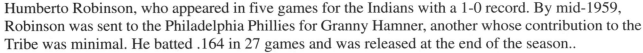
Mickey Vernon

Humberto Robinson, who appeared in five games for the Indians with a 1-0 record. By mid-1959, Robinson was sent to the Philadelphia Phillies for Granny Hamner, another whose contribution to the Tribe was minimal. He batted .164 in 27 games and was released at the end of the season..

Vernon, who broke in with the Senators in 1939 after a sparkling collegiate career at Villanova University, won his first batting championship with a .353 average in 1946.

When he came to the Indians in 1949, Vernon was quoted in a Cleveland *Plain Dealer* article that the deal would "add at least 20 points" to his average, which had fallen to .242 in 1948. "It's very simple," he said. "I won't have to bat against Bob Feller, Bob Lemon, Gene Bearden and the rest of the Cleveland pitchers anymore. Instead, I'll be batting against Washington pitching."

As it turned out, the trade added 49 points to Vernon's average, not just 20.

A seven time member of the A.L. all-star team, Vernon won his second batting title three years after leaving the Indians, narrowly beating former teammate Al Rosen by .001 percentage point on the final day of the season against the Philadelphia Athletics.

In that last game, Vernon went 2-for-4, raising his average to .337, lining out in what would be his final at-bat. The Senators had received word that Rosen had gone 3-for-5 against Detroit, giving him a .336 mark, and Vernon could have left the game at that point, but didn't.

However, he didn't bat again as the two players ahead of him in the Washington lineup were retired in base running blunders – which some suspected were intentional in order to protect Vernon's average.

Vernon ended his career as a player-coach for Pittsburgh in 1960, appearing in nine games, for a career average of .286 in 2,409 games.

He replaced Cookie Lavagetto in 1961 as manager of the Senators, a job he held until May 22, 1963, and later coached for several teams in the major leagues, and managed in the minors.

Old too soon, smart too late

They called him "Eatin' Ed," and the nickname was appropriate.

Then, in 1968, Ed Farmer was an 18 year old rookie pitcher for the Indians Only eight months out of high school, Farmer became a spring training legend.

Ed Farmer

Unfortunately for the Indians, however, Farmer became famous for his appetite, not his fastball, both of which were sensational.

To state it kindly, Farmer was eccentric, flamboyant and extremely immature. At least he was then, and through the first three or four years of his baseball career.

But after leaving the Indians, who gave up on Farmer and traded him in 1973 to Detroit for a couple of players who never did anything - and also after two arm operations that sidelined him for two years - Farmer became one of the best relief pitchers in the game for three seasons. He was credited with 54 saves from 1979-81 for the Chicago White Sox, and also pitched for Philadelphia, Baltimore, Milwaukee, Texas and Oakland, in addition to the Indians and Detroit.

Farmer retired in 1984 with an 11-year, 30-43 won-lost record and 75 saves.

After hanging up his spikes, Farmer became a scout, served as a special assistant to White Sox general manager Ron Schueler, and is an analyst for White Sox games on the radio – all of which further attests to the fact that he no longer is the irresponsible young man the Indians knew 24 years ago.

Then, as Farmer now knows better than anybody, though his arm was strong, he wasn't ready to face the challenge ahead. "Ed Farmer was supposed to be this young phenom," he said in an interview during the height of his success with Chicago. "He was with the Indians, a team that was desperately looking for a hero, and they picked Ed Farmer, at 18, to be that hero.

"At that time Ed Farmer could throw the ball as hard as anyone. But he was just a kid. He wasn't ready to be a hero. He wasn't ready for anything he was facing."

But Farmer tried. Oh, how he tried.

Once, while talking to a sportswriter during that first spring training, Farmer said his goal was to win both the Rookie of the Year Award and the Cy Young Award, because he'd promised his mother on her deathbed that he'd do it for her.

There also was the hamburger story. Farmer said he got hungry one night and ate 20 hamburgers in one sitting. And then, embellishing the story, he said he had been banned from several smorgasbord restaurants in Tucson because of his tremendous capacity for food.

Hence the nickname, "Eatin' Ed." It stuck with Farmer for a long time. "Too long," he said. "That hamburger story is like one of those fish stories. A guy catches a 20 inch fish and brags that it was, 'Oh, about 30 inches,' and the next thing it's like five feet. All of it made me look like a fool."

To set the record straight now, those "20" hamburgers really were only 18 of the small, White Castle variety, though being barred from the smorgasbords was true.

That was "Eatin' Ed" Farmer, a legend in his time, and a perfect example of somebody who got old too soon and smart too, late - at least for the benefit of the Indians.

They called it a "fadeaway" in his daddy's day, and once Jim Bagby Jr. learned the intricacies of the pitch – subsequently and currently known as a "screwball" - the Indians had quite a father-son combination.

The Bagbys, senior and junior, didn't pitch in Cleveland at the same time, of course. The father, known as "Sarge," won more games (31) in one season than any Cleveland pitcher did before or since (while losing 12) in 1920.

Jim Bagby Jr.

And without those victories the Indians would not have won their first pennant and World Series.

Unfortunately, Bagby Sr. never had another season like it and three years later was out of baseball and back on the family farm in Atlanta. His major league career record was 127-87 for nine years, 122-85 for the Indians.

Bagby Jr. got his start in the major leagues with the Boston Red Sox in 1938 when he won 15 games and lost 11. Then he was primarily a fastball pitcher, but in a 1942 article in the Cleveland *News*, Bagby said he learned a lesson.

"I had a good fast ball, but nothing else. As long as the hitters didn't know what stuff I had, I did all right," he said.

"But, by 1939 they had caught on to me. They knew I only had a fastball, so I had to learn the fadeaway if I wanted to stay in baseball. I worked with my dad and by the time I got to the Indians, I had the pitch down pretty good."

The Indians got Bagby in the winter of 1940-41 in a six-player deal that was one of the biggest in baseball at that time. Bagby came to Cleveland with catcher Gene Desautels and outfielder Gerald "Gee" Walker for catcher Frankie Pytlak, third baseman Odell "Bad News" Hale and pitcher Joe Dobson.

Tribe fans didn't like the trade at first because Pytlak and Hale were two of their favorites.

But Bagby soon captured their fancy by winning 17 games in each 1942 and 1943, though he often resided in Manager Lou Boudreau's doghouse.

In five seasons (through 1945) with the Tribe, Bagby's record was 55-54, giving the father-son combination a 177-139 won-lost mark.

While Bagby Jr. didn't enjoy the success his father did in 1920, he is often remembered as one of the two pitchers credited with stopping Joe DiMaggio's record consecutive game hitting streak at 56 on July 17, 1941 at the Stadium.

Southpaw Al Smith started the game and was the loser, as the Yankees prevailed, 4-3. Bagby took over in the eighth and faced DiMaggio in his final at-bat with the bases loaded and one out - and Bagby Jr. could credit Bagby Sr. for what happened next. So could the Indians.

Bagby threw DiMaggio his "fadeaway."

The same "fadeaway" he'd learned from his dad.

The Yankee star swung and bounced the pitch to Boudreau, who played the bad hop off his chest and turned it into a double play, which ended the inning and, as it turned out, DiMaggio's streak.

Thanks, at least in part, to Jim Bagby Sr.

The legacies of Joe Gordon

Joe Gordon helped create two of the most memorable legacies in Indians history, as both a player and manager.

Gordon was a leader with his bat and glove in the Indians drive to the American League pennant

Joe Gordon

and the franchise's World Series championship in 1948. He hit .280 with 32 homers and 124 runs batted in, and teamed with shortstop Lou Boudreau to form one of the best double play combinations in baseball.

It was Gordon who suggested to Boudreau, the player manager, that knuckleballer Gene Bearden should start the one-game playoff against Boston for the pennant, after the two teams finished the season in a tie. Boudreau took Gordon's advice and the Tribe won, 8-3.

Before joining the Indians in an Oct. 11, 1946 trade with the New York Yankees for pitcher Allie Reynolds, Gordon participated in five World Series. He retired as a player in 1950, then managed in the minors for several years.

In June of 1958, Gordon was asked by Indians General Manager Frank Lane if would like to return to Cleveland to replace Bobby Bragan as manager. According to newspaper accounts at the time, the conversation between Lane and Gordon was short.

Lane: "Would you like to manage the Indians?"

Gordon: "Hell, Yes."

Lane: "When can you come here and take over the team?"

Gordon: "Yesterday."

Lane: "What about (contract) terms?"

Gordon: "The hell with terms."

And with that, the second chapter - and without a doubt the most bizarre - in Gordon's career with the Indians began.

After completing the 1958 season, Gordon, in 1959, led the Indians to what would be their last serious run at the American League pennant for the next 35 years. They finished with an 89-65 record, though it wasn't good enough and Chicago finished five lengths ahead of the Indians.

Through it all, Gordon feuded in the clubhouse with players Jim Piersall and Billy Martin, and in the front office with Lane, who supported the two players against the manager. On Sept. 18, with only seven games remaining, Gordon announced his intention to resign at the end of the season. Lane, of course, was overjoyed and immediately started courting Leo Durocher as Gordon's successor.

Durocher, however, soon priced himself out of the job and Lane, given time to reconsider Gordon's performance (as well as Piersall's and Martin's), asked Gordon to return for 1960. Gordon, who'd also had time to reflect on the situation, agreed. and was introduced as the Indians' "new" manager at a press conference attended by members of the media who were expecting to greet Durocher.

But the reconciliation didn't last long. Only 95 games into the 1960 season, in fact.

On Aug. 3, Lane traded Gordon to Detroit for Tigers manager Jimmie Dykes.

It was the only time in baseball history that managers were traded.

It was the kind of deal only Frank Lane could dream up.

Aptly nicknamed "Frantic Frank" when he was general manager of the Indians from 1958 through 1960, Lane turned the team upside down with his trades.

The most notorious of them sent Rocky Colavito to Detroit, and Herb Score to Chicago on consecutive days in April 1960.

Lane's craziest deal, however, was made August 3, 1960 when - for the only time in major league baseball history - he traded managers with the Tigers.

Joe Gordon, who'd piloted the Tribe since June 28, 1958, when he replaced Bobby Bragan, was sent to Detroit for Jimmie Dykes, who was in his second season managing the Tigers.

Lane, who thrived on media attention, tried to credit - or blame - his counterpart with the Tigers, Bill DeWitt, for being the instigator of the Gordon-for-Dykes deal. He even claimed that Gordon pushed for it.

Frank Lane in effigy

"Two weeks ago," Lane said then, "DeWitt suggested that we trade managers. We laughed it off, but later I mentioned it to Joe (Gordon), and he said, 'It may not be such a bad idea.' And since Joe was so agreeable, I did it."

At the time, the Indians, a pre-season contender for the pennant, were fourth, 50-46 (.521), six games behind New York, and the Tigers were in sixth place, 45-52 (.464).

As it turned out, it was a deal that didn't help either team; the Indians went 26-32 under Dykes and finished fourth, 21 games behind the Yankees, and the Tigers went 26-31 under Gordon, winding up sixth, 26 games off the pace.

But never mind the result. Lane was delighted with the national notoriety he received. The deal also probably was made to placate one of Lane's favorites, Jim Piersall, who didn't get along with Gordon.

As the Cleveland *Plain Dealer* reported in the wake of the trade of managers: "Members of the Indians, equally confused and amused by the unprecedented development, voiced the belief that it was inevitable either Piersall or Gordon would go. Gordon … long felt that the outspoken outfielder (Piersall) tried to undermine his authority as manager."

By taking over the Detroit team, Gordon also was re-united with Colavito, which was ironic. Gordon reportedly had pushed hard for Lane to send Colavito to the Tigers at the start of the season, a deal that angered Cleveland fans.

And, trading Gordon for Dykes was further ironic in view of what Lane had done the previous season. When it had become evident in the waning days of 1959 that the Indians would not win the pennant, Lane fired Gordon with the intention of hiring Leo Durocher to pilot the team in 1960.

There was so much public criticism of Durocher, however, that Lane backed off and rehired Gordon, even gave him a raise.

But it didn't take long for Lane to change again.

And when the opportunity arose to unload Gordon - allegedly thanks to DeWitt's "suggestion" and Gordon's willingness to go - Lane jumped at what certainly was the craziest trade in Cleveland baseball history.

A very fortunate victory

It was only a gag, a promotion the Indians hoped would help sell a few additional tickets for a game that was played in the old Cleveland Stadium on June 4, 1951.

But it turned out to be even better – an 8-2 victory over the hated New York Yankees and longtime nemesis "Steady Eddie" Lopat, who had beaten them 11 consecutive times coming into the game.

Eddie Lopat

The Indians, then in fourth place, six lengths behind the front-running Yankees, were trying desperately to get back in the pennant race.

They were so desperate, in fact, that the Indians management, then under the direction of usually ultra-conservative General Manager Hank Greenberg, went along with a suggestion by a fan that "lucky" rabbits' feet be handed out to the fans, 20,217 of whom attended the game.

They were supposed to jinx Lopat, a southpaw "junk ball" pitcher whose won-lost record at the time was 8-0 in nine starts.

The good luck charms didn't work too well at the onset of the game as the Yankees scored twice in the first inning off Tribe right-hander Mike Garcia.

However, when Lopat took the mound in the bottom of the first inning, a fan jumped over the low railing in front of the box seats along the third base line and trotted toward Lopat.

"I was taking my tosses to start the inning and I got this feeling that someone was trying to sneak up on me," Lopat explained in a story that appeared in *The National Pastime* magazine published by SABR (the Society for American Baseball Research) several years later.

"I turned around and, sure enough, there's a guy coming at me, carrying a black kitten. He walked up to the mound and threw the kitten at me. I raised my hands – I didn't want its claws in my face – and (the kitten) hit me in the chest and clung there for a few seconds before I could brush it off.

"By that time a security guard came out and walked the guy – and the kitten – off the field and the game got started."

The "guy" was ejected from the Stadium, along with his black cat, but apparently his attempt to jinx Lopat and the Yankees was more effective than the rabbits' feet.

Luke Easter and Al Rosen reached base with two out in the first inning, and Bob Kennedy smashed a home run off Lopat, putting the Indians ahead, 3-2.

But their good fortune, for whatever reason, didn't stop there.

The Tribe scored two more runs before Lopat got out of the first inning, another run came home, for a 6-2 lead, in the second, and Lopat was sent to the showers, replaced by Tommy Byrne, who finished the game, giving up another run in the sixth.

Garcia, a.k.a. "The Big Bear," righted himself after struggling in the first inning and blanked the Yankees the rest of the way, en route to a 20-13 season record.

And when the game was over and he was asked about his success, Garcia grinned and reached into his back pocket.

"It was this," he said – holding a rabbit's foot in his hand.

The rebirth of 'Sudden Sam'

It was supposed to be only a stop en route to the Hall of Fame for Sam McDowell, back there in 1960.

He had everything, a blazing fast ball clocked in the 100 mph range, a curve ball that scouts said "fell off a table," and a tall, lean, muscular body.

But then, "Sudden Sam," as McDowell soon was nicknamed, ran into a road block.

Alcohol and drugs.

By McDowell's own admission, "I was the biggest, most hopeless and violent drunk in baseball," during his 15 years in the major leagues, the first 11 with the Indians.

Finally, after failing to reform - and to regain his blazing fast ball - with San Francisco, the New York Yankees and Pittsburgh from 1972 to mid-1975, McDowell was drummed out of baseball.

He has since turned his life around and now, as a certified alcohol and drug rehabilitation counselor, McDowell is trying to keep others from wasting their talents as he did his.

The former left-handed pitcher for whom the Indians had the highest hopes from the time scouts Hoot Evers and Bob Kennedy signed him for what was then one of the largest bonuses ever granted, worked for several teams in the employment assistance programs.

Sam McDowell

As for the problem that cost McDowell fame and fortune, he said, "I don't know if anybody could have helped me then," McDowell says, "but I wish they had." Certainly, so did the Indians.

Several major league teams were beating a path to McDowell's home during his outstanding high school pitching career.

McDowell signed for a $75,000 bonus in 1960 when he was considered another Sandy Koufax, and earned his nickname in his major league debut in September 1961.

Pitching in relief against Minnesota, McDowell cracked a couple of ribs while striking out Jim Lemon. When reporters asked Lemon's opinion of McDowell, the Minnesota slugger replied, "His fast ball sure gets up there all of a sudden."

From then on McDowell was "Sudden Sam."

McDowell won 20 games in 1970, led the American League with a 2.18 earned run average in 1965 when his record was 17-11, was No.1 in the A.L. in strikeouts five times, pitched four one-hitters, including two of them back-to-back in 1966, was selected to the All-Star team five times, and was voted the Indians' "Man of the Year" in both 1969 and 1970 by Cleveland baseball writers.

Sudden Sam's major contribution to the Indians, however, might have been the players he brought in trade - pitcher Gaylord Perry and shortstop Frank Duffy - when he was dealt to San Francisco in 1972.

After the Giants, Yankees and Pirates also gave up on McDowell because he wouldn't stop drinking, his record was 141-134 with 2,453 strikeouts in 2,492 innings.

Finally, McDowell reformed in 1980 after he nearly died from alcohol abuse, though by then it was too late to save his wasted baseball career.

McDowell dried out and went into rehab - which he says is a continuing process - and now works hard trying to prevent other young men from wasting their careers.

The Speaker-Cobb scandal

Two of baseball's greatest players - one of whom was former Indians player-manager Tris Speaker –
were involved in a 1926 gambling scandal that nearly ruined the careers and reputations of both.

Involved with Speaker was Ty Cobb, the so-called "Georgia Peach," who held the record for
making the most hits in a career (4,189), before Pete Rose surpassed it and retired with 4,256 after the 1986 season.

Tris Speaker/Ty Cobb

Cobb and Speaker, elected to the Hall of Fame in 1936 and
1937, respectively, and two other players, pitchers "Smoky Joe"
Wood of the Indians and Dutch Leonard of the Tigers, were accused
in 1926 of fixing the outcome of a game played in 1919 between
Cleveland and Detroit.

It was Leonard who made the allegation because he apparently
was resentful of the way he'd been treated by Cobb, who'd been
his manager with the Tigers. Leonard, who retired after the 1925
season, charged that the Indians, with second place locked up,
deliberately lost a game to the Tigers in 1919. He claimed that all
four players – himself, Cobb, Speaker and Wood, who retired in
1922 – had made, and won bets on the fixed game.

Leonard even produced letters from Cobb and Wood that
supported his allegations and implicated all four players.

According to a report published in the Chicago *Herald-
Examiner* and disseminated by the *Universal Press Service*, "The gist of Leonard's statement to (then-
Commissioner Kenesaw Mountain) Landis was that, following the game between Cleveland and Detroit
on Sept. 24, 1919, he, Cobb, Speaker and Wood met under the grandstand where the talk turned to the
game of the next day.

"'Don't worry about tomorrow's game,' Speaker said, according to Leonard's story, 'we (Cleveland) have got second place clinched and you will win tomorrow.'

"The four then agreed, Leonard says, that they might as well bet on the game. Cobb, Leonard al-
leges, was to put up $2,000; Leonard, Wood and Speaker $1,000 each."

Leonard also produced two letters published by the Chicago newspaper that he said were received
from Wood and Cobb. Enclosed in the first, from Wood, was the money that each had won on the game.
In Cobb's letter to Leonard, he acknowledged receipt of the money, although Cobb wrote that he was
"considerably disappointed in our business proposition" because he had expected to receive a larger
amount of money.

However, after an extensive investigation by Landis, the players were cleared on Jan. 27, 1927,
although Speaker and Cobb were subsequently required by American league President Ban Johnson to
resign as player-managers of their teams.

Speaker, who played for the Indians from 1916-26, and managed the team from 1918-26, went to the
Washington Senators in 1927, and to the Philadelphia Athletics in 1928, after which he retired with a
career batting average of .345 for 22 seasons (he played for the Boston Red Sox from 1907-15).

Cobb played for the Tigers from 1905-26, was their manager from 1921-26, and played for the
Athletics in 1927 and 1928, after which he retired with major league baseball's highest career batting
average, .366, compiled in 24 seasons.

As long as World Series highlight films are played and replayed, the scene will remain: Dale Mitchell at the plate.

He checks his swing against a pitch that appears high and out of the strike zone.

Umpire Babe Pinelli raises his right arm for strike three.

Bedlam breaks out in Yankee Stadium.

It was the final pitch of Don Larsen's perfect game - the only perfect game in World Series history - a 2-0 victory for the New York Yankees against the Brooklyn Dodgers in Game 5 on Oct. 8, 1956.

For Mitchell, pinch hitting for Sal Maglie, it was the second-last plate appearance of his 11 year major league career and, the truth be told, it's too bad it ended that way.

Too bad, at least, that the memory of Dale Mitchell to many fans might be of him taking that called third strike to climax Larsen's masterpiece. Better that Mitchell should be remembered as the great though oft-maligned hitter that he was for the Indians in the late-1940s and early-1950s.

As then-manager Lou Boudreau was quoted in 1949, the year Mitchell led the American League with 203 hits and 23 triples: "If anyone ever again hits .400, Dale Mitchell will be the man." And

Dale Mitchell

though Mitchell had his detractors, he was one of the best hitters in the game for most of his career.

He hit .300 or better six times, striking out only 119 times in 3,984 at bats, an average of less than 11 a season. Hank Greenberg and Al Lopez, in the early-1950s the Indians general manager and man-ager, respectively, often were critical of Mitchell because, they said, he didn't pull the ball enough.

"Home run hitters drive Cadillacs; singles hitters drive Fords," Greenberg - a one-time home run hitter himself - used to chide Mitchell in the hope of motivating him.

And Lopez nagged Mitchell to "swish" with his bat instead of "slapping the ball."

But nothing convinced Mitchell. Though he hit 13 homers in 1953 and 11 in 1951, he totaled only 41 for his career.

It didn't bother the fans either. Mitchell was one of the most popular players on the team.

Finally, after he slumped to .259 in 1955, and as he was hitting a lowly .133 after 38 games in 1956, the Indians sold Mitchell to Brooklyn for $10,000 on July 29.

Before he left the Stadium, Mitchell walked through the clubhouse, bidding his former teammates goodbye and good luck. He even went up to the press and radio boxes to thank the writers and broad-casters for their support.

But Mitchell refused to shake hands with Lopez.

He was quoted as saying, "Cleveland and its fans have been good to me, but it might have been better if I had been popular in other places," meaning, of course, the manager's and general manager's offices.

And then Mitchell joined the Dodgers to keep his date with destiny - and Don Larsen in the 1956 World Series. He finished with a career batting average of .312 in 11 major league seasons, but - un-fairly - is best remembered for striking out at the end.

Larry Doby's biggest victory

It might have been the most unpopular move by Bill Veeck, who didn't make many mistakes after buying the Indians in 1946.

But this one - signing Larry Doby, the American League's first black player – initially created an immediate storm of protest.

Helyn and Larry Doby

Veeck said he took "considerable heat, including an estimated 20,000 pieces of hate mail, much of it containing threats and obscenities," after he bought Doby for $10,000 from the Newark Eagles of the Negro National League on July 3, 1947.

Doby, then a second baseman who followed Jackie Robinson into major league baseball by 81 days, flopped that first half-season in Cleveland, going 5-for-32 (.156) in 29 games.

But in 1948 it was different. He was switched to the outfield and became one of the best center fielders in baseball then and since.

The addition of Doby also was met with disapproval by some members of the Indians. Veeck held a team meeting before Doby arrived and, according to Doby's biography, *Pride Against Prejudice*, told the players: "I understand that some of you said if a nigger joins the club you're leaving. Well, you can leave now because this guy (Doby) is going to be a bigger star than any guy in this room."

When Doby arrived, he was introduced to the players individually. The book said two refused to shake Doby's hand. Both were southern-born first basemen, again, according to *Pride Against Prejudice,* and believed to be Les Fleming and Eddie Robinson, though Robinson has denied that contention several times since it surfaced.

Doby struck out in his first plate appearance, July 5 in Chicago, establishing two relief pitchers as the answers to trivia questions, to wit: Doby was a pinch hitter for Tribe pitcher Bryan Stephens, and Earl Harrist of the White Sox was the hurler who fanned Doby on five pitches.

That strikeout brings up another interesting story, since contradicted in the Doby book.

Veeck, in a 1961 interview, recalled Doby's first at-bat: "He swung at three pitches and missed each by at least a foot. (Doby) was so discouraged ... he sat in the corner (of the dugout), all alone, with his head in his hands. Joe Gordon was up next ... and missed each of three pitches by at least two feet and came back to the bench and sat down next to Doby, and put his head in his hands, too."

It was a nice story but the fact is, Gordon was on third base when Doby batted.

Veeck said he personally answered all of those 20,000 letters of criticism, and within a year Doby completely won the fans over as he became a star of the first magnitude.

Doby helped lead the Indians to pennants in 1948 and 1954, made the American League All-Star team six times, and retired in 1959 with a 13-year major league batting average of .283 and 253 homers. He also played in the major leagues for the White Sox and Detroit, as well as in Japan. He was elected to the Hall of Fame in 1998.

And just as Doby was the second black player in the major leagues, he also was the game's second black manager with the White Sox in 1978, after coaching stints with the Indians and Montreal.

It happened nearly seven decades ago, on July 10, 1932 at old League Park, and is still a major league record: Nine hits - a week's worth, if you will - in just one game.

Johnny Burnett, an otherwise-undistinguished infielder for the Indians, lashed seven singles and two doubles in 11 trips to the plate in an 18 inning slugfest against Philadelphia. It once was called the "daffiest" baseball game ever played.

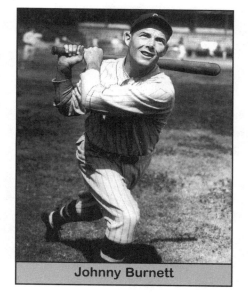

Johnny Burnett

Jimmy Foxx hit three homers as the Athletics prevailed, 18-17, despite the Indians getting 33 hits, which also remains a major league record, as were the 58 hits by both teams.

Ironically, Philadelphia's winning run scored - believe it or not - on a ground ball that was lost in the sun!

Here's how Sam Otis of the Cleveland *Plain Dealer*, reported the game:

"Out beyond the edges of a deepening shadow that had eked its way almost to the distant left field barrier of League Park - out in the lone patch of sunlight lingering to pester an unfortunate fielder - a crashing ground smash yesterday took a pesky hop into the setting rays of Old Sol to give the Philadelphia Athletics an eighteen inning triumph over a never-say-die band of Indians in the most dramatic diamond struggle in Cleveland history. The score was 18-17.

"An unlucky hop - a double for Eric McNair - a run for the great Jimmy Foxx, who already had crashed three home runs into the left field concrete stands - a feat never before accomplished - and the Indians had lost after five times rallying to erase leads acclimated by the enemy in a contest that extended four hours and five minutes, during which time not one of the 10,000 startled spectators even thought of departing ere the final verdict was sealed."

Burnett singled his first three trips, then doubled and singled again for 5-for-5, before striking out in the seventh. Then Burnett singled, doubled, and lined two more singles in his next four at-bats, and flied out in the 17th.

Another oddity was that winning pitcher Ed Rommel gave up 29 hits in the final 17 innings in relief of Lew Krausse. According to the newspaper account, Rommel remained in the game because A's manager Connie Mack brought only two pitchers - Rommel and Krausse - to the game.

The first two games of the series had been played in Philadelphia on Friday and Saturday, July 8 and 9, but this one had to be moved to Cleveland because Sunday baseball was outlawed in Pennsylvania at that time.

And this final oddity: it was the only game Rommel won in 1932, and was the final victory in his 171-119 career record. He later became an American League umpire.

Burnett, who joined the Tribe in 1927, achieved one more distinction before he was traded to the St. Louis Browns for outfielder Bruce Campbell on Nov. 20, 1934.

Burnett hit the first home run in the old Cleveland Municipal Stadium on Aug. 7, 1932, in a 7-4 victory over Washington. He played just one more season for St. Louis in 1935 and retired with a .284 lifetime average in 558 games - none bigger or better than the game he played on July 10, 1932.

The frantic wheeler-dealer

It began innocently enough, at the winter meetings in 1957, a couple of weeks after Frank Lane became the Indians general manager.

Lane, who'd been a very unpopular general manager of the St. Louis Cardinals because he'd traded Red Schoendienst and threatened to deal Stan Musial, replaced the fired Hank Greenberg in Cleveland.

Frank Lane

His first transaction was to draft minor league outfielder Gary Geiger. Two days later Lane struck big time.

Pitcher Early Wynn and outfielder Al Smith were sent to the Chicago White Sox, and Lane was off and running. In exchange for Wynn and Smith, the Indians received journeyman third baseman Fred Hatfield and veteran outfielder Minnie Minoso, a longtime favorite of Lane.

Between November 12, 1957 his first day on the job, and January 3, 1961, when he "resigned" and joined Charlie Finley in Kansas City, Lane made 49 transactions involving 108 players.

He always seemed to have a team coming, one going, and another on the field.

Lane also fired managers Bobby Bragan, hired Joe Gordon, fired Gordon, rehired him the next day, and four months later traded Gordon to Detroit for Tigers Manager Jimmie Dykes.

Lane once estimated he made more than 400 deals in his career, and claimed, "Every one I wanted to make, I made. The only deals that irked me are the ones I didn't make."

During his always-tumultuous career, Lane also was general manager of Cincinnati and the Chicago White Sox, in addition to the Cardinals, Athletics and Indians.

Despite his penchant for wheeling and dealing which often resulted in turmoil, Lane was considered a good judge of talent and turned several losing teams into winners.

He came close to doing that in Cleveland. The Tribe finished sixth in 1957, climbed to fourth the next year, and to second in 1959, losing the pennant to Chicago by five games.

But then Lane went overboard. In the space of six days in April 1960, Lane made three trades that backfired:

* Norm Cash (who became the American League batting champion in 1961) was sent to Detroit on April 12 for Steve Demeter, who wound up as a career minor leaguer;

* Rocky Colavito was dealt to the Tigers on April 17 for Harvey Kuenn; and

* Herb Score was traded to Chicago on April 18 for Barry Latman.

Cleveland fans were outraged, especially over the Colavito-Kuenn deal. The Indians dropped back to fourth place that season and, by the following January, Lane was gone.

Lane would never admit to having made a mistake in trading Colavito, even though he got rid of Kuenn at the end of 1960, sending him to the San Francisco Giants for pitcher Johnny Antonelli and outfielder Willie Kirkland, two players who contributed little to the Indians

At a dinner a few years later he again angered Tribe fans.

"I'd still trade that dago fruit peddler (Colavito) for Kuenn if I had to do it over again," said Lane, who died at 85 in 1981.

Frank Lane's failed leader

Even then, in 1958 as a 29-year old second baseman, Billy Martin was recognized for his combativeness - and leadership.

The same reasons George Steinbrenner gave for hiring Martin five times to manage the New York Yankees.

"Billy is not a Mickey Mantle, but I want him because he will take charge on the field," is the way Indians General Manager Frank Lane explained his acquisition of Martin.

Lane sent former relief aces Ray Narleski and Don Mossi, and minor league infielder Ossie Alvarez to Detroit for Martin and pitcher Al Cicotte on November 20, 1958.

"Martin was the man I wanted when I came to Cleveland a year ago. In fact, I tried to get him before I even hung up my hat here," Lane said then.

In his first 12 months in Cleveland, Lane made 17 deals involving 42 players - 21 coming and 21 going - earning for himself the nicknames "Frantic Frank" and "Trader Lane."

Lane said he was willing to "go high" to get Martin, a member of five Yankee championship teams and the World Series star in 1953, because, "We needed Billy more than anyone else ... he's better than anything we had at second base last year."

Billy Martin

Martin had well established a feisty reputation by the time he came to Cleveland. Ironically, it was the same factor in his being exiled by the Yankees that triggered Lane's determination to get him.

Martin fell from favor with the Yankees - and, they said, was an "evil influence" - when he and teammates Whitey Ford, Mickey Mantle and Hank Bauer brawled with other customers in a New York nightclub while celebrating Martin's 29th birthday, May 16, 1957.

Martin also had highly-publicized fights with St. Louis catcher Clint Courtney, Boston outfielder Jim Piersall (who would become his teammate with the Indians in 1959), and later with Chicago Cubs pitcher Jim Brewer, among others.

All of which seemed to make Lane want him more.

"The Indians have needed a leader, and I don't mean simply a holler guy," Lane said. "What we've lacked is a hustling, scrappy player who will keep the others on their toes.

"That's the sort of player Martin is. It's the intangibles that make him so valuable."

But, despite Lane's praise, those "intangibles" weren't enough for Martin to help the Indians in 1959, his only season in Cleveland. He played 73 games, hit .260, and the Indians failed to win the pennant again, though they finished second to Chicago by five games.

The following winter Lane traded Martin, his failed "leader," and two other players to Cincinnati for another second baseman, Johnny Temple, who also contributed very little.

As for Mossi and Narleski ... Mossi became a starter and compiled a 17-9 record for the Tigers in 1959, and 59-44 the next five years, while Narleski was 4-12 before retiring at the end of his only season in Detroit.

Martin spent his final season as a player in 1961 with the Reds and Minnesota Twins, after which he began his managerial career.

It was a 'phenomenal' play

It was the first ever in baseball history and was called "phenomenal" when shortstop Neal Ball made an unassisted triple play for the Cleveland team, then called the "Naps," in the opener of a double header against Boston at League Park on July 19, 1909.

Neal Ball plaque

Only nine unassisted triple plays have been made since then, including the second in baseball history – and the only one in a World Series game – by Indians second baseman Bill Wambsganss against Brooklyn on Oct. 10, 1920.

Ball's triple play occurred in the second inning of a 6-1 victory by the Naps and Cy Young over the Red Sox.

It came after Heinie Wagner led off with a single and Chick Stahl beat out a bunt, placing runners at first and second. Amby McConnell failed in two attempts to sacrifice, then hit a line drive toward center field.

The runners were off with the crack of the bat, and so was Ball. He turned to his left and leaped to catch McConnell's liner for one out, took two steps and stepped on second, doubling Wagner, and tagged Stahl, who had no chance to return to first base.

The crowd was momentarily stunned, then broke into wild cheering upon the realization of Ball's achievement.

As the Cleveland *Plain Dealer* reported, "Ball did not stop with this record breaking play. In addition he accepted eight other chances, having nine putouts … three more than went to the credit of first baseman George Stovall of the Naps. This is thought to be a fielding record.

"(Ball) was not content with carrying off the fielding honors. When he came to bat in the second inning after making his triple play, he was greeted with tremendous applause and responded to the cheers of the fans by hitting the ball over Tris Speaker's head in center field for a home run. (And) in the fourth inning he made a two-bagger.

"After the game Ball said, 'I never dreamed of making a triple play until I had touched second base with my foot and saw Stahl charging into me. He could not recover his balance in time to turn and chase back to first, so all I had to do was keep on going and touch him.

"'That was all there was to it. It all happened in about two seconds. It was a play made to order to fit the situation, and I am mighty glad that I happened to be the one who was right in the right spot and able to pull it off.

"'I don't suppose I will ever get the chance to make another such play, but I've got no kick coming. It's pretty fine to be able to make it once in a lifetime.'"

It is ironic that, of the 10 unassisted triple plays in the history of major league baseball, Cleveland players have been involved in five of them though the Indians were the victims three times.

Eleven years after Ball made his fielding gem, Wambsganss did the same in Game 5 of the 1920 World Series against Brooklyn's Clarence Mitchell; Red Sox first baseman George Burns made the third unassisted triple play against Frank Brower of the Indians on Sept. 14, 1923; Johnny Neun, a first baseman for the Tigers, retired three Indians upon catching Homer Summa's liner on May 31, 1927; as did Washington shortstop Ron Hansen against Joe Azcue and the Indians on July 30, 1968.

Another one who got away

There was no great outcry by Tribe fans when Roger Maris was traded by Frank Lane to Kansas City on June 15, 1958, although, in retrospect, maybe there should have been.

After all, Maris did hit more homers, 61, in a single season, 1961, than anybody in the history of baseball, including Babe Ruth, who had 60 in 1927, until Mark McGwire and Sammy Sosa eclipsed the record in 1998.

The Indians got first baseman Vic Power and shortstop Woodie Held for Maris and two others, pitcher Dick Tomanek and first baseman Preston Ward.

Roger Maris

The deal pleased Maris, who was "disgusted" with the Indians, he admitted in a 1964 interview, citing Lane and Manager Bobby Bragan as the reasons.

"I wasn't their sort of player and they made it clear," said Maris, who died at age 51 in 1985.

Ironically, Bragan was fired 12 days after Maris was traded, and Lane departed two years later.

Actually, the Maris deal wasn't all that bad for the Indians. Power hit .282 with 25 homers the next three seasons, and Held played in Cleveland through 1964, hitting .252 with 127 homers.

And in subsequent deals, Power brought pitcher Pedro Ramos from Minnesota, and the Indians got outfielder Chuck Hinton from Washington for Held.

But still, Maris's 203 homers over seven seasons also would have been great for the Indians.

Maris went to the Yankees in 1960 when he and two others were traded by Kansas City.

A year later, in 161 games, he astounded baseball fans - and angered many of them - by breaking the record Ruth had set in a 154 game season 34 years earlier.

Maris disdained a football scholarship to the University of Oklahoma to sign with the Indians in 1953 for a $5,000 bonus, plus $10,000 more if he made it to the big leagues.

He did, in 1957, when the Indians also had Rocky Colavito in right field.

But Maris hit only .235 with 14 homers in 116 games as a rookie, and his average was .225 when Lane sent him to Kansas City.

At the time, the K.C. franchise was still the Athletics and critics sneered that it was a New York farm team because of all the deals that were made between the two teams.

The Yankees got the best of most of them, but not necessarily in the package for Maris.

After showing signs of developing into a home run hitter, Maris, was traded to New York along with shortstop Joe Demaestri and first baseman Kent Hadley. The A's got pitcher Don Larsen, first baseman Norm Siebern and outfielders Hank Bauer and Marv Throneberry.

It proved to be a good deal for both teams - and, of course, also for Maris, whose record homer came in his second-last at-bat in the final day of 1961 off Tracy Stallard of Boston.

Thereafter, Maris never came close to duplicating the success he enjoyed in 1961.

In his seven subsequent seasons, Maris hit a total of 117 home runs, never more than the 33 he hit in 1962, and closed out his major league career with two final seasons with the St. Louis Cardinals in 1967 and 1968.

The 'Good Humor Man'

Leon "Daddy Wags" Wagner had a wiggle in his walk, talk and batting stance.

He was the Indians "Good Humor Man" - most of the time.

Once during a baseball clinic at the Stadium, a woman asked Wagner why he wiggled before he swung the bat.

Leon "Daddy Wags" Wagner

"What wiggle?" Wagner wanted to know. "Show me." The woman did and Wagner said, "Shall we dance?" Another time Wagner was asked at a luncheon how he got his "Daddy Wags" nickname. The explanation went on for 10 minutes or more. When it was over, nobody was quite sure what Wagner said.

But everybody enjoyed it.

In the winter of 1969, a year after Wagner had been traded to the Chicago White Sox for Russ Snyder, he was arrested in Los Angeles for driving while intoxicated.

Wagner claimed it was a case of mistaken identity.

"That wasn't me," he said, threatening a lawsuit. "Somebody borrowed my car and got drunk. He was stopped by police and gave 'em my driver's license, which was in the glove compartment.

"I'm going to sue for defamation of character. It would be the same thing as somebody being caught at a freak party saying he was Bing Crosby or Bob Hope.

"I got the same rights, don't I?" asked Daddy Wags, who was sometimes off the wall - even off the planet on occasion.

But always entertaining, and always unpredictable.

In 1967, Wagner and Rocky Colavito were negotiating contracts with Indians President Gabe Paul. Both were coming off seasons in which their performances had slipped.

Colavito said he was insulted by Paul's offer, which included a 25 percent cut. But Wagner settled for the same money he made in 1966, the year he hit 23 home runs with 66 RBI, while batting .279, seven points over his 12 year major league average.

"I've got too much pride to hold out for more money based on the kind of season I had," Wagner said then. "Besides, I'll make up for it next year. I'll just go along with the program this time. The way I figure it, I'm like a racehorse, like Buckpasser, you know?

"I mean, you've got to win or place to collect the big money. I just showed."

Daddy Wags played for the Tribe from 1964, when he was acquired from California in a deal for Barry Latman and Joe Adcock, until June of 1968.

After hitting .253 with 31 homers and 100 RBI in 1964, Wagner was upset when he was not elected "Man of the Year" by Cleveland's baseball writers.

It was explained to Wagner that his second half slump that season cost him the award, but his indignation persisted.

Finally it was suggested that Wagner might receive a "Man of the Half Year" trophy. "Great," said Daddy Wags, though no such award existed.

And when his career ended in 1970, Wagner had no regrets. "Don't worry about Daddy Wags," he said. "No matter what, he ain't going to starve."

Growing up in Vera Cruz, Mexico, even by the time he had become an engineering student at the University of Mexico, Roberto Francisco Avila y Gonzalez – better known as Bobby Avila, or by his Americanized nickname, "Beto" – wanted to be a matador.

"But intelligence and ability prevailed. Avila found it was easier to make the baseball team in college than fight bulls," according to a story in the Cleveland *News* on Oct. 28, 1954, announcing that he had been elected the Indians' "Man of the Year."

Bobby Avila

The Tribe's second baseman was then the reigning American League batting champion with a .341 average and, in the flush of his success, predicted he could become the first player to hit .400 since Ted Williams in 1941.

Avila was negotiating a contract for 1955 and reportedly was seeking a salary of $30,000 – that's no typo! – a raise of about $13,000 over the $17,000 he was paid in 1954 when the Indians won the pennant and set an A.L. record with 111 victories.

"(Rogers) Hornsby did it three times (hit .401 in 1922, .424 in 1924, and .403 in 1925) and he's just human," Avila said then. "If one people (player) can do it, why not another? That's only four hits in 10 tries. That's not impossible. I will try for .400 next year."

Needless to say, Avila fell short of his goal and, in fact, never even batted .300 again in his 11 year major league career that ended in 1959, after the Indians traded him on Dec. 2, 1958, to Baltimore (for pitcher Russ Heman and $30,000).

He wound up playing for the Boston Red Sox and Milwaukee Braves, as well as the Orioles in 1959, hitting a combined .227 in 93 games. It left Avila with a .281 career average when he retired and returned to Mexico where he owned the Mexico City Reds and played second base for the team.

Later, Avila became president of the Mexican League, and also was active in politics. At one time he was considered a possible candidate to become president of Mexico.

One of many Indians discovered by C.C. Slapnicka, who signed Bob Feller, Herb Score, Lou Boudreau, Mel Harder, Jeff Heath, Jim Hegan, Ken Keltner and Hal Trosky, among others, Avila started in professional baseball at age 21 in 1948 at Baltimore of the Class AAA International League.

Though he batted only .220 in 56 games at Baltimore, Avila was invited to spring training with the Indians and made the team as the backup second baseman to Joe Gordon in 1949 and 1950. He took over as the regular in 1951, after Gordon retired.

In his first season as the Tribe's starting second baseman, Avila became a marked man because of his aggressive play. After he scored the tying run in a game in Philadelphia by kicking the ball out of the catcher's glove, former Indians catcher Steve O'Neill, then manager of the Red Sox, was outspoken in his criticism of Avila.

O'Neill was quoted in the *News*: "From all I can hear around the league, (Avila) is asking for it. He'll be lucky if he doesn't have his legs cut out from under him before the season is half over. Everybody will be out to get him," though nobody ever did. He was too nimble.

And so, though Avila was never the most popular guy among his peers, Tribe fans loved him – even if he never hit .400.

A great trivia question

Ask one hundred baseball fans who Al Benton was and ninety-nine probably would shrug in wonderment and say they didn't know.

But Benton, whose full name was John Alton Benton, should be more familiar. He is, after all, the answer to one of baseball's best trivia questions.

Al Benton

A relief pitcher for the Indians in 1949 and 1950 when relievers were not glorified as they are today, Benton was the only man to face both Babe Ruth and Mickey Mantle in regular season games.

When Benton was a rookie with the Philadelphia Athletics in 1934 he pitched against Ruth, who was then playing his final season with the New York Yankees (he finished his Hall of Fame career with the Boston Braves in the National League in 1935).

And it was in Benton's final season in the major leagues, with the Boston Red Sox in 1952, that he faced Mantle, who was then playing his first full season with the Yankees, and beginning his trek toward the Hall of Fame.

During his 14 year major league career, from 1934-52, Benton, a huge right-hander from Oklahoma, appeared in 455 games for the Athletics (1934-35), Detroit (1938-48), the Indians (1949-50), and Red Sox.

Benton's won-lost record was 98-88 with a 3.66 earned run average, mostly coming out of the bull pen. His best season was 1941 with the Tigers, when he went 15-6 (2.97 ERA) in 38 games, 14 as a starter.

In those days baseball did not have a "save" statistic, otherwise Benton might have been better known and, certainly, better appreciated.

The Indians rescued Benton after one of his four trips back to the minor leagues, and his two-year record in Cleveland was a creditable 13-8 in 76 games, 11 as a starter. His 2.12 ERA in 1949 was best in the American League.

He owed his chance with the Indians to Steve O'Neill, then a Cleveland coach who had been manager of the Tigers when Benton pitched for them.

At the time the Indians were trying hard to repeat their pennant-winning season of 1948, though it wasn't to be. They fell to third place, eight games behind New York, and when they finished fourth in 1950, sweeping changes were made. Al Lopez replaced Lou Boudreau as manager, and Benton was waived.

But Benton wouldn't quit.

When no other big league club picked up his contract, Benton rejoined Sacramento of the Class AAA Pacific Coast League in 1951. There he earned another shot, this time with the Boston Red Sox for whom he went 4-3 with a 2.39 ERA in 24 appearances, all in relief, in 1952. Benton died in 1968 at the age of 57.

Records are unavailable as to how he fared against Ruth and Mantle.

But, considering that Benton had a fast ball that ranked with the best in baseball, and also that he was renowned for his tenacity, it's safe to assume he did OK, and probably deserves more credit than simply being the answer to one of baseball's best trivia questions.

Howdy Doodie or Jackie Gleason?

It had reportedly come down to a decision between "Howdy Doodie" and "Jackie Gleason," though nobody ever clarified who wanted to see which TV program that night in Washington, D.C.

All that surfaced was that Gary Bell and Jack Kralick, roommates and the best of friends, at least until then, got into a heated discussion over what to watch on television after a night game against the Senators, and before the Indians would fly to Los Angeles the next day.

The argument ended in a hurry, after Kralick reportedly threw a punch and Bell countered with one of his own.

"Aw, it was just one of those things that happens in August when the pressure is heavy and tempers are short," Tribe manager Birdie Tebbetts minimized the incident.

It happened Aug. 22, 1965, after the Indians had beaten the Senators, 8-5. Bell, who'd won the game in relief, along with his roommate, Kralick, had picked up a pizza and some beer, then went back to their hotel room to watch television.

Gary Bell

Which is when their disagreement began - and quickly ended.

The story came out the next morning when all the Indians but Kralick assembled at Washington's National Airport for the flight to Los Angeles to play the Angels that night.

Kralick was missing because he had an appointment with a dentist - to repair a tooth that had been broken by Bell's punch – which was typical of those daffy days of 1965, a season that began with great expectations, but quickly deteriorated. The Indians went into a tailspin and, by mid-August, were in free fall. They wound up in fifth place, with an 87-75 record, 15 games behind the Minnesota Twins.

Less than a year later, on Aug. 19, 1966, Tebbetts was out of a job.

Both of the pitchers involved in the two punch "disagreement" should have been much better than the career records they compiled, especially Bell. He showed great promise as a Tribe rookie in 1958, winning 12 games while losing 10, and was 16-11 in 1959.

But the fun-loving Bell never did that well again, although he was a key factor in Boston winning the American League pennant in 1967, after he had been traded to the Red Sox for first baseman Tony Horton and outfielder Don Demeter. The deal, made June 4, 1967, turned out to be one of the worst for the Indians - and one of the best for the Red Sox. Bell was 1-5 in nine games for the Indians before the trade, and 12-8 with a 3.16 earned run average for Boston.

Two years later Bell was finished, with a career won-lost record of 121-117, after going from the Red Sox in 1969 to the then-Seattle Pilots and later that season to the Chicago White Sox.

Kralick's career was even shorter. A classic southpaw, Kralick broke in with Washington in 1959, and went 13-11 in 1961 after the Senators moved to Minneapolis and became the Minnesota Twins. He was 12-11 the next season, and was acquired by the Indians on May 2, 1963, in a deal for pitcher Jim Perry. Kralick won 25 games while losing 16 for the Tribe the next two years. His record fell to 5-11 in 1965, and to 3-4 before and after that 1966 fight with Bell.

Three weeks into the 1967 season, after Kralick lost his first two starts, he was sold to the New York Mets. They sent Kralick to the minors and he never returned, retiring with a 67-65 record.

That 'fast and fuzzy' fast ball

It was late in the summer of 1935 and C.C. "Slap" Slapnicka, a tall, slim, balding and frail-looking man with a sharp nose, strolled into the semi-pro baseball park.

"It was in the outskirts of Des Moines (Ia.), not far from my home in Cedar Rapids, and I'd heard about a kid pitcher," Slapnicka, then a scout for the Indians, was quoted as saying several years later.

"I watched a couple of pitches from the first base line, and I got the funny feeling that this was something extra special.

"So I moved over behind the backstop and sat down on an automobile bumper.

"I sat there for six innings. It must have been uncomfortable, but I never noticed.

"All I knew was that this was a kid pitcher I had to get. I knew he was something special. His fast ball was fast and fuzzy, it didn't go in a straight line, it wiggled and shot around.

"I didn't know then that he was smart and that he had the heart of a lion, but I knew I was looking at an arm the likes of which you see only once in a lifetime."

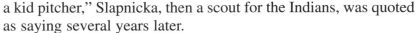

C.C. "Slap" Slapnicka

The arm Slapnicka talked about belonged to Bob Feller and, of course, Slapnicka "got" him for the Indians.

Back in Cleveland a few months later, Slapnicka raved about his discovery during a meeting of Indians directors.

"Gentlemen, I've found the greatest young pitcher I ever saw," he said. "I suppose this sounds like the same old stuff, but this boy will be one of the greatest pitchers the world has ever known."

And while Feller turned out to be Slapnicka's main claim to fame, he certainly wasn't the only gem discovered by the veteran talent scout.

During a front office career that began in 1923, Slapnicka also is credited with having signed for the Indians Herb Score, Earl Averill, Mel Harder, Hal Trosky, Sammy Hale, Jeff Heath, Ken Keltner, Bobby Avila, Jim Hegan and others.

Slapnicka got Feller for a $1 "bonus", plus a written promise that the young pitcher could visit his folks whenever he got lonely.

Score got enough money - $60,000 in 1952 - so that his family could visit him.

Upon his retirement at age 70 in 1957, Slapnicka said, "My only regret is that Feller and Score didn't come up together. Wouldn't that have been something?"

The "something" probably would have meant a pennant or two for the Indians in that period, 1936-41, when Slapnicka served as general manager of the team.

Slapnicka began in baseball as a pitcher himself, from 1906 to 1923, though he wasn't good enough to stick in the major leagues, despite brief trials with the Chicago Cubs and Pittsburgh.

Slapnicka was promoted from chief scout to general manager by owner Alva Bradley in 1935, and remained in that position until he resigned in 1941 to work for the St. Louis Browns.

He rejoined the Indians under Bill Veeck in 1946, still looking for another "fast and fuzzy fast ball," the likes of which he said Feller and Score threw in their prime.

But Slapnicka never found another one before he died in 1979 at age 93.

Twelve games Feller can't forget

Bob (Sugar) Cain never pitched for the Indians but the left-hander who made his home in Cleveland until he died at age 72 in 1997, was the principal in a game that Bob Feller can't forget.

Cain, then pitching for the St. Louis Browns, beat Feller on April 23, 1952 in St. Louis, in what was only the second double one-hitter in major league baseball history.

It well could have been - perhaps *should have been* - Feller's fourth no-hitter as the Browns' only hit was a routine fly ball to right field in the first inning that became a triple for second baseman Bobby Young.

It could have been - and probably *would have been* - caught by regular right fielder Harry Simpson, or Bob Kennedy, had either been in the game.

But on this day rookie Jim Fridley was the right fielder and broke the wrong way when Young's drive curved toward the foul line.

Fridley tried to cut back, but couldn't in time and the ball sailed over his head.

Marty Marion followed with a grounder to third baseman Al Rosen, who muffed it for an error, and Young scored with the game's only run.

It was the toughest to take of Feller's 12 one-hitters, although on another occasion he didn't yield a hit until the eighth inning.

Bob Feller

Two other bids by Feller for no-hitters were spoiled in the seventh inning.

Bobby Doerr, a second baseman for the Boston Red Sox who was voted into the Hall of Fame in 1986, spoiled two of Feller's no-hitters with singles in the second inning of games on May 25, 1939, and in the second inning on July 31, 1946.

On three other occasions former teammates of Feller were villains.

Infielder-catcher Billy Sullivan, then with the Browns, got the only hit in the sixth inning of a game on April 20, 1938; outfielder Earl Averill, then with Detroit, spoiled another no-hitter by Feller in the sixth inning of a game on June 27, 1939; and catcher Frankie Hayes, then with Chicago, singled in the second inning for the only hit off Feller on Aug. 8, 1946.

Another Hall of Famer, catcher Rick Ferrell, then with St. Louis, did it to Feller in the fifth inning on Sept.26, 1941.

Feller's five other bids for no-hitters were spoiled by Philadelphia first baseman Dick Siebert in the eighth inning of a game on July 12, 1940; Detroit outfielder Jimmy Outlaw in the fifth inning, Sept. 19, 1945; St. Louis outfielder Al Zarilla in the seventh inning, April 22, 1947; Boston shortstop Johnny Pesky in the first inning, May 2, 1947; and Boston catcher Sammy White in the seventh inning, May 1, 1955.

The three no-hitters Feller did pitch, which was a major league record until Sandy Koufax and then Nolan Ryan surpassed it, were masterpieces against Chicago, New York and Detroit.

The first one was especially noteworthy, on April 16, 1940, in Chicago, the only Opening Day no-hitter in baseball history, a 1-0 victory. Feller won his second no-hitter, also 1-0, on April 30, 1946, in New York, at a time when speculation was rife that he was "washed up," that his fastball was no longer as overpowering as it had been; and no-hitter No. 3 came on July 1, 1951, a 2-1 triumph over Detroit at the old Cleveland Stadium.

Was it Lane's worst deal?

It was a trade that Cleveland baseball fans long remembered, and long lamented.

Norm Cash for Steve Demeter.

It took place April 12, 1960, during the regime of Frank Lane, who went to his grave in 1981 being criticized for the deal.

Norm Cash

Actually, Lane agreed with his critics after a fashion - and after awhile. "If I knew then what I know now, I wouldn't have traded Cash," Lane said a few years before his death.

"But you've got to remember, at the time I made the deal, George Strickland, our utility infielder, was hurt, and Vic Power was our first baseman, which meant that Cash was going to be nothing more with us than a pinch hitter."

As it turned out, to Lane's eventual regret, Cash hit .286 with 18 homers as Detroit's regular first baseman in 1960, and won the American League batting championship in 1961, hitting.361, hammering 4l homers and driving in 132 runs.

Demeter, a slick-fielding third baseman, played in four games for the Indians, batted five times without getting a hit in that 1960 season, and his name never appeared in another major league box score.

But it's also true that Cash never had another season like his first two while playing for the Tigers through 1974, compiling a lifetime average of .271 with 377 homers in 2,089 games.

Little wonder Cleveland fans often lament the Cash-for-Demeter deal - except for another fact that's often overlooked.

Remember, Lane was the same guy who acquired Cash a year earlier from the Chicago White Sox in a deal that was as outstanding for the Indians as the Cash-for-Demeter trade was for the Tigers.

Not only did Lane get Cash, he also obtained John Romano, who became the Indians' regular catcher for the next five years, and Bubba Phillips, a very serviceable third baseman for three seasons, plugging two gaping holes in the Indians lineup.

To get Romano, Phillips and Cash from the White Sox, Lane gave up outfielder Minnie Minoso, who went on to have several good seasons in Chicago, and three other players who did not figure in the Indians' plans - backup catcher Dick Brown and pitchers Don Ferrarese and Jake Striker.

In retrospect, Cash's comments after he was acquired by the Indians, and before he was sent to Detroit are interesting: "Lane never made a bad deal," Cash was quoted during spring training of 1960. He added, "Who knows? Maybe I'll become another Tito Francona, and maybe I'll get another World Series check."

He proved to be right on both counts, although it didn't happen in Cleveland. Cash played in the 1968 World Series with the Tigers, hitting .385 as they beat St. Louis in seven games.

His reference to Francona pertained to the latter's sensational season in 1959, when he batted .363 after being obtained by the Indians from Detroit.

And, ironically, as it turned out, Cash himself did more than anybody to refute the claim that Lane never made a bad trade.

The 'fathers' of Chief Wahoo

Everybody knows Chief Wahoo, the red, white and blue caricature of a grinning red-faced Indian which is the official logo of the Cleveland Indians.

Emblazoned on the caps the Indians wear, as well as on virtually every item of apparel connected with the Tribe, Chief Wahoo probably is the most distinctive and popular logo in professional sports.

The origin of Chief Wahoo goes back to the early 1920s, several years after the team's nickname was changed in 1915 from "Naps" to "Indians." Some claim it was done to honor Louis Sockelexis, who was believed to have been the first native Indian to play in the major leagues, though that has been denied.

The first Chief Wahoo, drawn by an unknown artist, was simply a profile of an Indian with a feather in his hair. It was replaced in the 1930s by another profile of an Indian, this one wearing a full headdress.

Neither was particularly attractive, which probably was the reason an artist named Walter Goldbach, then 17 years old, created a new – and much more distinctive, as well as a more handsome – Chief Wahoo.

Bill Veeck, who owned the Indians at that time, liked Goldbach's Chief Wahoo. "Veeck was a real showman and wanted

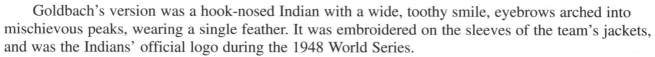

An early Chief Wahoo

to change the image of the team to something that would catch the attention of the public," Goldbach said.

Goldbach's version was a hook-nosed Indian with a wide, toothy smile, eyebrows arched into mischievous peaks, wearing a single feather. It was embroidered on the sleeves of the team's jackets, and was the Indians' official logo during the 1948 World Series.

Back in 1947, Goldbach never dreamed that American Indians would take offense to the image. He still doesn't understand what all the fuss is about. "That was the last thing on my mind when I created (Chief Wahoo), that I'd offend somebody. It was just a happy cartoon," Goldbach said.

A new Chief Wahoo came into being in the early 1950s, drawn by the late Cleveland *Plain Dealer* sports cartoonist Fred Reinert.

Though Reinert's Chief Wahoo always smiles now, his likeness is virtually the same as the first of four different happy versions he developed initially.

Then, and continuing through the 1950s and 1960s, a half-column engraving of Reinert's Chief Wahoo appeared on Page One of the *Plain Dealer* every morning during the baseball season.

If the Indians won the day before, Chief Wahoo smiled broadly and brandished a tomahawk. If they lost, he wore a black eye and downcast expression, with stars flying around over his head. If they played a double header and split the two games, a happy, but also beat up Chief Wahoo was displayed.

And if the Indians were rained out, Chief Wahoo appeared on Page One holding an umbrella instead of a tomahawk.

Reinert's Chief Wahoo was adopted by the Indians as their official logo in the 1950s and, despite criticism by certain special interest groups, it continues to be one of the most popular in professional sports.

'As smart a player as ever came along'

His career with the Indians was brief and forgettable, consisting of only 10 games in 1931, during which he batted .077 with one hit in 13 at-bats, and 29 more in 1934, after his July re-acquisition from the then-Washington Senators, when he batted .258.

Moe Berg

But there's much that's memorable about Moe Berg, a catcher who played most of his 15 year major league career elsewhere, with Brooklyn in 1923, the Chicago White Sox from 1926-30, Washington from 1932 through mid-1934 (before he returned to Cleveland), and the Boston Red Sox from 1935-39.

While Berg, originally a shortstop, was never a great hitter – his career batting average in 663 major league games was .243 - he was considered an excellent catcher, with a strong throwing arm and, especially, a good head for handling pitchers.

Berg also was very intelligent. At Princeton University where he'd been a star first baseman, he majored in languages - four years of French, two of Latin, two of Spanish, three of Italian, one of Greek, and one of German - before graduating *magna cum laude* in 1923.

After joining the Dodgers his first year out of college, Berg read books and studied Latin, Sanskrit (the ancient language of Hinduism) and Medieval French, often in the bull pen. During off-seasons he studied at the Sorbonne, and obtained a law degree at Columbia University. Later in life he practiced law. Most notable, however, was Berg's experiences after retiring from baseball, as revealed after his death at 70 in 1972 in the book, *Moe Berg: Athlete, Scholar … Spy.*

Though Berg always refused to discuss his espionage activities, the authors of the book traced his labors back to a post-season tour of Japan in 1934. He was a member of an American League team that included Earl Averill and Clint Brown of the Indians, and Babe Ruth, Lou Gehrig and Lefty Gomez of the New York Yankees.

Berg was with the team, managed by Connie Mack, not because of his ability as a player. It was because he had picked up the language two years before when the Japanese invited him, along with his friends, Ted Lyons of the Chicago White Sox and Lefty O'Doul of Brooklyn, to do some teaching among promising young collegians in Japan.

While there, Berg broke away from time to time from the other players and, once, on a ruse, got to the top of a hospital in central Tokyo. From there he took motion pictures that were used, years later, in Gen. Jimmy Doolittle's famous air attack on Tokyo in World War II.

Upon retiring from baseball after the 1939 season, and after the United States' entry into World War II, Berg was with the OSS (Office of Strategic Services, forerunner of the CIA) in Switzerland and Norway to ferret out Nazi progress in the race for the atomic bomb.

According to the book, Berg had much to do in the closing days of the war with pinpointing for the Allies the whereabouts of German scientists, and with helping to bring many of them to work in the United States.

And so, while Moe Berg might not have been a major league star, he was, as Casey Stengel once was quoted, "as smart a ballplayer as ever came along." You could look it up.

Precisely the right place

If ever a man was in precisely the right place at precisely the right time it was Bill Wambsganss, better known in baseball history as Bill Wamby.

Wamby's right place at the right time was about three strides to the right of second base at Cleveland's old League Park on Oct. 10, 1920.

It was during the fifth game of the World Series between the Indians and Brooklyn Dodgers. Each team had won two games and now, in the top of the fifth inning, the Dodgers were threatening to cut into the Indians' 7-0 lead.

As Wamby described it before his death in 1985 at 91, the Dodgers Pete Kilduff had singled, and so did Otto Miller, bringing relief pitcher Willie Mitchell to the plate.

What happened next brought undying fame to Wamby, a second baseman for the Indians from 1914 through 1923. He also played for the Boston Red Sox and Philadelphia Athletics before retiring in 1927 with a lifetime batting average of .259 in 13 major league seasons.

In that fifth inning of the fifth game of the 1920 World Series, with Kilduff on second and Miller on first, Mitchell hit a line drive to Wamby, who turned it into an unassisted triple play, the first - and still the only - unassisted triple play in World Series history.

Bill Wambsganss

"You'd have thought I was born the day before and died the day after," Wamby said of the play that gained him lasting fame. "The only credit I deserve is for being in the right place at the right time."

The famous play developed as Wamby made a leaping stab of Mitchell's liner, then, in three strides, stepped on second base to double Kilduff, who had broken for third, and turned toward first base only to find Miller a few feet away, trying to stop.

"I intended to throw the ball to first to nail Miller, but when I saw him so near, I instinctively tagged him (for the third out)," he said. "It was no big thing."

Not at the time, anyway.

"After the game I had one newspaper interview. A guy from Brooklyn talked to me. He asked how it felt to make an unassisted triple play. I said it was the chance of a lifetime, which it was."

The Indians won that game, 8-1. It also featured Elmer Smith's bases-loaded home run in the first inning, the first grand slam ever hit in a World Series game, and a home run by Jim Bagby Sr., the first by a pitcher in a World Series.

The Indians went on to defeat Brooklyn, five games to two in what was then a best-of-nine World Series.

For Wamby, whose name was shortened by a printer who couldn't fit Wambsganss into the box score, 1920 was the highlight of his career - but not because of the triple play.

It was winning the World Championship of baseball, even though it wasn't that big a thing back then, he said.

Maybe not.

But as long as the game is played, Wamby will be remembered for making an unassisted triple play in a World Series game - by being precisely in the right place at precisely the right time.

The good, bad and ugly deals

The Rocky Colavito-for-Harvey Kuenn deal in 1960 probably was the most unpopular trade the Indians ever made. But was it the worst in Cleveland baseball history? Hardly.

For that distinction we dust off the archives and go all the way back to the winter of 1898-99. It was then that the Cleveland Spiders traded Cy Young - yes, *that* Cy Young! - to the St. Louis Cardinals for somebody so obscure his name isn't even in the records anymore.

Bruce Ellingsen

Another deal made by the Cleveland team that deserves mention was that which sent "Shoeless Joe" Jackson, one of baseball's best hitters, to the Chicago White Sox in 1915. Cleveland received Ed Klepfer, Bobby Roth and Larry Chappell for Jackson, who gained notoriety as a key figure in the "Black Sox Scandal" of 1919.

"Shoeless Joe" was one of eight players barred from baseball for life for participating in the conspiracy to throw the 1919 World Series to Cincinnati.

Some of the other deals that didn't turn out well for the Tribe:

- Minnie Minoso, Sam Zoldak and Ray Murray to the Philadelphia Athletics for Lou Brissie in 1951.
- Cal McLish, Billy Martin and Gordy Coleman to Cincinnati for Johnny Temple in 1959.
- Norm Cash to Detroit for Steve Demeter in 1960.
- Sonny Siebert, Joe Azcue and Vicente Romo to Boston for Juan Pizarro, Dick Ellsworth and Ken Harrelson in 1969.
- Pedro Guerrero to Los Angeles for Bruce Ellingsen in 1974.
- Neal Heaton to Minnesota for John Butcher in 1986.

However there also were some very good acquisitions, again beginning in the early days of baseball in Cleveland.

- Napoleon Lajoie, perhaps the best player in the history of the franchise, and Elmer Flick, also a Hall of Famer, purchased from the Philadelphia Athletics in 1902.
- Tris Speaker from the Boston Red Sox for Sad Sam Jones, Fred Thomas and $55,000 in 1916.
- The same Norm Cash, along with Bubba Phillips and John Romano from the Chicago White Sox for Minnie Minoso, Don Ferrarese, Jake Striker and Dick Brown in 1959.
- Dick Donovan, Gene Green and Jim Mahoney from Washington for Jim Piersall in 1961.
- Gaylord Perry and Frank Duffy from San Francisco for Sam McDowell in 1971.
- Andre Thornton from Montreal for Jackie Brown in 1976.
- Mike Hargrove from San Diego for Paul Dade 1979.
- Len Barker and Bobby Bonds from Texas for Jim Kern and Larvell Blanks in 1978.
- Brook Jacoby, Brett Butler, Rick Behenna and $150,000 for Barker in 1983.
- Joe Carter, Mel Hall and Don Shulze from the Chicago Cubs for Rick Sutcliffe, Ron Hassey and George Frazier in 1984.
- Sandy Alomar Jr. Carlos Baerga and Chris James from San Diego for Carter.

And the ugly: Manager Jimmie Dykes from Detroit for Manager Joe Gordon in 1960.

The loss of Chris Chambliss

Chris Chambliss was the Indians' first draft choice in January 1970, and won "Rookie of the Year" honors twice, in the Class AAA American Association, when he played for Wichita (Kans.) in 1970, and in 1971 in the American League, after he'd been promoted to the major leagues.

However, by his own admission, the highlight of Chambliss's career in baseball came in 1976, when he was a member of the New York Yankees.

It was Chambliss's leadoff home run in the bottom of the ninth inning of the fifth and final game of the A.L. Championship Series that beat Kansas City, 7-6, and won the pennant for the Yankees, their first in 12 years, since 1964.

Chambliss was wearing Yankee pinstripes then – unfortunately – after being dealt in a controversial trade to New York on April 27, 1974. The Indians, desperate for starting pitchers, sent Chambliss and relief pitchers Dick Tidrow and Cecil Upshaw, for starters Steve Kline and Fritz Peterson, and relievers Tom Buskey and Fred Beene.

Recalled from Wichita by the Indians and installed as their regular first baseman in early-May of 1971, Chambliss hit .275 that season, becoming only the second player in the 71 year history of the Cleveland franchise to win the rookie award. Herb

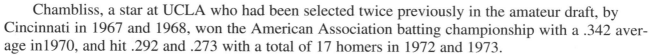

Chris Chambliss

Score was the first, in 1955, and two others won it after Chambliss – Joe Charboneau in 1980, and Sandy Alomar Jr. in 1990.

Chambliss, a star at UCLA who had been selected twice previously in the amateur draft, by Cincinnati in 1967 and 1968, won the American Association batting championship with a .342 average in1970, and hit .292 and .273 with a total of 17 homers in 1972 and 1973.

Chambliss was batting .328 in 17 games when he was traded by then-General Manager Phil Seghi to the Yankees, whose president at that time was Gabe Paul. Yes, the same Gabe Paul who had been the Indians chief executive from 1961-73, and was in charge when Chambliss was drafted. Paul had joined the Yankees when George Steinbrenner bought the franchise, and returned to head the Indians in 1978 after F.J. "Steve" O'Neill purchased the club.

Chambliss's home run, one of the most dramatic in postseason play, was drilled off the first pitch by Kansas City reliever Mark Littell. "It was a high fast ball and I just reacted," said Chambliss. "I wasn't trying to hit a home run … the ball went just far enough into the stands."

It set off a near riot in Yankee Stadium as fans stormed the field. "The fans were coming on to the field and I was basically just trying to get around the bases and get back to the dugout."

As he reached second base, the bag had already been ripped from the ground, and before it was carried away by a fan, Chambliss touched it with his right hand. He had to zig-zag between more fans as he ran between second base and third, and on his way home, he recalled, "I ran right over one guy."

It was sheer bedlam - but a wonderful experience for Chambliss.

He played for the Yankees through 1979, and Atlanta from 1981-86, compiling a career .279 batting average. Chambliss managed in the minor leagues from 1989-92,, and was a coach for St. Louis from 1993 until he rejoined the Yankees as their hitting instructor in 1996.

He was 'super' for one season

They called him "Super Joe" and wrote a book about him after his first season in the big leagues, that's how quickly Joe Charboneau's career peaked.

But his star burned out even quicker, and three years after he was the American League's Rookie of the Year, Charboneau was playing semi-pro baseball in Buffalo, hoping to get one more chance with another professional team - which he never did.

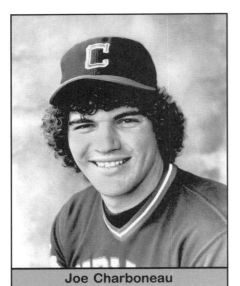

Joe Charboneau

Ah, but in Cleveland in 1980, Charboneau really was super.

The flamboyant outfielder hit .289 and led the Indians with 23 homers and 87 RBI. One of his homers was among the three longest ever hit in Yankee Stadium. It flew into the third deck, reached previously only by Frank Howard and Hall of Famer Jimmy Foxx.

Cleveland fans, desperately seeking a hero, fell in love with Charboneau and his well-publicized idiosyncrasies - drinking beer through his nose, eating cigarettes, claiming to have pulled his own teeth, and more.

Charboneau reveled in the attention.

"I never wanted to be an ordinary major leaguer," he said. "When I was a kid and 1 dreamed about playing in the majors, I always saw myself as a star."

And, despite his shortcomings, Joe never was ordinary.

The Indians got him from Philadelphia in a minor league deal in 1978, and Charboneau slugged his way to the varsity, hitting .352 with 21 homers at Class AA Chattanooga in 1979.

But, after he burned up the American League as a rookie, nothing was the same for Charboneau in 1981. He slumped to .210 with only four homers in 48 games, then was demoted to Class AAA Charleston, where he continued to struggle,

When the season ended, Charboneau underwent back surgery, and embarked on a strenuous rehabilitation program, hoping that would help him recapture the glory he'd known.

Unfortunately, it didn't. After 22 games in 1982, hitting only .214 with two homers, Charboneau was released.

Gabe Paul, then president of the Indians, called it a "tragedy."

"Joe had a lot of talent. Maybe this will be good for him. He always talked about going somewhere else to play. Now he'll have a chance," Paul said.

Perhaps to soothe his own ego, Charboneau agreed.

"I've wanted to be released since last year. Now, maybe I can hook on with a Class AAA team. I still want to get back to the majors. If nothing else, maybe I can play in Japan, Mexico or Holland," Joe said.

But nothing - except that opportunity to play on the sandlots in Buffalo - came Charboneau's way. He soon gave up trying to make it back to professional baseball and retired.

Now Charboneau operates a school in Cleveland for young, aspiring ball players, teaching them to play the game which he loved so fervently, and played so well - if only for that one great season when he was rightfully known as "Super Joe."

Buddy's battles with adversity

It was January 1974 and Buddy Bell was playing a charity basketball game with a team of Indians baseball players.

He leaped for a rebound, landed on the side of his right foot, and crumpled to the floor, his knee throbbing with pain.

Before that season ended, Bell would spend two stints on the disabled list, and before his career was concluded in 1989, he would undergo seven knee operations.

As it was, Bell played 18 years in the big leagues - seven in Cleveland where he was one of the fans' all-time favorites - and it's always interesting to speculate how much better he might have been if not for the knee problems that plagued him.

Bell broke in with the Indians in 1972 as their Opening Day center fielder, even though third base was his position through his previous three minor league seasons.

At the time, Graig Nettles was the Tribe's third baseman.

Buddy Bell

But not for long. Nettles was traded the following winter and Bell returned to his natural position where he went on to win six Gold Gloves and five All-Star rings.

Something else that was happening during Bell's career with the Indians from 1972 until he was traded in December 1978 further illustrates the determination that made him a star.

Shortly after Bell rejoined the Tribe in 1990 as a minor league coach and roving infield instructor (a position he held for one year, though he returned again in 1994 as a coach under Mike Hargrove until becoming manager of the Detroit Tigers in 1997), he talked about how he played most of his career with epilepsy. It was a story that should provide inspiration to others so afflicted.

Bell admits he was terrified when he was first diagnosed following a seizure in 1974. So were his mother and father Gus, who had been a major league outfielder with Pittsburgh, Cincinnati, New York Mets and Milwaukee, from 1950 through 1964.

"But as soon as we heard that most cases were controllable by medication, we all pulled together," said Buddy.

"I worried whether I could still play, but once I got used to the (medication) ... pretty soon I was back on my game."

In his 18 seasons with the Indians, Texas, Cincinnati and Houston, Bell compiled a lifetime average of .279, with 2,514 hits and 201 homers - also in spite of his aching knees.

Bell was traded by the Indians to Texas for Toby Harrah at the 1978 winter meetings in a deal they came to regret.

But another Bell came along recently - Buddy's son and Gus's grandson David.

David, who was born in 1972, was drafted by the Indians in 1990 and, after six seasons in the minor leagues, was traded to the St. Louis Cardinals in a deal for pitcher Ken Hill. The Indians re-acquired David in 1998, but later that season traded him to Seattle. Another of Buddy's sons, Mike, also is playing professional baseball in the farm system of the Anaheim Angels.

And Buddy took over as manager of the Colorado Rockies in 2000.

The Indians most popular player?

Down through the years many Cleveland players have been idolized by the fans, primarily for their achievements on the field, but also for their demeanor out of uniform.

One whose character was as impeccable as his statistics is still considered by some old-timers to have been the most popular player to ever wear an Indians uniform.

Charley Jamieson

No, it wasn't Rocky Colavito or Lou Boudreau or Bob Feller - this most popular player was on the scene long before they came along. It was Charles Devine "Jamie" Jamieson, who also has been called the best player not in the Hall of Fame.

A swift outfielder who played 18 years in the major leagues, all but four in Cleveland, Jamieson was one of the team leaders in 1920 when he batted .319 in 108 games to help the Indians win their first pennant and World Series.

Jamieson hit .300 or better eight times, his lifetime batting average of .303 was higher than 49 of the 121 non-pitchers in the Hall of Fame, and he played in 1,779 games, more than 38 of the certified "immortals."

Still, Jamieson never received much consideration by voters for the Hall of Fame, and his name - and solid credentials - are still constantly overlooked by the Veterans Committee, which is supposed to evaluate and select old-timers who belong at Cooperstown.

"Jamie," as the fans called him, also was an excellent outfielder who came to the Indians in 1919 in what proved to be one of the best deals of that era. He was acquired from the Philadelphia Athletics with third baseman Larry Gardner and minor league outfielder Elmer Myers for outfielder Braggo Roth.

Myers never made it out of the minors, but Gardner was the Indians regular third baseman from 1919-22, and a member of the team through 1924. Roth was sent by the Athletics to Washington later in the 1919 season, and played for the Senators in 1920 and the New York Yankees in 1921, his last season in the major leagues.

Jamieson put together five of the greatest seasons anybody could want, from 1920-24 when he hit .319, .310, .323, .345 and .359 as the Indians' leadoff batter.

When Jamieson retired in 1932, Gordon Cobbledick, then the baseball writer for the *Plain Dealer* wrote the following tribute to the longtime star:

"Jamieson fell short of the stature of Napoleon Lajoie and Tris Speaker, but he has been accurately called the most popular ball player in Cleveland history.

"An incident in 1929 may explain why. It was Jamieson Day at League Park, the day set aside to honor the ball hawk. Fans had subscribed to a purse of $3,200 as a gift to their favorite.

"The Indians were playing the Athletics and Lefty Grove was pitching. Jamie had made two hits and batted in one important run, but he came up in the ninth with the winning runs on base and bounced out to the third baseman.

"A few minutes later Indians owner Alva Bradley met the veteran at the door of the clubhouse. Jamie was nearly in tears. "Mr. Bradley, I'm Scotch and I like money as well as the next guy, but I'd have given this whole $3,200 for one more hit off that big monkey," he said.

The decision Vosmik lived to regret

No doubt about it, Sept. 29, 1935 was a day Joe Vosmik would never forget - and the decision he made then was one he undoubtedly regretted the rest of his life.

Signed off the Cleveland sandlots, Vosmik made it to the Indians in 1931 and quickly became one of their most popular players, with good reason.

He hit.320 as a rookie, .312 in 1932 and .341 in 1934, while playing a very solid left field.

Vosmik got off to a torrid start in 1935 and never cooled off, challenging for the American League batting championship almost from the beginning of the season.

But he couldn't shake one player, second baseman Buddy Myer of the then-Washington Senators.

On the morning of Sept. 29, the final day of the season, Vosmik had a three point lead over Myer as the Indians went into a double header against the St. Louis Browns at League Park while the Senators were playing the then-Philadelphia Athletics.

To protect what he thought was a safe lead over Myer, Vosmik asked Indians Manager Steve O'Neill if he could sit out the double header.

O'Neill consented. The Indians were lodged in third place with neither a chance to move up nor fall back in the standings.

Joe Vosmik

Vosmik pinch hit in the ninth inning of the opener of the Indians double header and made an out.

Then, after receiving word from Philadelphia that Myer had gone 4-for-5 to boost his average to .349 - and into the lead by one point – Vosmik replaced Walter "Kit" Carson in the early innings of the Indians' second game against St. Louis.

Vosmik singled in his first three trips to the plate, climbing to within less than a full percentage point of his Washington rival. But he never got any closer.

The game was called after six innings because of darkness as, in those days, baseball under the lights was only a farfetched dream.

Thus, Vosmik's final average was .348 - rounded off from .348387.

Myer finished with .349 - rounded off from .349025, meaning he beat out Vosmik by .000638, concluding one of the closest batting races in major league baseball history.

Adding to Vosmik's frustration was that, had he not sat out the opener of that double header, he might have beaten Myer.

Just one more hit by Vosmik would have given him a batting average of .349436, and the 1935 American League batting championship by .000419 over Myer.

As it turned out, neither Vosmik nor Myer enjoyed that kind of success again, though Myer hit .336 in 1938. He retired in 1942 with a 17-year average of .303.

Vosmik, who was traded to St. Louis in 1937, then to the Boston Red Sox, Brooklyn Dodgers and Washington, ended his career in 1944. He hit.325 in 1937, and. 324 in 1938, but also never again challenged for the batting championship.

He wound up with a .307 lifetime average for 13 seasons, which was very good – but would have looked so much better with a batting crown in 1935.

The reluctant (no-hit) pitcher

For a guy whose father wouldn't let him pitch, Sonny Siebert sure did become a very good pitcher.

"I guess it was because my dad threw his arm out as a pitcher when he was young," Siebert explained in a Cleveland *Plain Dealer* story in 1966, after he'd hurled the 12th no-hitter (of 15) in the history of the Indians.

Sonny Siebert

Siebert blanked the Washington Senators on June 10, 1966, allowing only two base runners, one on a walk in the fifth, and the other on an error in the eighth. Neither advanced past first base.

The no-hitter was the high point of Siebert's 12 seasons in the big leagues. He went 16-8 with a 2.80 earned run average in 1966 and was elected the Indians "Man of the Year" by the Cleveland baseball writers.

Siebert came close to pitching two more no-hitters, one for the Indians on May 19, 1968, the other for Boston on July 31, 1970. Curt Blefary spoiled the first one with a seventh inning double in a game in which the Tribe beat Baltimore, 2-0, and two years later Jay Johnstone singled in the third inning off Siebert in Boston's 2-0 victory over California.

Because of his father's advice, Siebert, who also was an accomplished basketball player - he had a tryout with the St. Louis Hawks of the NBA when he got out of college - started in professional baseball as an outfielder-first baseman. The Indians gave him a $35,000 bonus, which was a lot of money in 1958, and Siebert started his career at Batavia (N.Y.) of the Class D New York-Penn League, the lowest rung in professional baseball. The day before the season started, Siebert collided with a teammate and was sidelined for two months. Six weeks later he broke an ankle.

He reported for winter ball but couldn't run full speed so he was asked to pitch batting practice. The Indians liked what they saw, but Siebert still resisted switching to the mound.

After another season playing first base and the outfield - and earning a reputation as a "singles hitter" - Siebert was convinced to defy his dad. But only because he knew if he didn't turn to pitching, he would soon he looking for another job. A job outside of baseball.

It was a very smart decision, though it took Siebert five more minor league seasons to make it to Cleveland. And even then, in 1964, Siebert made it tough on himself.

Most rookies - at least then - would be so happy to get a chance in the majors, they'd jump at the first contract offered them. Not Siebert. He was a holdout for three weeks in spring training.

But once he reported to camp, Siebert opened everybody's eyes with a 90-plus mph fast ball, and a crackling curve that had the hitters leaning back on their heels.

The reluctant pitcher was a regular starter from 1965 until April 19, 1969, when he was the key man in a six-player deal with Boston that turned out to be among the worst in Tribe history.

Siebert was sent to Boston with Joe Azcue and Vicente Rome, for Ken Harrelson, Dick Ellsworth and Juan Pizarro. Siebert had three more good seasons with the Red Sox, who traded him to Texas in 1973. After pitching for St. Louis in 1974, and San Diego and Oakland in 1975, Siebert retired with a 140-114 lifetime record.

Not bad for a guy whose father didn't want him to be a pitcher.

Mike Hargrove called it "the worst game I've ever been associated with" – and it also might have been the game that cost him his job as manager of the Indians when they lost to the Boston Red Sox, 23-7, on Oct. 10, 1999.

Five days later Hargrove was fired, ending a 21 year career with the organization that began on June 14, 1979, when he came to the Tribe from the San Diego Padres in a trade for outfielder Paul Dade.

Despite that 16 run differential in what Hargrove said was the worst game with which he'd ever been associated, the Indians suffered an even more lopsided defeat earlier in 1999, and though it also was humiliating, it wasn't nearly as costly. On July 24, in their 97th game of the season, they were blown away by the New York Yankees, 21-1, in Yankee Stadium.

However, the game that Hargrove designated as the "worst" was particularly devastating because it was administered by the Red Sox in the American League Division Series. It came after the Indians had taken a two-games-to-none lead and needed only one more victory to advance to the A.L. Championship Series against the New York Yankees.

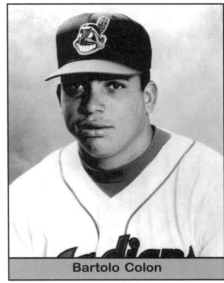
Bartolo Colon

Instead, they lost the third game, 9-3, when the bull pen failed, and then, apparently still reeling, the Indians were blown out in Game 4 in Boston.

The Red Sox's 23 runs and 24 hits (of which four were homers) were the most ever scored in a postseason game. They scored in every inning except the sixth against six Cleveland pitchers. John Valentin hammered two of Boston's four homers, and the others were delivered by Jason Varitek and Jose Offerman.

Bartolo Colon, working with three days' rest, started for the Indians but was kayoed in the second inning, charged with seven runs and the loss. He was followed by Steve Karsay, Steve Reed, Sean DePaula, Paul Assenmacher, and Paul Shuey, none of whom pitched with much greater success. The next day it was all over as the Tribe lost Game 5, 12-8, and was eliminated by the underdog Red Sox, ending the season and, ultimately, Hargrove's managerial tenure which began on July 6, 1991.

While the 16 run differential in the playoff game against Boston was, as Sandy Alomar Jr. called it, "embarrassing … humiliating," it was only the sixth worst in the history of the Cleveland franchise, which began in 1901. In that first season, the Indians – then known as the "Blues" – lost to Detroit, 21-0, on Sept. 15, which has the dubious distinction of being the all-time worst.

Second worst was the afore-mentioned, 21-1, shellacking by the Yankees, in which Mark Langston was bombed early, charged with nine runs, including seven in the fifth inning when he was banished to the showers.

Worst loss No. 3 was handed the Indians by the Red Sox, 24-5, on Aug. 21, 1986, when Greg Swindell, who'd been drafted No. 1 only two months earlier, made his major league pitching debut.

Two losses, 17 years apart, were tied for the fourth-worst in franchise history, the first, a 21-3 defeat at the hands of the Yankees on July 14, 1904, and the second, also by a 21-3 score, was administered by the then-Philadelphia Athletics on July 25, 1921.

The consummate professional

He wasn't flamboyant, a loud mouth or a braggart, which might be reasons so many good things Andre Thornton did for the Indians during an era when they were not very successful often went unnoticed.

In the history of the Cleveland franchise only four players hit more homers than Thornton's 214 - and the then-leader, Earl Averill, was only 12 ahead when Thornton retired.

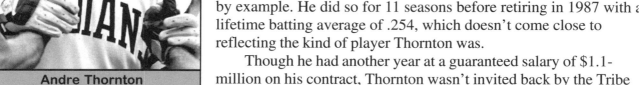

Albert Belle holds the franchise record with 242 homers, followed by Averill's 226, Hal Trosky's 216, and Larry Doby's 215.

What's more, only eight players drove in more runs than Thornton's 749, only nine had more extra base hits than his 419, only ten hit for more total bases than his 1,954, and only ten had higher slugging averages than his .453.

Thornton's batting statistics probably will soon be overtaken by Manny Ramirez and Jim Thome, but that won't lessen his past contributions to the Indians.

Always the consummate professional, Thornton led the Indians by example. He did so for 11 seasons before retiring in 1987 with a lifetime batting average of .254, which doesn't come close to reflecting the kind of player Thornton was.

Though he had another year at a guaranteed salary of $1.1-million on his contract, Thornton wasn't invited back by the Tribe in 1988.

Andre Thornton

Despite his disappointment, Thornton accepted the decision with grace, which always was his style.

Included in Thornton's contributions to the Tribe were two serious knee injuries, that required operations (for a total of four), and a dislocated shoulder that also required surgery.

Unfortunately, seldom during Thornton's career with the Indians did he have the luxury of being surrounded by many other good hitters, a team weakness that pitchers usually exploited, as Jim Palmer admitted before both retired.

"Whenever I faced the Indians, I only worried about one thing," Palmer once said. "I didn't want to face Thornton in the late innings. If I did (face him), I walked him. He could change a 1-0 win into a 2-1 loss in one swing."

A year after he arrived in a 1976 trade with Montreal for pitcher Jackie Brown, Thornton was faced with the ultimate adversity.

His wife and daughter were killed in an automobile accident on the Pennsylvania Turnpike on Oct. 17, 1977. Thornton and his son also were injured, but survived.

The loss devastated Thornton, but his religious faith carried him through the ordeal and he followed with one of his beat seasons in 1978: 33 homers, 105 RBI and a .262 average.

It was typical of the man's inner strength and stability.

So was Thornton's comment when the Indians didn't invite him to return for another season, either on the field or in their front office.

"We can part company feeling very good about the fact I certainly tried to uphold my end of the bargain," he said. "I gave the Indians the best I could for as long as I could."

Indeed he did, which nobody can dispute - and which, unfortunately, not every player can say at the end of a career.

Daytime soap opera fans knew John Beradino as "Dr. Steve Hardy" of "General Hospital" on the ABC television network weekday afternoons.

But fans of the Indians, when they won the American League pennant and World Series in 1948, knew him better as Johnny Berardino - and, yes, in those days he had an extra "r" in his last name.

Beradino, who played Dr. Hardy since the serial began in 1963, was an insurance policy for the Indians the year they beat the Boston Red Sox in a historic one-game playoff, and then beat the Boston Braves in the World Series.

How valuable was Beradino then? Well, disregard his .190 batting average in 66 games as a utilityman playing every infield position.

Beradino was acquired in the winter of 1947-48 in a trade with the St. Louis Browns and was paid the then-handsome salary of $80,000.

Johnny Berardino

What's more - which perhaps better explains his value to the Indians - owner Bill Veeck insured Beradino's face for $1-million, in case he suffered an injury on the field.

Beradino, whose big league career began with the Browns in 1939, played for the Indians until he was sent to Pittsburgh in 1950. He went back to the Browns in 1951 and finished with the Tribe in 1952.

Beradino's lifetime batting average was a respectable .249 for 11 seasons.

Shortly after retiring from baseball Beradino got his start in the movies and television and promptly changed the spelling of his name, making it easier to pronounce - as well as to fit on a marquee or billboard.

"Actually, I had been contemplating leaving the game as early as 1947 to concentrate on acting," he said in a newspaper interview in 1989, promoting the 25th anniversary of "General Hospital."

"Most people don't realize that I was an actor long before I was a ball player. I was one of those brat actors in the 'Our Gang' comedies ... I always loved acting as a kid."

With the Indians in their pennant-winning season of 1948, Beradino did just about everything; he played 20 games at second base behind Joe Gordon, 18 at first base behind Eddie Robinson, 12 at shortstop behind player-manager Lou Boudreau, and three at third base behind Ken Keltner.

"I'll never forget that year," Beradino recalled. "It was a tremendous race, right down to the wire. Then Boudreau personally took care of the Red Sox in the playoff game (hitting two homers and going 4-for-4).

"Nobody likes to sit on the bench, and I certainly didn't either. But it was easier, considering the caliber of the guys who were playing ahead of me."

As Dr. Hardy, Beradino appeared in one or two segments of General Hospital each week, prior to his death at the age of 79 in 1996.

And, all the time he appeared in the soap opera, Beradino – a.k.a. Dr. Steve Hardy – wore the World Series ring he earned as a valuable utility infielder, helping the Indians win baseball's most coveted prize.

'My God, Bill, what happened?'

There was nothing very special about Don Black and if ever the description, "journeyman pitcher," aptly described anybody, it did Black.

He was purchased by the Indians during the winter of 1945-46 after three undistinguished seasons with the Philadelphia Athletics, for whom he posted records of 6-16 in 1943, 10-12 in 1944, and 5-11 in 1945.

Don Black

Black won one game and lost two for the Tribe in 1946, then hit his peak on July 10, 1947, pitching a no-hitter to beat the A's, 3-0. It was one of his 10 victories, to go with 12 losses that year.

In 1948, as the Indians fought to keep pace with Boston, New York and Philadelphia in the torrid American League pennant race, Black was a nonentity, though he became the center of attention on the night of Sept. 13.

Then, in a game against the St. Louis Browns at the Stadium, with the Indians four games out of first place, Black stepped into the batter's box in the second inning and swung viciously, fouling off a pitch from Bill Kennedy.

According to a newspaper account, "Black staggered slightly as he finished his swing, then walked away from the plate and turned in a small circle in back of umpire Bill Summers.

"'My God, Bill, what happened?' Black muttered to Summers. Then he sagged to a kneeling position. Summers bent over Black and asked, 'What's wrong?'

"'It started,' Black explained, 'on that last pitch I made to (Eddie) Pellagrini.'

"It was a curve ball for a third strike and the physical effort expended in that pitch, plus the full-bodied swing at the plate a few minutes later, snapped an aneurysm.

"Blood flooded Black's brain and spinal cord. He was rushed to the hospital and surgery was considered, but dismissed because Black's condition was too serious. Doctors gave him only a 50-50 chance to live."

Black survived, but never pitched again.

On Sept. 22, 1948, nine days after Black was stricken, Indians owner Bill Veeck staged a "Don Black Night" at the Stadium. He pledged that the Indians' entire share of the gate receipts would go to Black.

However, Veeck's motives were not entirely altruistic.

The Indians that night were to play Boston, one of their rivals for the pennant, and Veeck was well aware that any additional moral support would be most important.

And so, a massive crowd of 76,772 fans stormed the Stadium to honor Black - and, as it turned out, to spur the Indians on to a 5-2 victory behind Bob Feller.

Once again Veeck's promotional sagacity had paid huge dividends, this time for Black as well as the Indians.

The victory over the Red Sox proved to be especially important as the two teams finished the season tied for first place, then the Tribe won the pennant in an unprecedented, one game playoff.

Black also shared in the World Series payoff but, unfortunately, didn't live long to enjoy it. Only 11 years later, on April 21, 1959, he died at age 43.

Back in 1963, two young players, Tony Martinez and Vic Davalillo, were expected to become the cornerstone of an Indians dynasty.

Martinez, a Cuban refugee, was the key man because of the position he played - shortstop. Davalillo, a Venezuelan, was a left-handed hitting center fielder who could do everything, especially fly on the bases.

"Everybody tells me there's no way these two guys can miss," chirped Birdie Tebbetts, then Indians manager.

But they did miss, especially Martinez.

And no way were they the answer to the Indians' problems.

Oh, Davalillo played 16 seasons in the major leagues, the first 5 1/2 with the Indians before they traded him to California on June 15, 1968, for outfielder Jimmie Hall. But he never lived up to the lavish expectations predicted for him.

It was theorized that Davalillo had lost his ... well, *intestinal fortitude*, that he was intimidated by pitchers, especially left-handers, after suffering a broken right arm when hit by a fast ball from Detroit's Hank Aguirre in 1963.

"I am not afraid," Davalillo would insist.

But the critics were unconvinced, especially Joe Adcock, the Indians manager in 1967. "Stay in there and swing. Don't bail out," Adcock would scream at Davalillo in batting practice.

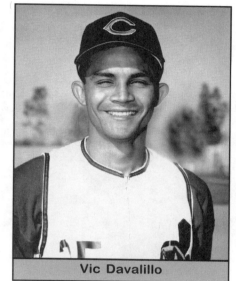
Vic Davalillo

Unfortunately, Adcock's advice only embarrassed Davalillo. He went on to play for St. Louis in 1969, Pittsburgh in 1971, Oakland in 1973, and Los Angeles in 1977, and wound up with a creditable .279 lifetime average when he retired in 1980.

Not bad, but far short of expectation. Martinez fell even shorter.

He was sensational both in the field and at the plate in three minor league seasons (1960-62), but never flashed that kind of ability in trials with the Tribe the next four years.

Martinez hit only .156 in 43 games in 1963, and was returned to the minors. He was tried again - and found wanting again - in each of the next three seasons, during which he batted a total of 34 times with three hits 30 games.

Finally the Indians gave up on Martinez.

They sold him to Tulsa of the Class AAA American Association when, as then Tribe General Manager Gabe Paul explained, "We tried to deal Martinez to another major league club, but nobody was interested.

"It's one of those mysteries in baseball," Paul said of the failure of Martinez and, to some extent, Davalillo, when so many had expected so much of both.

At the time of his demotion, Martinez shrugged and said, "I disappointed the Indians too many times and I don't think I ever would have received another real opportunity with them.

"I guess I'll have to start all over again and earn another chance. I've done it before and I can do it again," he said.

But he never did. A few years later Martinez was out of baseball.

It was, as Paul had said, "One of baseball's great mysteries."

The 'House' that Burns opened

It was April 18, 1923, Opening Day in New York, and the first game was played in the "House That Ruth Built" - Yankee Stadium.

But it wasn't Babe Ruth who got the first hit in the new ballpark.

George Burns

That honor was claimed by a former and soon-to-be future member of the Indians, George Burns.

Burns, who played for the Indians in 1920 when they won their first pennant and World Series, and would play for them again from 1924-28, was the first baseman of the Boston Red Sox, the Yankees' Opening Day opponent in 1923.

A right-handed batter, Burns lined a single to left field in the second inning – the first hit of the game - though Ruth homered later in the game.

But that first hit wasn't the only distinction attributed to Burns, who many historians believe belongs in the Hall of Fame.

Their argument has merit: Burns appeared in 1,866 games for five major league teams, compiling a 16-year career batting average of .307. He hit .300 or better eight times, including a lifetime high .361 in 1921.

Burns broke in with Detroit in 1914, was traded to the Philadelphia Athletics in 1918, was sold to the Indians in May 1920, was dealt to Boston with two other players in December 1921 for Stuffy McInnis, came back to Cleveland in January 1924 in a seven-player package that sent Steve O'Neill and Bill Wambsganss to the Red Sox, was sold to the Yankees in August 1928, and went back to the Athletics the following season. He retired in 1930.

Despite being a right-handed batter, Burns "owned" the friendly right field wall at old League Park, especially in 1926 when he whacked 64 doubles for the Indians – second most in baseball history.

That also was the year Burns batted, .358, led the American League with 216 hits and drove in 114 runs. It won for Burns the AL Most Valuable Player Award.

To put that in proper perspective, the runner-up for the MVP that year was Babe Ruth, who batted .372 with 47 homers and 146 runs batted in. That was the season the Yankees won the pennant, and the Indians finished second, three games out of first place.

Burns hit .268 for the Indians when they won the 1920 pennant, and was one of their stars in the World Series, when they beat Brooklyn in seven games. Burns drove in the only run of the sixth game with a sixth inning double off Sherry Smith as the Indians beat the Dodgers, 1-0, on a three-hitter by Walter (Duster) Mails.

Burns, who was born and raised in Niles, O., made an unassisted triple play in 1923, and also played in the 1929 World Series for the Athletics.

After his retirement, Burns managed in the minors for nine years, and then became a deputy sheriff in Seattle from 1939-68. He died in 1978 at the age of 84.

And though Burns' career records are remembered by few, they undoubtedly would make Burns a millionaire by today's standards.

It was during the 1930s and early-1940s that Cleveland was called the "graveyard of managers," perhaps with good reason.

It began when popular Roger Peckinpaugh was fired midway through the 1933 season and replaced by Walter Johnson. But Johnson proved to be no more successful and he, too, was dismissed on Aug. 5, 1935, as the Indians continued to flounder.

Steve O'Neil

Into that tempest stepped Steve O'Neill, who came out of the coal mines of Minooka, Pa. to catch for the Tribe in 1911, and soon became a star with the team through 1923. O'Neill hit .321 in 149 games in 1920 when the Indians won the pennant and World Series, and was a favorite of the fans.

As Gordon Cobbledick wrote in the Cleveland *Plain Dealer* after O'Neill died at age 69 on Jan. 26, 1962: "Stephen Francis O'Neill's career in Cleveland, as a player and resident, spanned more than half a century.

"In his baseball youth O'Neill played with such Cleveland greats as Napoleon Lajoie, Ray Chapman, Terry Turner, Doc Johnston, Jack Graney and Vean Gregg, and he was still around, as manager and later as coach, in the days of Lou Boudreau, Bob Feller, Ken Keltner, Ray Mack, Larry Doby and Mel Harder.

"He was a contemporary of Ty Cobb, Walter Johnson, Tris Speaker and Eddie Collins ... and he was an established star when a rookie pitcher named Babe Ruth broke in with Boston."

Traded to Boston on Jan. 7, 1924, O'Neill played four more years with the Red Sox, New York Yankees and St. Louis Browns. Few players were better liked than O'Neill, which - as it developed during the 2 1/2 seasons he managed the Tribe - might have been the genial Irishman's biggest fault.

The Indians didn't fare any better under O'Neill, finishing third after he replaced Johnson, and fifth in 1936 and fourth in 1937. Ed McAuley, columnist for the Cleveland *News*, wrote an open letter to O'Neill after the Indians lost 11 of 13 games in 1936. "Get Mad, Steve," the headline admonished the easy-going manager. It apparently convinced then-owner Alva Bradley.

When the Indians finished 19 games out of first place in 1937, Bradley hired Oscar Vitt - which subsequently made matters worse - while O'Neill went on to bigger and better things. He took over as manager of the Detroit Tigers in 1943, and proved that it wasn't necessary for him to "get mad" to be successful.

The Tigers won the AL pennant and World Series in 1945, after finishing second in 1944, and were second again in 1946 and 1947. O'Neill managed the Red Sox in 1950 and 1951, and the Philadelphia Phillies from 1952 through the first 77 games in 1954. His 14 year record as a manager was 1,040 victories and 821 defeats for a creditable winning percentage of .559.

Shortly after O'Neill retired he was lauded by McAuley, who was no longer critical of him for being too soft. "(O'Neill) played with one world championship club and managed another. Not many men in all the history of the game have been as lucky - if that's the word for it - as O'Neill has been, and no one begrudged him his happy fortune.

"Stephen Francis O'Neill is one of the genuinely good guys of our time."

'I'm going to kill myself'

The date was Aug. 3, 1935, and the Tigers were batting against the Indians in the 10th inning of the opening game of a double header in Detroit.

Bruce Campbell, then the Indians' 25-year old right fielder who was one of their best hitters with

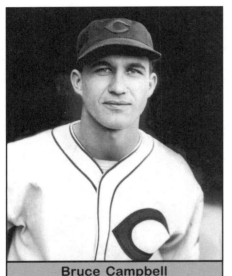

Bruce Campbell

a .325 average, called for time as Tigers pitcher Schoolboy Rowe went to the plate to bat against Lloyd Brown.

Campbell walked slowly to the side of center fielder Earl Averill and told him, "I can hardly see … if (Rowe) hits the ball my way it'll have to go for a hit."

Averill summoned Indians manager Walter Johnson and trainer Lefty Weisman, and a few minutes later they escorted Campbell to the dugout. Although the initial concern was that Campbell was only suffering the effects of a bad cold, it turned out to be much more serious.

According to a story that appeared in the Cleveland *Plain Dealer*, after Campbell went to bed that night, he awoke in a "delirium," and was rushed to the hospital. He was diagnosed as suffering "cerebral spinal fever, a form of spinal meningitis," and doctors gave him "only a 50-50 chance to recover."

It was Brown who probably was responsible for saving Campbell's life. They were roommates and, as the story reported, "About 4 a.m., Brown said, he awoke to find Campbell pushing him from the bed.

"Alarmed, the pitcher asked Campbell what was the matter. He got no response, other than moans. Apparently (Campbell) was delirious and did not recognize Brown.

"Brown saw that Bruce was feverish, took him to the bathroom, washed his face, gave him some water and put cold towels on his head. For a half hour, Campbell would sit down, get up, walk around with his hands in front of him as if he couldn't see, frequently vomiting.

"At one point, he went to the open window and put his head out as if to jump. Brown thought he heard Campbell mutter, 'I'm going to kill myself.' Brown slammed down the window and pulled him away. An ambulance was summoned and Campbell was taken to the hospital," where he would remain for several weeks, finished for the season.

Despite the seriousness of the illness, Campbell recovered and went on to play seven more years in the major leagues, although a recurrence of the debilitating illness ended his playing career in 1943.

In 1,360 games for five teams from 1930-42, Campbell batted over .300 three times, compiling a .290 career batting average that included 106 homers and 766 RBI.

Campbell played for the Indians from 1935-39, after being acquired from the St. Louis Browns (for infielder Johnny Burnett and pitcher Bob Weiland). He also played for the Chicago White Sox, from 1930 until early-1932, the Browns from 1932-34, and after his five seasons with the Indians, was traded (for outfielder Beau Bell) to the Tigers, for whom he played in 1940 and 1941, and the then-Washington Senators in 1942.

Campbell attempted a comeback with Buffalo of the Class AAA International League in 1946, but by then his skills had eroded and he returned to his home in Ft. Myers, Fla. where he operated a successful real estate business until his death on June 17, 1995.

One of the Indians' most blatant attempts to rediscover the road to the World Series - and to bolster attendance - was Gabe Paul's trade for Ken Harrelson on April 19, 1969.

Harrelson, nicknamed "The Hawk" because of his nose, which was very hard to miss, had become a cult hero in Boston in 1968 when he hit .275 with 35 homers and 109 RBI for the Red Sox. Paul figured The Hawk was exactly what the Indians needed.

So did Tribe skipper Alvin Dark, who'd been Harrelson's manager in Kansas City in 1966 and 1967, before Charlie Finley fired the flamboyant first baseman for insubordination.

Harrelson signed with the Red Sox as a free agent and the Fenway Faithful loved him.

Harrelson wore his hair long like the Beatles, dressed like a wealthy hippie and had his own television program, of which he was the emcee, of course.

Ken Harrelson

Paul and Dark were so eager to capitalize on Harrelson's style - and, they thought, his ability to hit baseballs great distances, with regularity - they made what turned out to be one of the Indians' worst-ever trades.

They sent starting pitcher Sonny Siebert, catcher Joe Azcue and reliever Vicente Romo to the Red Sox for Harrelson and two aging left-handed pitchers, Juan Pizzaro and Dick Ellsworth, neither of whom accomplished anything of note for the Tribe.

And to make matters worse, Harrelson - ostensibly broken-hearted about leaving Boston - refused to report to the Indians unless his contract was re-negotiated and, naturally, his salary increased.

Paul had no choice but to comply, and when Harrelson finally came to Cleveland, he made an entrance befitting a movie star.

Greeted at the airport by a throng of teenagers, Harrelson, wearing love beads over his Nehru jacket, led the kids like the Pied Piper to his waiting limousine.

He quickly got another television show called "The Hawk's Nest," and his apartment on Cleveland's Gold Coast resembled something out of a Playboy magazine.

When asked what kind of women he preferred, Harrelson thought for a moment, then replied, "breathing."

Though The Hawk's batting average was a lowly .221 in 1969, neither Paul nor Dark complained. Harrelson had hammered 30 homers and driven in 92 runs in 159 games, and even more was expected of him in 1970.

But then disaster struck. On March 19, 1970, in a spring training game against Oakland in Mesa, Ariz., Harrelson slid into second base and broke his right leg.

"My spikes caught in the dirt and my foot turned backwards," he described what happened. "I heard it pop. I knew it was broken." Harrelson returned in September for 17 games, and played in 52 in 1971, hitting .199 with five homers. But he couldn't run well and retired by mid-season.

It ended one of the most colorful eras in Indians' history, and nullified Gabe Paul's grand intention to hype the team's attack - and, perhaps more importantly, its appeal at the gate.

The 'Polish Spitballer'

No man is an island, though Stan Coveleski made a pretty good try at being one.

The "Polish Spitballer," as Coveleski was nicknamed, came out of the Pennsylvania coal mine fields and always let his pitching speak for itself, usually very eloquently.

Stan Coveleski

"Covey loved the outdoors and loved to pitch, but he hated to talk," said Bill Wambsganss, a teammate of Coveleski's with the Indians from 1916 through 1923.

At the time of Coveleski's death on March 20, 1984, George Uhle, another former teammate, recalled one of the few times Covelski expounded on a subject. "Covey liked to take a belt (of whiskey) every night," Uhle said. "One year when we trained in Hot Springs (Arkansas) he had a jug of moonshine in his trunk.

"But the guys on the railroad had a trick.

"They'd hold a stethoscope to the baggage and if they heard a gurgling sound, they'd open the trunk and steal the whiskey. Remember, it was Prohibition days then.

"When Covey got to Hot Springs and discovered his jug was gone, he cussed those baggage guys something terrible. It was the only time I ever heard him say more than a few words."

The highlight of Coveleski's career was 1920, when the Indians won their first pennant and World Series. He went 24-14 and beat the National League Brooklyn Dodgers three times. Coveleski allowed the Dodgers just two runs and 15 hits in 27 innings, winning the first, fourth and seventh games.

After the spitball was banned at the end of the 1919 season, two pitchers on each team were allowed to continue to throw the pitch as long they'd used it previously.

Obviously, the spitball was Coveleski's best pitch - though not his only one - and it's interesting to speculate what might have happened if he had not been permitted to use it the last nine years of his career, through the 1928 season.

Coveleski wound up with a 215-142 major league lifetime record, but 133 of those victories (and 89 losses) were recorded after the spitball was ruled illegal.

After Coveleski won only 15 games and lost 16 in 1924, the word got around that he was tipping off his spitball.

It led to the Indians' decision to trade him to Washington on Dec. 12, 1924 for pitcher Byron Speece and outfielder Carr Smith, neither of whom made an impact with the Indians.

But the deal gave Coveleski one more chance at World Series glory. He bounced back in 1925 for his fifth and final 20 victory season, leading the Senators to the pennant, though he lost two games to Pittsburgh in the World Series.

When Coveleski was inducted into the Hall of Fame in 1969, he probably was more talkative than at anytime in his career.

"I'd love to be pitching today with the stuff we had back when I pitched," he said. "Today they only use three pitches. We had six - spitball, curve ball, fast ball, screwball, shine ball and emery ball."

Coveleski was the master of them all - and they all spoke eloquently for the guy who never otherwise had much to say.

Baseball's most bizarre game

The Indians have been involved in their share of weird games, but few – probably none – was more bizarre than the one they played at League Park on May 23, 1901.

"Never in the history of the national game has there been a more sensational finish," is the way the Cleveland *Plain Dealer* reported the Indians' 14-13 victory over Washington the next day.

Not only was the game a gem, so was the newspaper's story.

"It was a case of hopeless defeat turned into glorious victory ... and never before did an audience show as much inclination to go totally insane or give a better oral demonstration," the story continued.

Then called the "Blues," the Cleveland team was losing, 13-5, going into the bottom of the ninth.

"Cleveland faced what seemed to be the inevitable ... (and) the people had left the stands by scores, disgusted with such a one-sided game. The few who remained did so to scoff, but soon stayed on to cheer."

Sounding much like a rendition of "Casey at the Bat," the story reported that the first two Cleveland batters were retired in the ninth as, "Hoffer struck out and Pickering was thrown out at first."

Manager Jim McAleer

Then: "McCarthy sent a clean single to right field and the spectators were offended. It seemed like a useless delay. Bradley hit another one safe and the opinion was that the players were only trying to help their batting averages.

"But LaChance, after going after two bad ones, pounded a single to center and McCarthy crossed the plate. Wood was hit by a pitched ball and the bags were full, but no one had the slightest hope of pulling the game out of the fire.

"Scheibeck, however, hit the ball square on the nose for a double. Genins cracked out a single and (opposing pitcher) Patton was taken out of the box and Lee substituted.

"Egan took four bad ones and Beck, who batted for Hoffer, sent the ball so close to the left field fence that Foster could not handle it and the runner took two bases.

"In the meantime, seven runs had been scored in the inning and one more would tie the game.

"Then Pickering singled and Beck went home.

"By this time the audience gave a life-sized picture of pandemonium let out for recess. A crowd of Indians on a red hot warpath could not have been more demonstrative.

"They roared, they jumped, they shouted. They threw everything within reach in the air. Hats, umbrellas, canes, cushions went up as if a cyclone had struck that part of the landscape. They rushed on the field and came close to losing the game for Cleveland by forfeit.

"McCarthy was the man who was given the opportunity of batting in the winning run and he accepted. A single to left sent Pickering across the plate, he having gone to second on a passed ball.

"The demonstration that followed may be imagined – it cannot be described."

And wasn't, except for this last statement.

"Cleveland's ninth inning ... will be remembered until the last person who saw it can remember no more.

The Tribe's 'apathetic' outfieder

Early in John Lowenstein's career with the Indians, which began in 1970 and continued through 1977, someone asked him if he'd like to see a banner in his honor hung at the Stadium.

Lowenstein reacted as if he'd been shot.

John Lowenstein

"Basically, I'm against all banners," he said. "If somebody puts up a sign about me, I'd immediately disqualify myself from the game. Signs have no ethereal value."

Still, when he was pressed on the subject, Lowenstein did offer a description of what he considered the perfect baseball banner - about himself.

It would be a huge white sign hung in the center field bleachers at the Stadium where fans are not allowed to sit. There'd be no writing on the banner and it would be displayed only when the Indians were on the road.

Yes, John Lowenstein was a little different. In many ways.

When some fans wanted to start a fan club for him, Lowenstein said no. Instead, he formed the "Apathy Club." Nobody knew how many members the club had because nobody was interested enough to show up for meetings. Which is the way Lowenstein liked it.

Lowenstein was delighted when he hit .242 in consecutive seasons (1974 and 1975). Not only did it show consistency, but also the middle-of-the-road anonymity Lowenstein craved.

"I have no desire to be an everyday player," Lowenstein made clear during his career, which continued through 1985.

But, the truth be told, a pretty good player was hiding behind that nonchalant facade.

Lowenstein played every position but pitcher and catcher.

The Indians liked Lowenstein so much, after sending him to Toronto (with Rick Cerone to reacquire Rico Carty, who'd been lost in the expansion draft) in November 1976, they traded Hector Torres to get him back in March of 1977.

But they didn't keep him long. Only until February of 1978, when Lowenstein was dealt with Tom Buskey to Texas. A year later the Rangers traded Lowenstein to Baltimore where he was perfectly-utilized by Orioles manager Earl Weaver.

Suddenly - whether he liked it or not - the unpretentious infielder-outfielder no longer was merely an average player with above-average quotes.

Now there were impressive statistics behind his name. In the nine seasons before going to Baltimore, Lowenstein hit .238 with 48 homers and 204 RBI in 723 games. In the seven seasons he spent with the Orioles, Lowenstein hit .274 with 68 homers and 237 RBI in 645 games.

Not bad for a guy who spawned the Apathy Club in Cleveland.

Weaver employed Lowenstein almost exclusively against right-handed pitchers. But unlike so many players, Lowenstein did not object to being platooned.

"You could say I went from playing a lot, to playing a little, to being used sometimes, to playing on a platoon basis," said Lowenstein.

Only the inimitable John Lowenstein could say it - and mean it.

It's hard to believe that anybody could - or even *would* - try to do what some insist Bobby Bragan did.

But then, considering all the frustrations the Indians suffered after Bragan was drummed out of Cleveland, one has to wonder. Many people do.

Legend has it that Bragan put a "curse" on the Tribe after he was fired by Frank Lane on June 28, 1958.

"Aw, that's not completely true ... but if folks in Cleveland want to believe it, let 'em," Bragan said several years ago during an old-timers game at the Stadium.

Again, many people do.

Bragan's tenure was the shortest of any non-interim manager in Cleveland baseball history - 67 games, only 31 of which were victories. He was hired in the winter of 1957-58 by Hank Greenberg who, shortly thereafter, was bought out as a part owner of the team, and Lane came in as general manager.

The Indians did better after Joe Gordon took over for Bragan, finishing with a 77-76 record, but only eight times in 35 years, from 1958 through 1993, did they win more games than they lost.

One of those times was 1959, and the way they fell apart in September of that season might have been the first indication that the Indians were indeed cursed.

Bobby Bragan

They were running virtually neck-and-neck with Chicago entering the final month, but then collapsed, losing a weekend series to the White Sox and falling out of the race for good. They wound up with an 89-65 record, five lengths behind Chicago.

A month or so after Bragan was fired, he took a minor league managing job with Los Angeles, then in the Pacific Coast League, and proceeded to blame the media for the problems he had with the Indians.

"You never read in a Cleveland paper anything that encourages attendance," Bragan was quoted as saying, apparently believing he lost his job because only 663,805 fans came through the turnstiles in 1958. In reality, a more significant factor in Bragan's demise were some questionable personnel decisions, and several intemperate and unwise statements he'd made a couple of weeks before he was fired.

The Indians were badly beaten by the Athletics in a game in Kansas City. A big reason was that Bragan played a rookie outfielder, Gary Geiger, at third base. The A's quickly "found" Geiger, slapping several "hits" past and through him.

After that game, Bragan, by his own admission to the media, "lectured the players for not trying."

It was a bad rap, and from that point on a fire smoldered within Lane, an impatient man even when things were going well, which they definitely weren't in those trying times.

Finally, Lane could take no more of what he considered Bragan's ineptitude and fired him.

It would have been then that Bragan, angry and embittered, placed his curse on the Indians - if he really did.

But who's to say he didn't, everything considered – at least until 1995, when the Indians won their first pennant in 41 years, and at that time only the fourth in franchise history.

The farm boy who arrived too late

When he was a teenager at Northwestern High School near Wooster, O. there was almost no doubt among his admirers that Dean Chance would end up in the Baseball Hall of Fame.

By the time he graduated Chance had a 51-1 record, and had led Northwestern to the state championship in 1959. He pitched a four-hitter in the only game he lost in three years.

Dean Chance

Chance's idol then was Bob Feller and his burning ambition was to play for the Indians, though he didn't get the opportunity to do so until it was nearly time for him to leave the game.

Selected by Baltimore in the amateur draft of 1959, Chance signed for what was then a large bonus - $30,000. He pitched two seasons in the Orioles minor league system, and was claimed by the then-Los Angeles Angels in the expansion draft in the winter of 1960-61.

Chance made it to the Angels late in 1961, and two seasons later blossomed into the most overpowering pitcher in the major leagues.

With a 20-9 record and 1.65 earned run average, Chance won the Cy Young Award in 1964 (that was before the American and National leagues each selected a winner), pitching 11 shutouts, including six that he won by a score of 1-0.

But then the former Ohio farm boy who was considered one of the best young pitchers in baseball – and who reveled in the faster-paced L.A. lifestyle - suffered arm trouble. His record slipped to 15-10 in 1965, and to 12-17 in 1966.

Chance was traded to Minnesota where he enjoyed a brief resurgence, going 20-14 with 2.73 E.R.A. in 1967, which helped him win the A.L. "Comeback of the Year" award.

One of his victories, 2-1, was a no-hitter against the Indians at the old Cleveland Stadium on Aug. 25, and another was a five inning (rain-shortened) perfect game, 2-0, against Boston on Aug. 6.

But again his record slumped, first to 16-16 and then to 5-4 the next two seasons, which led to his acquisition – finally – by the Indians on Dec. 10, 1969. In addition to Chance, the Indians received two regulars, third baseman Graig Nettles and outfielder Ted Uhlaender, as well as relief pitcher Bob Miller, for pitchers Luis Tiant and Stan Williams.

However, by then another comeback was beyond Chance's reach and, with a 9-8 record as a starter and reliever in 1970, his $55,000 salary was too much for the Indians to afford. His contract was sold by the financially-strapped team to the New York Mets for $100,000.

"If it weren't for leaving Cleveland, this would be the greatest thing to happen to me," Chance said of the deal that was to give him a new start in the National League. But the Mets finished third in the N.L. East and Chance failed to win a game. He wound up in Detroit where his career ended with a 4-6 record in 31 games in 1971.

Chance's bottom line reads: 128 victories and 115 losses, with a 2.92 E.R.A. in 406 games, 294 as a starter, and 1,534 strikeouts and 739 bases on balls in 2,147 1/3 innings.

Unfortunately – for both Chance and the Indians - only one of his 11 seasons and nine of those victories were in Cleveland.

A wonderful year to remember

Every ball player has one game he will always remember.

But John Patsy Francona, better known as Tito, has 122 games he'll never forget.

That's how many games Francona played for the Indians in 1959, the last time they were a legitimate pennant contender until their "re-awakening" 35 years later.

Francona spent 15 years in the big leagues, drawing paychecks from nine different teams. But he never had a season before - or after - that compared to 1959, although it didn't begin as anything special. Francona spent the first two months on the bench before manager Joe Gordon gave him a chance to start in center field.

The next thing Indians fans knew, Tito was hitting the ball all over the place. It was amazing. He even flirted with a .400 average much of the season.

Although Francona didn't wind up with enough plate appearances to qualify for the American League batting championship, he ended the season with a solid .363 average that included 17 doubles, 20 homers, 68 runs and 79 RBI.

Unfortunately for Tito - and the Indians - it wasn't the same in 1960. Francona's average fell 71 points, closer to his lifetime .272 mark than his career high.

Tito Francona

"I remember that season (1969) very well," Francona said several years ago while visiting Cleveland for an old-timers game. "We had a lot of fun, but we should have won the pennant. That was my best year. Everything went right. Nobody could throw a fastball by me. I'd go one-for-three and my average would drop. I don't think I ever went two games without a hit."

During that sweet season, Gordon told reporters, "Francona will be playing for this club the next 10 years."

Gordon was almost right, as it turned out. Francona spent six seasons in Cleveland, a lifetime for a ballplayer, though he never duplicated the success he enjoyed in 1959.

Francona said he loved playing in Cleveland, but every winter returned to his home in Pennsylvania. He was admittedly fearful of buying a home in Cleveland because, at that time, Frank Lane - notorious as "Trader Lane" - was the Indians general manager.

As did so many of his teammates, Francona wondered every winter if he'd still be an Indian the following spring.

Before coming to Cleveland in exchange for Larry Doby on March 21, 1959, Francona had bounced from Baltimore to the Chicago White Sox to Detroit.

There was no indication that his career season was bubbling just beneath the surface; in 1958 Francona hit .258 for the White Sox and .246 for the Tigers in a total of 86 games.

"I never thought Tito would come through the way he did," Lane said back then. "It was a matter of wanting to get rid of Doby and I figured Tito might have a chance.

Francona's final season in Cleveland was 1964 and, 24 years later, another Francona surprised the Indians with a good year. This one was Terry Francona, Tito's son. He hit .311 in 1988, a good year to be sure.

But not nearly as good as his father had in 1959.

When Gomer batted '4.000'

No doubt about it, Gomer Hodge was a very good pinch hitter.

But he certainly was a terrible mathematician.

Gomer, whose given name was Harold, came up to the Indians as a 27-year old rookie in 1971 after spending eight seasons in the minor leagues.

Gomer Hodge

Hodge was nicknamed "Gomer" because of his uncanny resemblance in speech to actor-singer Jim Nabors, who starred in the then popular television program, "Gomer Pyle, U.S.M.C."

On Opening Day, against the Boston Red Sox, Hodge delivered an eighth inning pinch single, then stayed in the game and stroked a game-winning hit in the last of the ninth as the Indians prevailed, 3-2.

A couple of games later Gomer got his third straight pinch single, and the next day did it again, making it 4-for-4, after which he told a group of reporters interviewing him:

"Gollee, fellas, I'm hittin' 4.000!"

Well, sort of.

Unfortunately - for Hodge and the Indians – Gomer's ability to hit turned as bad as his ability to figure his batting average.

After that wonderful start, which captivated Tribe fans, as well as Manager Alvin Dark, Hodge reverted to the form that had kept him in the minors so long.

After those first four hits - for what Gomer considered a 4.000 average - he went just 13-for-79 and finished the season with a .205 batting average in 80 games, with one homer and nine runs batted in, nearly all of his game appearances coming as a pinch-hitter.

The following winter the Indians demoted Hodge to Portland, their Class AAA farm club in the Pacific Coast League, and he never made it back to the major leagues.

Ah, but those first few weeks of 1971 will never be forgotten by Gomer, whose humility was captivating - and unusual - in a sport composed mostly of individuals with massive egos.

"I asked the Good Lord for help everytime I went to the plate," he said when asked for the secret to the success that enabled him to hit "4.000" in his first week with the Indians.

"Sure, I was nervous, but not as nervous as I am talking with you guys. I never got attention like this," he said, smiling - and blushing - as usual.

His hitting, and his humility, made Hodge a favorite of the fans.

Hodge - or Gomer, if you prefer – signed with the Indians in 1963, prior to the advent of the amateur draft. He climbed slowly but surely through the minor league system, despite never hitting more than .291, his average at Savannah of the Class AA Southern League in 1970, which earned his promotion to the Indians.

After he was demoted to Portland in 1972, Hodge played a couple more seasons in the minors, but was never able to earn a return trip to Cleveland. Since the late 1970s, Hodge has been a minor league coach for several organizations.

He was quoted recently as saying that he'd always remember those first few weeks in Cleveland, in 1971, when his batting average soared to "4.000."

And anybody who was ever around Harold Hodge, better known as "Gomer," will never forget him, either.

James Timothy Grant II, a.k.a. "Mudcat," said he always wanted to pitch his entire career in Cleveland. "It's where I started, where I got my first chance, and the only place I liked almost as much as Lacoochie," he said in an article in the Cleveland *Plain Dealer*.

"Lacoochie" was I.acoochie, Fla. where Mudcat and brother Julius, a.k.a. "Swampfire," who also was a pitcher, grew up and learned to play - and love - baseball.

Mudcat Grant

But Mudcat also said he was glad to be traded in 1964, to Minnesota for pitcher Lee Stange and a player to be named later, third baseman George Banks.

And if that sounds incongruous, listen as Grant explains.

"The reason I was glad to go to the Twins," he said, "was because of Johnny Sain. That man is the greatest."

Sain, a former star with the Boston-Milwaukee Braves in the National League, was the Twins' pitching coach who refined Grant's curve ball which, until then, did little more than spin.

Still, as a member of the Indians - even without a great curve ball - Grant became one of their most consistent pitchers from the time he joined them in 1958, until he was dealt to Minnesota six years later.

Signed by the Indians in 1954, Mudcat's four-year minor league career record was a spectacular 70-28, though he was only 67-63 in 6 ½ seasons in Cleveland.

But Grant's career took a definite turn for the better once he joined Sain.

In 1965, Mudcat became the first black pitcher to win 20 games when he was voted American League "Pitcher of the Year," and led the Twins to the pennant with a 21-7 record. He also beat the Los Angeles Dodgers in two of the three games the Twins won in the World Series that year.

However, Grant's career went downhill thereafter.

He was traded to the Dodgers in 1968, then was selected by Montreal in the 1969 expansion draft, was dealt to St. Louis later that season, and spent 1970 and 1971 with Oakland and Pittsburgh.

Grant had a spring trial with the Tribe in 1972 but by then his fast ball was gone. So was the curve ball that Grant learned from Sain, the pitch that made Mudcat one of the best pitchers of his time.

He retired with a 145-119 record in 14 major league seasons.

Unfortunately for Cleveland fans, most of those games were won elsewhere as Grant was traded away, along with other established players, including Jim Perry, Pedro Ramos and Gary Bell, because the Indians were suffering a severe economic crisis in the 1960s. Simply stated, the Indians couldn't afford Mudcat and other highly - paid players then.

When Mudcat failed in that 1972 comeback attempt, he became a television voice of the Indians, teaming up with Harry Jones while working part-time in community relations for the Indians.

Grant subsequently embarked upon yet another career, this one in show business.

"I just obey my impulses, do what comes natural and have fun," he once explained his penchant for singing and dancing. "I love to entertain people."

And, as he also made clear, Mudcat loved to pitch in Cleveland for the Indians.

It's too bad he couldn't have done more of it in his prime.

Terrible tempered Alex

There were two defining characteristics about Alex Johnson, who played for the Indians - though not very well - in 1972, and usually was the center of a storm of controversy.

First: He was an excellent natural hitter, having won the American League batting championship with a .329 average for the California Angels in 1970.

Alex Johnson

Second: He had a violent temper, often defied then-Manager Ken Aspromonte and many times refused to run out ground balls to the infield.

He also usually played with abject indifference, and constantly maintained a cold war with the media.

Before coming to Cleveland - perhaps the reason he was traded to the Tribe - Johnson had been suspended more than half of the 1971 season by the Angels for "not giving his best effort," and also for threatening Manager Lefty Phillips on several occasions.

In a rare interview during his suspension, Johnson said, "I had justifiable reasons for not being in the spirit for playing properly. There was indifference on the whole team in working together. I felt the game of baseball wasn't being played properly, so my taste wasn't there," the Associated Press reported that Johnson said.

The moody outfielder also claimed that his problems stemmed from his relationship with sports writers covering the Angels.

"I rejected them because of what they wrote about me," Johnson was quoted as saying. "The more I rejected them, the worse they wrote about me. It caused a bad feeling on the club. Things were magnified, not properly told.

After he was traded to the Indians, along with catcher Gerry Moses, for outfielders Vada Pinson and Frank Baker, and pitcher Alan Foster, Johnson's problems on the field and with the media resumed in Cleveland.

Not only did he feud with Aspromonte, Johnson also had a running battle with umpire Ed Runge that eventually required the intervention of American League President Joe Cronin.

Several times, in games that Runge worked at first base, Johnson seemed to go out of his way to intentionally crash into the umpire.

It was unfortunate that Johnson's temperament caused him so much trouble because he was truly gifted as a hitter.

The brother of former Cleveland Browns and New York Giants running back Ron Johnson, Alex made it to the big leagues with the Philadelphia Phillies in 1964, hitting .303 in 43 games.

He was traded to the St. Louis Cardinals in 1966, Cincinnati Reds in 1968, and to the Angels in 1970, before joining the Indians.

After Johnson hit .329 with eight homers and 37 RBI in 108 games for the Tribe in 1972, he was peddled to the Texas Rangers for a couple of minor league pitchers, but didn't last long with them either. The Rangers sent Johnson to the New York Yankees in 1974, and he wound up his career with Detroit in 1976.

In 13 controversy-marred seasons, Johnson compiled a lifetime .288 average which, for many players, would have been commendable.

But not for one with the great natural ability of Alex Johnson.

'Almost beyond comprehension'

"I'm so excited and jubilant and happy, I can't put it all into words. This is the greatest thrill of my life. It is a magnificent moment, a fairy tale. I'm not even sure it is real."

Those were the words spoken by Steve Dunning – then appropriately nicknamed "Stunning Steve" – after making his major league debut with the Indians on June 14, 1970.

Dunning, then 21, was the first player in the nation to be picked in the amateur draft, and 11 days later started his first professional baseball game, against the Milwaukee Brewers. He beat them, 9-2, at the old Cleveland Stadium.

Steve Dunning

"It was overwhelming to be drafted No. 1 (out of Stanford University), then to be given the opportunity to pitch in the big leagues immediately, and to win. It was almost beyond comprehension," Dunning later said of his introduction by the Indians.

"It was something I'll never forget as long as I live … a dream come true."

Unfortunately for Dunning and the Indians, that stunning debut turned out to be the high point of his baseball career that lasted less than nine years. Dunning won 18 games and lost 29 in three-plus seasons with the Indians. He was 4-9 in 1970, 8-14 in 1971, 6-4 in 1972, and was 0-2 when he was traded to Texas (for pitcher Dick Bosman and outfielder Ted Ford) on May 10, 1973.

On July 1, 1978, Dunning walked away from the game and returned to college, Loyola University in Los Angeles, and earned a law degree. "I didn't last as long as I would have liked, but I wouldn't trade my experiences in baseball for anything," Dunning said. "I have absolutely no regrets."

Especially not when in recalling that first game, played in front of a "Bat Day" crowd of 25,380 fans who, in effect, helped pay the $60,000 signing bonus the Indians gave Dunning.

He struck out the first big league batter he faced, Tommy Harper, on a 3-and-2 pitch. "It was a high fast ball that Harper swung at and missed, and the crowd roared like nothing I ever heard before," said Dunning. "I was never so pumped up in all my life." He blanked the Brewers in the first two innings, but a walk and Harper's two out homer broke the ice in the third. But it didn't matter as the Indians tied the score in their half of the inning, and added three more runs in the fourth.

Dunning left after five innings with a 5-2 lead on a yield of five hits and two walks, with three strikeouts. Reliever Bob Miller took over and held the Brewers scoreless while the Indians were adding single runs in the sixth and eighth innings.

"That (victory) provided me with such an ironic impression of major league baseball," Dunning said. "I thought to myself, 'This can't be that tough. I only have to pitch five innings, my team scores five runs, I give up only two and I win.'"

He pitched another memorable game for the Indians in 1971, to beat the then-Washington Senators, 1-0, on April 18. Tom McCraw singled in the second inning for the only hit Dunning allowed.

Thereafter, however, it wasn't that easy for Stunning Steve, and he won only five games, while losing 12 with four teams – the Rangers, California, Montreal and Oakland - in parts of four seasons after leaving the Indians.

The game 'Sudden Sam' can't forget

"**I**'ll never know for sure what might have happened if I hadn't said anything to George Strickland that night, or if he hadn't taken me out of the game.

"That's the reason I'll never forget that game in Detroit in 1966," Sam McDowell easily recalled one of the most vivid memories of his 15 year major league pitching career that ended in 1975.

George Strickland

The date was Sept. 18 and the Indians were trying to climb into fifth place in what was then a 10 team American League race. Strickland was the interim manager, having replaced Birdie Tebbetts, who'd resigned under fire a month earlier.

"I often wonder if I could have struck out 18 (and tied what was then the major league record) if I could have gone all the way in that game," said McDowell.

"One thing I know, I had everything that night. My fast ball was as good as it ever was, and my control was nearly perfect. I got 14 strikeouts in only six innings. No matter what pitch I threw, I could put it anywhere I wanted. I was at my all-time best, and I don't think I was ever that good after that night.

"I went back to the dugout at the end of the sixth inning and told Strickland my arm was beginning to tighten. I only said it because I wanted him to have somebody ready, just in case. We were winning (5-1) and I didn't want to take any chances.

"I remember telling George, 'I'm OK, and I want to stay in there. But maybe you should keep somebody ready just in case.' Just like that he took me out. I'd had some shoulder trouble early that season and Strick probably wanted to be sure I didn't hurt myself again.

"Nobody will ever know for sure what might have happened. But I only needed four more strikeouts to tie the record and five to break it, and I had three innings to get them. That's why, of all the games I pitched, it's one I'll never forget," McDowell said.

At that time the single game strikeout record was shared by Bob Feller, who set it in 1938, and Sandy Koufax of Los Angeles in 1962 (and subsequently equaled by Don Wilson of Houston in 1968 and Koufax again in 1969).

It was broken by Steve Carlton of St. Louis with 19 strikeouts on Sept. 15, 1969 (and equaled by Tom Seaver of the New York Mets in 1970 and Nolan Ryan of California in 1974). Then Roger Clemens, pitching for Boston, fanned 20 batters on April 29, 1986, and again in 1996, as did Kerry Wood of the Chicago Cubs in 1998.

As it turned out, McDowell didn't even get credit for the victory over the Tigers that night in 1966. Reliever John O'Donoghue blew the lead in the eighth and the Indians had to rally for a run in the 10th to win, 6-5, behind Luis Tiant. Ironically, Tiant struck out five Tigers in his 2 1/3 inning stint, and O'Donoghue fanned two in 1 2/3 innings, to go with McDowell's 14, giving the Indians 21 for the game.

In that game, before he was taken out, McDowell struck out the first five batters he faced, and nine of 10. He was awesome, and nobody will know if he was at his all-time best. If not, he certainly was close.

McDowell went on to win only nine games while losing eight that season, and in 194 innings he still led the league with 225 strikeouts - 14 of which he'll never forget.

Ray (Slim) Caldwell's first game for the Indians, on Aug. 24, 1919, came very close to also being his last.

Instead, he pitched for the Indians in 1920, and without his 20-10 record they couldn't have won the pennant.

Caldwell also hurled a no-hitter on Sept. 10, 1919, beating the New York Yankees, 3-0.

But it was that game 2 1/2 weeks earlier that established Caldwell's reputation as a battler.

In his Cleveland debut Caldwell was beating the Philadelphia Athletics, 2-1, with two out in the ninth inning when a violent thunderstorm hit League Park and he was struck by a bolt of lightning.

As the Cleveland *Plain Dealer* reported the next day: "Thousands of spectators were thrown into a momentary panic by the bolt which came without warning and made as much noise as the backfiring of a thousand autos or the explosion of a dozen shells from a battery of big berthas.

"Fully half of those in the stands were affected while every player felt the electrical current through his body, the spiked shoes they wore attracting the juice.

Ray Caldwell

"Caldwell and shortstop (Ray) Chapman were affected the most. Chapman almost slipped because of the numb feeling in one leg, but recovered and was one of those to run to the rescue of Caldwell, who lay stretched out in the pitcher's box.

"The pitcher, though, arose unassisted and in a minute or so the effects of the electrical storm passed off and he was able to resume work.

"He had to pitch to but one man, (Joe) Dugan, and forced him to hit a grounder to (Larry) Gardner just as the clouds broke and the rain came down heavily."

Caldwell, who was signed by the Indians after he'd been released by Boston, pitched for the Yankees from 1910 through 1918, compiling a 96-99 record in nine seasons. The Red Sox had acquired Caldwell in a seven player deal prior to the 1919 season, but became disenchanted despite his 7-4 record through the first half of the season.

Tris Speaker, then the Indians' player-manager, jumped at the chance to sign Caldwell, as *Plain Dealer* Sports Editor Gordon Cobbledick wrote in an Aug. 23, 1961 column.

"In the old League Park office, Speaker thrust at (Caldwell) a previously prepared contract. 'Read it,' said Speaker. 'Gimme a pen,' said Caldwell. 'Read it first. You don't even know how much money it calls for; Speaker told the pitcher, 'Gimme a pen,' Caldwell repeated.

"On that day, to all intents, Cleveland won its first American League pennant, though it didn't become official until nearly a season and a half later.

"In 1920 the Indians nosed out Chicago, which had been riddled by the Black Sox scandal, in the last week of the season. Their margin was only two games.

"Without the 20 victories contributed by Slim Caldwell they wouldn't, of course, have come close, and it is entirely likely that we'd have waited until 1948 for our first championship."

'The best since Joe Jackson'

When Oscar Vitt, the new manager of the Indians in 1938, first saw Jeff Heath in the batting cage in spring training, he called the rookie "the best natural hitter I've seen since Joe Jackson."

Vitt's admiration seemed appropriate as Heath, a handsome, muscular outfielder, was coming off a pair

Jeff Heath

of minor league seasons in which he hit .383 at Zanesville of the (Class C) Mid-Atlantic League in 1936, and .367 for Milwaukee of the (Class AA) American Association in 1937.

Later in the 1938 season Cy Slapnicka, then Tribe general manager, embellished Vitt's praise of Heath.

"If every man on this ball club had showed the determination and hustle that Jeff has showed me since the season started, we'd be so far ahead you'd think we were in another league," said Peckinpaugh.

But it turned out that the tributes were greatly exaggerated, and very premature.

Oh, Heath batted .343 with 21 homers and drove in 112 runs in 1938, and had a couple more good seasons during his next seven years in Cleveland. But flaws soon appeared in both his performance and temperament.

When Heath's average slumped to .219 with 14 homers and 50 RBI in 1940, he was accused of loafing and was blamed for the Indians losing the pennant by one game to Detroit. He responded by threatening his critics.

According to a newspaper account at the time, Heath issued an ultimatum to Ed McAuley, columnist and baseball writer for the old Cleveland *News.*

Heath took exception to an article in which McAuley suggested that he ought to be a better team man, and should start giving 100 percent effort all the time.

Heath said he would physically throw McAuley out if the writer ever showed his face in the locker room or dugout again.

McAuley dutifully reported the incident in the *News* the next day, then went to the dugout just before game time. A horde of reporters and cameras were on hand to record the event. The worst was expected because of Heath's well - known temper.

But no blood was shed, nor were any punches even thrown. Instead, Heath greeted McAuley with a big grin and a ready handshake. Ostensibly, all was forgiven and forgotten.

It was revealed later, however, that Alva Bradley, then the owner of the Indians, had sent a message to the clubhouse: "Tell Heath that if he touches one hair on McAuley's head, I will see to it that he never plays one more inning in Organized Baseball."

Obviously, Heath played on. He rebounded to hit .300 three more times, but was traded to Washington on Dec. 14, 1945 for speedy but light hitting outfielder George Case.

Heath wound up with the Boston Braves in 1948 and would have gleefully faced his former teammates in the World Series, but suffered a severely-broken ankle near the end of the season.

He played only 36 games for the Braves in 1949 and retired, ending a 14-year major league batting average of .293, 194 homers and 887 RBI, which was creditable - but far short of the brilliance predicted for him by Vitt.

Appropriately nicknamed 'Little Stormy'

His nickname was "Little Stormy," and it was not just a play on Roy Weatherly's name or physical stature.

The Indians center fielder from 1936 through 1942, Weatherly might have been the first - and perhaps still is the only - major league baseball player granted a bonus for not being ejected from a game in a season.

That was in 1940 after Weatherly had been banished by umpire Bill McGowan and, allegedly, was "blacklisted" by the American League. Then Indians owner Alva Bradley promised Weatherly $500 at the end of the season if he stayed out of further trouble.

No doubt about it, Weatherly was little - 5-6, 170-pounds in his prime - and stormy. There also was no doubt where Weatherly's temper came from.

Roy Weatherly

"An umpire baiter from way back, Roy has had his troubles with the men in blue since his earliest days with the Indians," according to a July 4, 1940 story in the Cleveland *News*.

"Weatherly comes by this aptitude naturally. One day in 1936 his father was at League Park. Roy was called out by umpire Brick Owens on a close play at first base. Weatherly's white-haired dad came hopping out of a field box to register his protest with the startled arbiter."

Roy's father was restrained before he could reach the umpire - but the elder Weatherly certainly made clear the basis of Little Stormy's stormy temperament.

But it wasn't just his temper that made Weatherly famous. He was a great outfielder and a pretty good hitter. Weatherly hit .335 in 84 games as a rookie in 1936, .310 in 1939 and .303 in 1940, when he incurred the wrath of many of his teammates, according to another newspaper account.

The players were angered by Weatherly's reluctance to sign their petition demanding that Manager Oscar Vitt be fired.

When Weatherly said he wanted time to consider the merits of the rebellion, one (whom Weatherly wouldn't identify) told him, "You're either for us or against us." Weatherly said he replied, "If you feel that way about it, just count me out," and didn't join the revolt.

Weatherly was traded to the New York Yankees, along with infielder Oscar Grimes for catcher Buddy Rosar and outfielder Roy Cullenbine, on Dec. 17, 1942. He hit .264 in 77 games in 1943, then went into the Army for two years.

Little Stormy - who by then had mellowed considerably - came out of the service in 1946 and rejoined the Yankees. But he played only two games before breaking his leg, which effectively ended his major league career.

Oh, true to his nature, Weatherly wouldn't quit. He went back to the minors and earned a chance with the New York Giants, hitting .261 in 52 games in 1950. But that was it and he ended his career with a .286 average in 811 major league games.

Some old-timers insist that Weatherly was one of the best outfielders of all-time. They might be right. One thing sure. Few were hotter-tempered than the man who was appropriately nicknamed "Little Stormy."

He thought he was dreaming

Only Gene Bearden's victory over Boston 47 years earlier in an unprecedented one game playoff in 1948, giving the Indians their second American League pennant, was singularly more important in franchise history than one by Dennis Martinez on Oct. 17, 1995.

Dennis Martinez

Pitching in what was then called the "Kingdome mausoleum," Martinez beat the Seattle Mariners, 4-0, in the sixth and deciding game of the A.L. Championship Series, vaulting the Indians into the World Series.

In beating the A.L. West Division champion Mariners in front of 58,489 partisan fans, Martinez out-pitched – and out-gutted – Randy Johnson, the Cy Young Award winning southpaw. Johnson won 18 games and lost only two, with a league-best 2.48 earned run average and 294 strikeouts in the regular season.

When the game was over, wrapped up in two hitless inning relief stints by Julian Tavarez in the eighth and Jose Mesa in the ninth, Manager Mike Hargrove said what most Tribe fans also had to be thinking: "I had to pinch myself to be sure I wasn't dreaming."

"Dennis Martinez wanted this game, and then he went out and showed why he's one of the best pitchers in baseball," is the way Carlos Baerga praised the crafty, 40-year old right-hander who allowed only four hits through seven innings. He left out of sheer exhaustion with a 1-0 lead.

Then Tavarez and Mesa extended the shutout while their teammates – especially Kenny Lofton – were providing a more comfortable cushion.

"After all I've been through in my career, this was the game I was looking for," said Martinez, a recovering alcoholic. "Finally I did something we can all remember. The people of Cleveland have been waiting for this for such a long time."

Lofton set an ALCS record by hitting .458 on 11-for-24 in the series, with four runs and three RBI, and also stole five bases in as many attempts.

Not only did Lofton drive in the first run in the fifth inning of the deciding game, he also scored the run that seemed to break the spirit of Johnson and Mariners in the eighth.

The inning began with a double by Tony Pena, after which Lofton used his great speed to beat out a bunt single, sending pinch runner Ruben Amaro to third.

Then, with Omar Vizquel at the plate, Lofton stole second, and a few moments later Dan Wilson, Seattle's catcher, committed a passed ball.

Amaro scored easily from third and, amazingly, so did Lofton from second. All the red-faced Wilson, and the startled and angry Johnson could do was talk to themselves.

"I wasn't going to try and score at first," said Lofton. "I was just bluffing (by rounding third). But Wilson kind of took his time getting to the ball, so I just came home." He slid in easily for a 3-0 lead, and two batters later Carlos Baerga homered.

Not only did the victory clinch the Indians' first pennant since 1954 (after which they were swept in the World Series by the then-New York Giants), it also gave the city of Cleveland its first championship since the Browns won the NFL in 1964, 31 years earlier

When the 'Big Mon' complained

It was a stunning acceptance speech Rico Carty delivered upon being introduced as the Indians "Man of the Year" for 1976.

It capped one of the most bizarre episodes in Indians history, and nobody was more stunned than Manager Frank Robinson, seated next to Carty at the head table.

All the players on the team were there in front of 600 fans at a Wahoo Club luncheon as Carty – appropriately nicknamed "Big Mon" - unleashed a verbal swipe at Robinson. "They talk about the leader of the team," he said. "They mention this player and that player. But who is the best leader of the team?

"It's the manager. When he leads, we got a ball club. Believe me, I'm telling this with all my heart," Carty continued, as Robinson winced.

So did General Manager Phil Seghi, seated next to the manager, and virtually all of the players.

It was amazing - but in retrospect, that's the way it was in those days of transition, when free agency had just come into being. It was the first year on the team for Wayne Garland, who had just signed a $2.3 million, 10-year contract after gaining his free agency from Baltimore. The average major league salary was $55,300 that year.

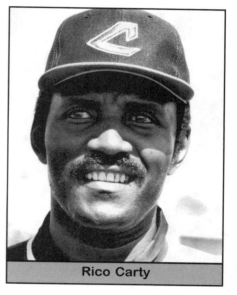

Rico Carty

Carty wound up his remarks with a plea to Robinson: "We need your help, Frank. If you don't help, we'll all be in trouble."

Again in retrospect, Carty's remarks did more harm than good. Two months later, on June 7, Carty and Robinson had a nasty confrontation that led to the Big Mon's suspension for 15 days for "insubordination."

And before Carty was reinstated, Robinson was fired on June 19 and replaced by Jeff Torborg.

But the change in managers had no effect on the fortunes of the Indians. They finished fifth with a 71-90 record.

Until his startling denunciation of the manager, Carty was indeed a Big Mon. After seven seasons with the Milwaukee-Atlanta Braves, during which he won the National League batting championship with a .366 average in 1970, Carty played for Texas, Oakland and the Chicago Cubs in 1973, and was purchased by the Indians from the Mexican League in August 1974.

Carty hit .308 and .310 for the Indians the next two seasons, then was lost to Toronto in the 1977 expansion draft. But Seghi wouldn't let him go. A month after the Blue Jays claimed Carty, Seghi got him back in a deal that proved very costly.

To retrieve Carty from Toronto, the Indians traded Rick Cerone and John Lowenstein and the Big Mon responded by hitting .280 and driving in 80 runs in 1977.

It turned out to be Carty's swan song. When F.J. "Steve" O'Neill re-purchased the Indians in the winter of 1977-78, his first move was to rehire Gabe Paul as president and chief executive officer.

And one of Paul's first moves was to unload the Big Mon.

Carty was traded back to Toronto, ending what certainly was one of the most bizarre episodes in Indians history.

The 'peerless second baseman'

You could call it "divine intervention," though that would be stretching it a little.

But certainly the Indians, then known as the Cleveland Bronchos, got help from above, in this case the Supreme Court of Pennsylvania, in the 1902 acquisition of the man many have called the best player in the history of the franchise.

Napoleon Lajoie

That would be Napoleon Lajoie, the "peerless second baseman," who was elected to the Hall of Fame in 1937 after a 21 year major league career in which he compiled a .338 batting average.

Lajoie started with the Philadelphia Phillies of the National League in 1896, but in 1901 jumped to Connie Mack's Philadelphia Athletics in the newly-formed American League.

The Phillies were so irate that Lajoie would not live up to the terms of his contract, they filed suit to prohibit him from playing for the hated cross-town Athletics.

While the Phillies and Athletics wrangled in court over which team owned Lajoie, he terrorized the A.L., winning the batting championship with a .422 average.

Finally, early in 1902, the court ruled that Lajoie had to play for the Phillies, which set off more legal maneuvering.

After much squabbling, it was decreed that the ruling only pertained to the Commonwealth of Pennsylvania, which meant that Mack had to trade Lajoie to another team, or return him to the Phillies.

It was then that Cleveland got lucky.

Charles W. Somers, who then owned the Cleveland franchise, was friendly with Mack and offered to buy Lajoie, who was enjoined from playing in Pennsylvania, except for the Phillies.

As former Cleveland *Press* sports editor Franklin Lewis wrote in his 1949 history of the Cleveland Indians: "Somers approached Mack and asked for Lajoie. Connie considered the case, recalled the many favors Somers had done, and said the Bronchos could have Lajoie if a satisfactory salary could be worked out.

"The news that Lajoie might come to Cleveland resulted in an overnight revival of interest in baseball in the Forest City. Somers sat down with Lajoie, and a price was agreed upon. One report said the Frenchman (Lajoie) was to be paid $25,000 for three years, another insisted he would receive $30,000 for four years.

"The Phillies sued to prevent Lajoie and (Bill) Bernhard (who also had jumped from the Phillies and was being traded to Cleveland) from playing with the Bronchos, but the suit was thrown out of court. The restraining order against (Lajoie) appearing with any team other than the Phillies in Pennsylvania was upheld, and for the next two years Cleveland played in Philadelphia without Lajoie.

"The Bronchos perked up considerably after Lajoie joined them in June," Lewis wrote, and unmistakable proof of his popularity surfaced the following season.

"The Cleveland *Press* ran a contest to select a new nickname for the team and the winner was "Napoleons," or "Naps."

The name was chosen in honor of Lajoie. In 1915, when Lajoie was sold back to the Athletics for whom he was then allowed to play, the Cleveland team's nickname was changed again, this time to "Indians."

A fascinating baseball odyssey

His is a story that only the oldest and staunchest Indians fans would remember. But the fascinating odyssey of Billy Evans, a very principled man, is worth retelling.

As was written in 1956, two years before he died at age 72: "Baseball and Billy Evans were and are synonymous. The sport never had a better booster. He wrote it, umpired it, and administered it.

"Most important, he loved the game, and sold it everywhere he went."

Evans started as a sportswriter for the Youngstown *Vindicator* in 1903, quit to become a minor league umpire in 1905, and was promoted to the American League in 1907 when he was only 23.

He remained an A.L. umpire - and was rated one of the best - for 26 years, during which he also wrote a syndicated column for Newspaper Enterprise Association.

Evans took over as general manager of the Indians in 1928, when Alva Bradley and associates bought the team, and remained in that position for eight years.

Billy Evans

In 1935, in the midst of the Great Depression, Evans resigned in protest when the directors of the club wanted to cut his salary from $12,500 to $7,500.

He was unemployed for less than a year, however.

Boston hired Evans as farm director, but he left that job after seven years - again as a matter of protest - to become general manager of the Cleveland Rams of the National Football League in 1941.

But baseball was in Evans' blood and a year later he returned to the game he loved as president of the Southern Association.

It was a position Evans held until 1946 when the Detroit Tigers named him their vice president and general manager. It was Evans' last job. He retired in 1954.

The Indians didn't win any pennants under Evans, but he is given credit for signing and developing some of their best players of the past, including Joe Vosmik, Hal Trosky and Roy Hughes. Also acquired under Evans' stewardship were Sammy Hale, Earl Averill, Dick Porter and Monte Pearson.

When he was with the Red Sox, Evans also was instrumental in the development of many fine young players, including Pee Wee Reese, who wound up as a star for the Brooklyn-Los Angeles Dodgers.

It was the deal for Reese, then a Red Sox farmhand, to the Dodgers that led to Evans' departure from Boston in 1940.

Evans wanted to keep Reese. But Red Sox manager Joe Cronin, then the team's shortstop himself, allowed the sale of Reese, who starred for the Dodgers 16 years, and was elected to the Hall of Fame in 1984. He died in 1999 at age 81.

It was a similar disagreement with Walter Johnson, then manager of the Indians, that finalized Evans' resignation as Cleveland general manager in 1935.

Johnson had demanded that catcher Glenn Myatt be released, and that another favorite, third baseman Willie Kamm, be suspended "for the good of the team."

Evans resisted both moves. But when Bradley supported Johnson, on top of the pay cut Evans was asked to take, he quit. Not only was it a matter of economics, it also was a matter of principle to Billy Evans.

Truly a victim of circumstances

If ever a guy was a victim of circumstances, it was Steve Demeter - and if the name doesn't immediately ring a bell, well, it's probably because he was such a victim.

Anyone old enough to remember when Norm Cash won the American League batting championship in 1961, and continued to be a productive first baseman-power hitter for Detroit through 1973, should remember Steve Demeter.

Steve Demeter

He is, and probably always will be a footnote in Cleveland baseball history, even though Demeter appeared in only four games and batted just five times without getting even one hit for the Indians.

Demeter, then a 25-year old third baseman, one of the best prospects in the Detroit farm system, was traded to the Indians for Cash on April 12, 1960 - five days before General Manager Frank Lane dealt Rocky Colavito to the Tigers, and six days prior to sending Herb Score to the Chicago White Sox.

In retrospect, the Demeter-for-Cash trade must rank with some of the all-time worst.

However, at the time, there was reason to support Lane's judgment.

Cash, 26, had just been acquired as a throw-in from the White Sox in a deal that featured outfielder Minnie Minoso to Chicago for third baseman Bubba Phillips and catcher John Romano.

Veteran Vic Power, a good hitter, was the Indians' first baseman, making Cash expendable, and Demeter looked like a budding star, based on his impressive minor league credentials.

But Demeter never cut it with the Tribe, though he never really got a fair opportunity after being demoted to Toronto, then a Cleveland farm club, early in the 1960 season.

Demeter didn't get another opportunity in the big leagues, though he continued to play - and play very well - in the high minors for another eight years.

Finally he retired, turning to coaching and then to scouting, which he still does.

Cash, on the other hand, was a sensation upon joining Detroit.

He hit .286 with 18 homers in 1960, .361 with 41 homers the following season, was a key to the Tigers winning the 1968 American League pennant and World Series. He finished a 17-year major league career with 377 homers and lifetime average of .271.

As for Demeter, who still makes his home in Parma, O., he said at the time of Cash's accidental drowning death in 1986 that he has no regrets over what was, or might have been.

The only thing that bothers him, Demeter said, "Is the inference that I was a bum. I don't have any illusions that I was a great ball player, but I could hit with men on base. Nobody who ever saw me could dispute that.

"To be traded for a player who was as outstanding as Cash, to be considered to be on par with him at one time, is kind of an honor."

And though Demeter might have been a victim of circumstances, in his opinion, "I was a success because I was able to make a living out of something I really wanted to do."

When the 'Big Train' derailed

They called Walter Johnson the "Big Train" when he was winning 416 games for Washington in the early 1900s. It was an appropriate nickname, writers said, "Because Johnson was always pulling his teammates to victories without too much support."

Those 417 victories (with 279 losses) established the Big Train as the second winningest pitcher of all-time, behind Cy Young, who won 511 games from 1890-1911.

Johnson won 20 games 12 times, including 36 in 1913 and 33 in 1912 in a 21-year career that began in 1907. He was elected to the Hall of Fame in 1936, the year the shrine opened.

Until Bob Feller came along, nobody ever threw a baseball with greater velocity than Johnson. No doubt about it, Johnson was sensational, magnificent - choose any superlative - as a pitcher.

After he retired in 1927, the Big Train turned to managing and discovered to his chagrin that it was a much tougher job than pitching.

Walter Johnson

Johnson became the Indians' 12th manager in 1933, and quickly incurred the wrath of Cleveland fans and media. Ed Bang, then sports editor of the Cleveland *News,* was especially critical in a column on July 17, 1934:

"Johnson showed anything but mental alertness and managerial ability. Truth be told, he fell so far short of what a wide-awake manager should do that the fans who were wont to cheer him … as a great pitcher, groaned in despair and booed him."

It proved to be only the beginning. In July 1935, fans began circulating petitions demanding that Johnson be fired.

They were enraged because Johnson had released popular catcher Glenn Myatt, and sent another favorite, third baseman Willie Kamm, home from a series in Philadelphia "for the good of the team."

Johnson's explanation for disciplining Kamm: "He was second guessing me," according to newspaper accounts.

Kamm demanded a chance to clear his name and, with the help of Indians owner Alva Bradley, received a hearing before Commissioner Kenesaw M. Landis.

The "trial," as it was called by the *News,* was held a few days later. "The commissioner ruled, in effect, that, 'They (Johnson and Kamm) are both nice boys of excellent character and reputation, but they just can't get along together. It's too bad, but I can't do anything about it," the *News* reported that Landis said.

While Landis couldn't do anything about it, Bradley wouldn't - at least not immediately. Finally, however, he had to take action; the pressure was too great.

As Bradley had said earlier in the season, "The owner of a ball club can hire a manager, but the public fires him."

And so, the "Big Train" became a former manager on August 4, 1935. Though the official word from Bradley was that Johnson "resigned," there's no doubt he was fired - by the public, if not by Bradley himself.

It ended one of the most tumultuous periods in Cleveland baseball history, though the Indians' fortunes didn't change in the seasons that followed, until Bill Veeck bought the team from Bradley 11 years later.

A little man with a big heart

Unfortunately, the Indians didn't realize how big a man they had in little Dick Howser, a 5-8, 150-pound infielder, until it was much too late.

They had a desperate need for a shortstop in 1963 and, on May 25, traded catcher Doc Edwards and $100,000 to the Kansas City Athletics for Howser, who'd made the 1961 American League All-Star team as a rookie, and catcher Joe Azcue.

Dick Howser

Three years later Howser was dealt to the New York Yankees for pitcher Gil Downs, who never got out of the minors.

Howser's brief career with the Indians was nothing special. He hit .256 in 162 games in 1964, but was injured much of 1965 and lost his starting job to Larry Brown, and played in only 67 games in 1966, hitting .229.

But it was Howser's latent leadership ability that the Indians could have utilized if he'd been given the chance.

Instead, it was with the Yankees and then, especially, with the Kansas City Royals that Howser surfaced as a manager; as a brilliant tactician, and expert handler of players.

It was in his final days as manager of the Yankees in 1980 that Howser's impeccable character became abundantly clear, and even more so six years later when he was dying of brain cancer.

After retiring as a player following the 1968 season, Howser served as a coach for the Yankees for 10 years, then coached baseball at Florida State University in 1979.

Howser returned to manage the Yankees in 1980 and led then to the American League East championship with a 103-59 record, their best in 17 years.

However, after the Yankees lost to Kansas City in the playoffs that year, owner George Steinbrenner wanted to fire third base coach Mike Ferraro, one of Howser's closest friends.

Howser would have none of it. When Steinbrenner insisted, Howser resigned in respect to Ferraro, and in August of the following season he took over as manager of the Royals.

Three years later Howser led Kansas City to the AL West championship. The Royals repeated in 1985, this time beating Toronto for the pennant and St. Louis in the World Series, each time coming back from 3-1 deficits.

It was during the 1986 All-Star Game, in which Howser served as AL manager, that his illness became evident. Players and coaches noticed Howser was often forgetful, had trouble recognizing people, and complained of headaches.

Ferraro, who had rejoined Howser as a K.C. coach, recalled, "Once when I asked Dick how he felt, he told me he'd had a stiff neck for two weeks. I knew that something was wrong."

Howser was examined and a tumor was discovered in the left frontal lobe of the brain. He underwent surgery three days later, on July 22, and the tumor was found to be malignant.

Howser underwent three more operations and treatment - all the while maintaining a brave, even cheerful attitude - and vowed to return as the Royals' manager in 1987. Which he did.

But three days into spring training, Howser had to resign, though he never gave up until two months later, when he died on June 17 at the age of 51.

He was called the 'Iowa Assassin'

Baseball players are driven from the grand old game for many reasons. In addition to advanced years and diminished skills, bad arms get some, aching knees get others.

But none of the above forced Hal Trosky into early retirement when he should have been at the peak of his career. It was migraine headaches that drove him out.

The Tribe's third leading home run hitter of all-time (behind Albert Belle and Earl Averill) was only 29 when, as Franklin Lewis of the Cleveland *Press* wrote on Feb. 18, 1942, "Harold Arthur Trosky put his baseball career in the medicine cabinet."

There was something else that plagued the power-hitting first baseman, which many believed caused the headaches. He was cursed with a too fragile psyche. It seemed that Trosky never recovered from charges that he was the leader of a player revolt against Manager Oscar Vitt.

On June 13, 1940 - the same day the Nazis captured Paris in World War II - ten Indians met with team owner Alva Bradley armed with a petition demanding that Vitt be replaced. Trosky was not among them; he'd gone home to Norway, Ia. because of the death of his mother.

Hal Trosky

Probably because of his prominence as a veteran member of the team, Trosky was burdened with the brunt of the abuse the Indians received in the wake of the rebellion.

They were taunted and called "Cleveland Cry Babies" after news of the meeting with Bradley was reported the next day as the lead story on Page One of the Cleveland *Plain Dealer* - above, even, the news from Europe telling of Hitler's major victory.

Trosky acknowledged that he'd been a member of the "Vitt Rebellion," but adamantly denied being the leader. "For what I've done, I offer no apologies ... but I've been blasted for something I haven't done," Trosky said near the end of the 1940 season, when the Indians lost the pennant by one game to Detroit.

The fans wouldn't accept Trosky's denial. They continued to boo him throughout the 1941 season and - for whatever reason - Trosky developed migraine headaches that affected his performance on the field. He was never the same thereafter.

In 1934, his first full season with the Tribe, Trosky - nicknamed the "Iowa Assassin" - hit .335 with 35 homers and 142 RBI. Three years later he improved to .343, 42 homers and 162 RBI.

But the booing became too much for Trosky to bear. The Indians sent him home early in 1941 when he was hitting .294 with 11 homers and 51 RBI, a sub-par season for him.

"They've got me down," Trosky said of the fans. "I'm all right until I get on the field. Then my head starts hammering."

The Indians kept hoping Trosky would return, but he didn't. Not to Cleveland.

He attempted a comeback with the Chicago White Sox in 1944, hitting .241 with 10 homers in 135 games. He didn't play in 1945, but returned again in 1946, when he appeared in 88 games, with a .254 average and two homers.

But the headaches persisted, and Trosky went home to Iowa, not the Hall of Fame.

The remarkable 'Bionic Man'

It was so bad for left handed pitcher Tommy John in 1975 that he couldn't use his left hand to even feed himself.

But he never gave up hope that he'd pitch again, and neither did his wife Sally.

Tommy John

This was after John underwent radical surgery, now called a "Tommy John operation," to replace a ruptured ligament in his elbow.

Not only did he pitch again, John won 164 more games, giving him 288 career victories, establishing him as a legitimate candidate for the Hall of Fame.

The surgery performed on John was so radical that even his doctors didn't know what to expect - except they didn't think the southpaw would be able to resume his baseball career.

"Essentially, we took a piece of ligament from (John's) right arm and replaced it in the left, then asked it to come alive again and perform," explained Dr. Frank Jobe, who operated on the pitcher in September 1974.

"It was a questionable procedure that had never been tried before. It was the only thing we could come up with that left even a remote possibility of Tommy's return to baseball. I told Sally that, on a scale of one-to-ten, Tommy's chances of pitching again were less than one," added Dr. Jobe.

But John persevered; refusing to concede that his career was finished.

And since John's operation and his remarkable comeback, other pitchers have undergone the same surgical procedure, most of them also with remarkable results.

Unfortunately, of John's 288 career victories, only two were registered in a Cleveland uniform.

It's unfortunate because John came up through the Indians organization and had to be ransomed off in a 1965 deal that Gabe Paul felt compelled to make to keep the franchise afloat.

It was to regain Rocky Colavito, who was traded five years earlier by Frank Lane, a deal that angered and embittered most Cleveland fans.

Paul, who replaced Lane, packaged John with catcher John Romano and outfielder Tommie Agee in a three-way deal with Chicago and Kansas City to get Colavito back. The Indians also received light hitting catcher Camilo Carreon.

It was a deal that turned out very bad for the Indians, especially in view of the success that John had in Chicago, and Agee, who became a star for the New York Mets.

John pitched well for the White Sox, winning 82 games through 1971. He was traded to Los Angeles where he went 40-15 in three seasons, then suffered the elbow injury late in 1974.

The only "pitching" John did the next year was to toss a ball with Sally, but it helped him launch a comeback in 1976, and in the next three seasons he won 47 games while losing 27.

He went to the New York Yankees as a free agent in 1979, was traded to California in 1982, returned to the minors in 1985 to prove he could still pitch, rejoined the Yankees in 1986 and won 29 more games before winding up a splendid career in 1989 at the age of 45 with 288-231 record.

A career that, unfortunately, could have been in Cleveland.

Ken Keltner always considered the Indians' 1948 playoff game, when they beat Boston, 8-3, for the American League pennant, the highlight of his 13-year major league career.

In the fourth inning of that pressure-packed game in Fenway Park, Keltner delivered a three-run homer that broke a 1-1 tie.

It got the Indians off and running into the World Series, which they also won against the Boston Braves in six games.

There was another game in Keltner's career in which he played a key role, and because of it he'll be remembered as long as baseball continues.

The date: July 17, 1941. The place: Cleveland Municipal Stadium.

That's when, in front of 67,468 fans, Joe DiMaggio's consecutive game hitting streak was stopped at 56, a record that probably will endure as long as any in the book.

Ken Keltner

Keltner turned two potential hits into outs with back-handed stabs of DiMaggio shots down the third base line. He fielded both well behind the bag and retired the famed Yankee Clipper with laser-beam throws to first base.

The first was in the first inning, the second in the seventh. Keltner was able to make each because he played DiMaggio so deep, with good reason. Keltner said he knew DiMaggio wouldn't bunt, and that, because it had rained the night before, batters had trouble getting out of the box quickly.

There also was another reason, which illustrates the competitive spirit that burned within Keltner. He said he wasn't thinking about DiMaggio's streak, "All I was concerned about was winning the game because we still had a chance (in the pennant race)."

Between those two plays by Keltner, DiMaggio walked, then, in his final plate appearance, grounded to shortstop Lou Boudreau who turned it into a double play.

But the Indians lost the game, 4-3, and any hopes that Keltner and his teammates had for staying in the race soon evaporated. The Tribe finished in a tie for fourth place with a 75-79 record, 26 games behind the Yankees, which is reason enough for Keltner choosing to forget the entire 1941 season, as well as DiMaggio's streak.

Something else Keltner would prefer to put out of mind - and wished others would, too -was what he did the winter of 1939.

That was the season, his second with the Tribe, Keltner hit .325 and was paid $7,000, not a bad salary in those days.

Keltner applied for unemployment compensation during the off-season, and the newspapers quickly got the story.

Keltner argued, with some logic, that unemployment compensation was "insurance," not "relief." He claimed he was entitled to it because the Indians had paid the premiums.

The application was rejected, however, after which Keltner called it a "gag," though the fans weren't amused and he was booed throughout the league.

But eventually Keltner's booming bat and splendid fielding won the fans over again, and he retired in 1950 with a lifetime average of .276 and 163 homers.

Hank's failed theory

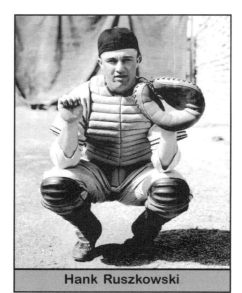

Hank Ruszkowski

A bright future was predicted for Hank Ruszkowski, who caught Allie Reynolds in the 1945 season opener and drove in both of the Indians runs in a 5-2 loss to Chicago.

A graduate of the Cleveland sandlots, Ruszkowski was a baseball, basketball and football star at South High School, and always dreamed of playing for the Tribe.

But something happened to Hank and his dream after that grand debut.

Maybe it was the year and a half Ruszkowski spent in the Army. He was drafted in 1945 after he played 14 games with the Indians. Or maybe it was the shoulder injury he suffered in the minors that required surgery in 1948.

Whatever, Ruszkowski - the "can't miss" prospect - never was the same after getting another chance with the Indians in 1949.

That was the year Ruszkowski reported to spring training with a theory that he believed would make him a powerful, long ball hitter, though then-Manager Lou Boudreau disagreed. Vehemently.

As reported by Ed McAuley in the Cleveland *News* that spring, Ruszkowski checked in with an assortment of new bats that weighed 48 ounces. At the time, the heaviest bat in the major leagues was one that weighed 44 ounces swung by muscular Johnny Mize.

Ruszkowski was quoted by McAuley as saying, "Babe Ruth used a 54-ounce bat and Riggs Stephenson (a .336 career hitter who played in the major leagues from 1921-34) swung 56 ounces. I know I'm strong enough to use a 50-ounce bat, and I think it will give me more power to all fields."

Ruszkowski's theory: "Most hitters use an unnatural and unnecessary motion when they bring their bats from their shoulder at the start of their swings. The only part of the swing that counts is the level sweep through the ball. So why not start the swing in that plane?"

Why not indeed.

Except that Boudreau - a very good hitter himself - didn't agree, and wouldn't go along with Ruszkowski's stubbornness. When Ruszkowski insisted upon proving his theory, Boudreau delivered an ultimatum, that Hank return to his conventional batting style, or return to the minors.

And so it was that Ruszkowski was optioned first to San Diego of the Pacific Coast League, then to Oklahoma City of the Texas League, but didn't last long with either team and was released by the Indians on May 3, 1949, his dream unfulfilled.

It was a shame because, at one time in his early days in the minors, Ruszkowski was considered as good a catcher-prospect as Jim Hegan who played 17 seasons for the Indians.

Ruszkowski hit .204 in 14 games in 1945 before Uncle Sam beckoned, and he appeared in 23 games with a .259 average for the Indians in 1947.

After his release by the Indians, Ruszkowski returned to Cleveland to complete his education at Baldwin-Wallace College and went into coaching.

Cincinnati gave him a tryout in 1954, but that didn't work out for Ruszkowski either and, sadly, his playing career was ended.

Sadly, it was a much-too-brief career.

Baseball's 'smartest pitcher'

They called George Uhle the "smartest pitcher in baseball" during his 17-year major league career that began in 1919, directly off the Cleveland sandlots.

But Uhle, who'd pitched the Cleveland Standard Parts team to the world amateur baseball championship in 1918, enjoyed a couple other distinctions while compiling a 200-166 record, including 147 victories (and 119 losses) for the Indians.

He was the best hitting pitcher in baseball with a career average of .289.

And, as proof of his offensive prowess, Uhle batted .361 (52-for-144) in 1923, and was the only player to ever pinch hit for Hall of Fame center fielder Tris Speaker, whose lifetime average was .345, seventh best in history.

Uhle and Speaker were teammates for eight years when Speaker was player-manager of the Indians from 1919-26.

Uhle also was called by Babe Ruth the best pitcher he ever faced. In a newspaper article before his death in 1985, Uhle talked about his success against Ruth.

George Uhle

"Early in the Babe's career he hit a pop fly homer off me in the (New York) Polo Grounds," said Uhle.

"But he never got another off me until after I was traded to Detroit (in December 1928 for pitcher Ken Holloway and shortstop Jackie Tavener).

"The way I pitched to Ruth, I'd give him a lot of slow breaking stuff, then try to blow the fast ball by him. None of the great hitters like slow stuff ... it throws their timing off. They all want to hit fast balls," he said.

On the other hand, Uhle freely admitted having trouble pitching to two relatively unknown players - Fatty Fothergill of Detroit, and Bib Falk of Chicago. "They hit me like they owned me," he said.

Uhle, who pitched for the Tigers from 1929 until 1933 when he was sold to the New York Giants, was raised on Cleveland's west side and came up through the sandlots.

The New York Yankees and Chicago White Sox also were interested in Uhle, but he signed with the Indians and never spent a day in the minors until he pitched briefly for Toledo at the end of his career.

Uhle went 10-5 as a rookie, and 4-5 the following year when the Indians won the 1920 pennant. Their first four starters then were Jim Bagby, Stan Coveleski, Guy Morton and Ray Caldwell.

But Uhle quickly became a star and three 20-victory seasons followed. In 1926 he was the American League's winningest pitcher with a 27-11 record as the Indians finished second, three games behind the Yankees.

The only Cleveland pitcher to win more games in one season was Bagby, who was 31-12 in 1920, though Addie Joss (1907) and Bob Feller (1940) also were 27 game winners.

Uhle went from the Giants to the Yankees in 1933, and returned to the Tribe in 1936, making seven appearances for the Indians, all in relief, and was credited with a victory he had long coveted. It was the 200th of his career to go with his 3.99 earned run average in 17 seasons.

But that was it. By then, at age 38, his fast ball was gone and without it, Uhle's smartness wasn't enough and he retired.

171

When Veeck couldn't say no

Bill Veeck was faced with a momentous decision.

The 1946 season had just ended and Veeck, who'd bought the Indians four months earlier, knew the team desperately needed a second baseman to replace Ray Mack and Dutch Meyer, both of whom were at the end of mediocre careers.

Allie Reynolds

Veeck knew the second baseman he wanted: Joe Gordon of the New York Yankees, who was available because he'd been feuding the previous season with General Manager Larry MacPhail.

The Yankees had Snuffy Stirnweiss waiting in the wings to replace Gordon, and were anxious to get another pitcher. Veeck had offered Red Embree, a 29-year old right-hander who was 8-12 in 1946, and was thought ready to blossom into stardom.

But MacPhail, after conferring with Joe DiMaggio, wanted another right-hander from the Tribe staff - Allie Reynolds, who was two years older than Embree, and whose 11-15 record in 1946 had been better. Veeck resisted and tried to restructure a package, but MacPhail would have none of it. He wanted Reynolds or there'd be no deal.

Finally Veeck reluctantly agreed. He really wanted Gordon. It proved to be just what the Indians needed as Gordon blended beautifully with shortstop Lou Boudreau defensively, and hit .272 with 29 home runs and 93 RBI in 1947.

Gordon was even better in 1948, driving in 124 runs with 32 homers and a .280 average, and the Indians won the pennant – though Reynolds also was something special for the Yankees.

The part Creek Indian, who was nicknamed "Super Chief," became the first American Leaguer to pitch two no-hitters in one season - one of them against Cleveland on July 12, 1951 - and helped the Yankees win six pennants in the next eight years.

Reynolds also fired a no-hitter against Boston on Sept. 28, 1951. That was the game Yogi Berra dropped Ted Williams' pop foul with two out in the ninth, but Reynolds came right back and retired the Red Sox slugger with his next pitch.

Though Reynolds was a 20-game winner only in 1952 when he was 20-8 with an AL-leading 2.06 earned run average, he averaged more than 16 victories and fewer than eight losses a year. Reynolds retired with a bad back in 1955 with a career 182-107 won-lost record, plus a 7-2 mark in 15 World Series games.

Obviously, MacPhail and his advisor, DiMaggio, knew what they wanted when they insisted upon getting Reynolds for Gordon. Still, the Indians probably wouldn't have won the 1948 pennant and World Series without Gordon, who retired in 1951.

But not before he figured in one more big deal. Gordon was hired to manage the Indians in 1958 and, on Aug. 3, 1960, was swapped to Detroit for Jimmy Dykes. It was the only time in major league baseball that managers were traded.

As for Embree, he went 8-10 for the Tribe in 1947 and, ironically, on Dec. 11 that year, finally was traded to the Yankees, this time for outfielder Allie Clark.

Embree won five and lost three for the Yankees in 1948, was traded to the St. Louis Browns, for whom he posted a 3-13 record in 1949, and was released at the end of the season.

Outfielder Al Smith thought he knew what kind of a pitcher the Indians were getting in 1964, even if nobody else was quite sure.

"If this kid is half as good as his father was, we've got a helluva pitcher," said Smith, who'd played against Luis Tiant Sr. in the Negro Leagues in 1946 and 1947. Suffice to say, Luis Jr. was more than "half as good" as his father, and the Indians did indeed have a "helluva pitcher."

Tiant hurled his first game in the major leagues on July 19, 1964, at Yankee Stadium, and fired a four-hit shutout, striking out 11 in a 3-0 victory.

The Indians had called up Tiant from their Portland farm of the Class AAA Pacific Coast League, where his record was 15-1. To make room for Tiant, another rookie pitcher named Tommy John was demoted - the same Tommy John who would eventually win 288 major league games.

Tiant arrived in New York on July 18 and was told by Manager Birdie Tebbetts that he'd face the Yankees the next day. "I fly all night to get here," Tiant said. "I get no sleep on the plane, none in the hotel. But I am too happy to be tired."

Bobby Avila, who was the Indians' second baseman from 1949-58, discovered Tiant in Cuba in 1959. Avila, who then owned the Mexico City Tigres, signed Tiant to pitch in the Mexican League. The Indians purchased Tiant after the 1961 season. Thus, while Tiant was called a rookie in 1964, he was far from inexperienced, and he already knew one of baseball's primary lessons: "If you have luck, you win," Tiant said the day he made his Tribe debut. "If you do not have luck, you lose. But I try hard."

Tiant went 10-4 with a 2.83 earned run average that first season, and when you add those 15 victories in Portland, the rookie's record in 1964 was 25-5. He pitched for the Indians the next five years and was appreciated, not only for his ability on the mound, but also for having a marvelous sense of humor.

In addition to a sizzling fast ball, a curve that scouts said "fell off a table," and a sharp breaking slider, Tiant often distracted batters with a wind up in which he turned his back to the plate while rolling his head as though he were looking for a hot dog vendor in the stands..

Tiant's record was 21-9 and he led the American League with a 1.60 earned run average in 1968, but struggled in 1969, losing 20 games while winning only nine. The Indians, thinking he was washed up, traded Tiant, along with pitcher Stan Williams to Minnesota for pitchers Dean Chance and Bob Miller, third baseman Graig Nettles and outfielder Ted Uhlaender in what appeared to be a great deal for the Tribe.

Initially it was. When Tiant went 7-3 in 1970, the Twins also feared he was finished and released him. But Looie proved them wrong.

He won a tryout with Boston in 1971, made the team and went on to win 122 games while losing 81 for the Red Sox the next seven seasons, and pitched for the New York Yankees in 1979 and 1980, Pittsburgh in 1981, and California in 1982.

He ended a 19 year major league career with a 229-172 won-lost record, which many believe – with sound logic – should qualify Tiant for election to the Hall of Fame.

Luis Tiant

'Conked out' in the bull pen

The Indians had just returned from a road trip to play a crucial, three game, final weekend series of the season against the Detroit Tigers at the old Cleveland Municipal Stadium with the American League pennant hanging in the balance.

Birdie Tebbetts

Which is when Birdie Tebbetts, who would become manager of the Indians 23 years later, was introduced to the intensity of Cleveland's long-frustrated baseball fans.

The date was Sept. 27, 1940. The Indians trailed the first place Tigers by two games and needed to sweep the series to win the pennant.

Bob Feller, then the best pitcher in the A.L., took the mound for the Indians, whose record was 87-64, while Manager Del Baker of Detroit (89-62) gave the assignment – surprisingly – to Floyd Giebell, a rookie who'd won only two major league games (and afterward would never win another).

Tebbetts, a 28-year old catcher in his fourth full season with the Tigers, didn't play that day. Instead, he spent the afternoon in the visitors bull pen, situated in foul territory behind the left field line.

Cleveland fans were not in the best of moods as most were aware of the treatment their team had received in Detroit a week earlier. Then Tiger fans taunted the Indians, meeting them at the train station with baby carriages and bottles, and calling them "Cry Babies" because of their publicized, but failed rebellion against Manager Oscar Vitt earlier in the season.

Here's how Franklin Lewis described it in his 1949 history of the Indians.

"It was Ladies Day and 45,533 persons were in the stands. Thousands of the fans were armed with throwable objects. Sitting in an upstairs box directly over the (Detroit) bullpen was an ice peddler. He had gone to the park equipped with a basket of bottles and fruit. "He calmly dropped a bomb of groceries over the side, and they landed on the head of Tebbetts, who was conked out."

Birdie was not seriously injured – but he was seriously angered. He caught up with the fan and took a swing at him as the guy was being escorted out of the Stadium by police.

It wasn't funny, though Tebbetts often chuckled about the incident later, when he played for the Indians in 1951 and 1952, and during his managerial career in Cleveland from 1963 until mid-August 1966. "I would've killed the guy if the cops had let me at him," said Tebbetts, as feisty then as when he managed Cincinnati (1954-58), Milwaukee (1961-62), and the Indians.

As for the game that was interrupted when Tebbetts was "conked out," Birdie and the Tigers had the last laugh – and laughed all the way to the World Series.

As Lewis reported after Tebbetts had taken a swing at his tormentor: "Rudy York also took a swing. He picked on one of Feller's pitches and hit a high fly ball to left field.

"This one was right down the 320-foot line and fell into the seats for a home run, a freak round-tripper in the toughest park in the game in which to hit for the circuit! Charley Gehringer was on base, but the one run would have been enough.

"Giebell, the rookie, beat Feller, 2-0, and the maddest pennant race in Cleveland's history was ended."

When McLish couldn't buy a steak

Cal McLish, the Indians winningest pitcher in 1959, and one of the American League's best that season, was distinctive for a reason other than his baseball ability.

It was his name: Calvin Coolidge Julius Caesar Tuskahoma McLish.

"All I know is that it was my father who named me," McLish tried to explain in a 1956 interview, after the Indians had purchased his contract from San Diego, then of the Pacific Coast League.

"I don't know where the 'Calvin Coolidge' part of it came from; my dad wasn't even a Republican," he said in reference to the 30th president of the United States. "I guess he just liked the name, the same as he probably liked Julius Caesar."

As for "Tuskahoma," McLish said it was the name of a town in the Indian territory of Oklahoma where his parents were born.

"Dad was one-quarter Chickasaw, and Mom was one-sixteenth Cherokee, which makes me one-eighth Chickasaw and one-thirty second Cherokee," said McLish, who also is part Scotch, English, Irish and Dutch.

Cal McLish

McLish won 35 games and lost 16 for the Indians in 1958 and 1959, then became part of what turned out to be one of Frank Lane's worst trades. He was packaged with second baseman Billy Martin and a minor league first baseman named Gordy Coleman, and sent to Cincinnati for second baseman Johnny Temple, who was a bust in Cleveland.

But McLish pitched five more seasons for the Reds, Chicago White Sox and Philadelphia Phillies, and Coleman was one of Cincinnati's most productive hitters for the next seven seasons.

Something else that distinguished McLish was that, as a rookie with Brooklyn in 1944, he undoubtedly was the lowest paid major league player in modern baseball history. He signed with the Dodgers out of high school and was placed on the major league roster. McLish went 3-10 in 23 games.

"All that mattered when I signed was the $1,500 bonus they gave me," he said. "About three weeks into the season Charley Dressen, a coach on the team, came to me and said, 'Eat a big steak tonight and put plenty of butter on it because you're starting tomorrow.'

"I told him, 'I can't afford steak on my $150 salary.' He said, 'You can eat steak on $150 a week.' I said, 'Yeah, but I get $150 a *month*, not a week.'"

This, of course, was long before the formation of the Major League Baseball Players Association, and there was no such thing as a minimum salary.

"Dressen nearly flipped when I told him. So he talked to Leo Durocher, the manager, who called Mr. (Branch) Rickey, the general manager."

And with that, Calvin Coolidge Julius Caesar Tuskahoma McLish was granted a new contract. For $150 a *week,* not a month.

After a year in the Army, McLish spent the next three seasons in the minors until the Indians rescued him in 1956. He retired in 1964 with a 15-year major league record of 92-92, which wasn't sensational, but not bad, either. It would have earned him big bucks in today's market.

But McLish pitched in yesterday's market and his peak salary was $19,500 in 1959, when he won 19 games for the Indians, losing only eight.

The man who wouldn't quit

When it happened on April 30, 1951, Saturnino Orestes Minoso sat down and bawled his eyes out.

Minoso - better known as "Minnie" - had just been sent by the Indians to Chicago in a three team deal that brought left-handed relief pitcher Lou Brissie to Cleveland.

Minnie Minoso

The trade also involved the Philadelphia Athletics and was engineered by Frank Lane, then general manager of the White Sox.

While Minoso was crying in the clubhouse because he didn't want to leave Cleveland, Tribe General Manager Hank Greenberg was asking sportswriters to evaluate the deal.

The consensus was that it "stunk," as the Cleveland *Plain Dealer* reported in no uncertain terms the next day – which proved to be a very accurate appraisal.

Minoso, then 28 but just reaching his prime, went on to hit .300 in five of his next seven seasons for the White Sox - and for Lane, whom he soon came to call "Papa," for obvious reasons.

Brissie went 7-5 with 13 saves in three years with the Indians, and retired after the 1953 season.

It was no surprise, then, that one of the first moves by Lane after he replaced Greenberg as general manager of the Indians on Nov. 12, 1957, was to reacquire Minoso.

But instead of helping, it turned out to be another costly deal for the Tribe. In this one Lane sent pitcher Early Wynn and outfielder Al Smith to Chicago for Minoso and third baseman Fred Hatfield.

Wynn and Smith proved to be key players for the White Sox, who went on to win the pennant in 1959, while Hatfield played but three games for the Tribe in 1958 and was peddled to Cincinnati.

Minoso hit .302 for the Tribe in each 1958 and 1959, with 24 and 21 homers respectively, but the years were beginning to take their toll on the popular Cuban, or so Lane feared.

And thus - living up to his "Frantic Frank" nickname - Lane swung into action again. He traded Minoso back to the White Sox on Dec. 6, 1959.

It was a seven-player deal in which the Indians received catcher John Romano, first baseman Norm Cash and third baseman Bubba Phillips for Minoso, pitchers Don Ferrarese and Jake Striker, and catcher Dick Brown.

Again Minoso proved he was far from finished, even though he was approaching 40. He hit .311 and .280 for Chicago in 1960 and 1961, and went on to play for St. Louis in 1962, Washington in 1963, and returned once more to Chicago in 1964, when he played 30 games and batted .226, then "retired."

However, as a White Sox coach in 1976, Minoso pinch hit in three games - and singled once in eight at-bats - and was 0-for-2 in two games in 1980, giving him a career average of .298 in 1,835 games.

Considering that he had appeared in nine games for the Indians in 1949, it gave him the major league record for "playing" in five decades. It also was Minoso's intention to appear in one more game in September 1990, his sixth decade, at age 68.

But Commissioner Fay Vincent said no, ending once and for all the playing career of the man who wouldn't quit.

They called him 'Silent George'

When he played for the Indians there never was any doubt about George Hendrick's ability.

He could hit for average and power, run, throw and catch a baseball with the best of them - all of which are qualifications for superstardom.

But shortly after he was acquired from Oakland in a 1973 trade (with Dave Duncan for Ray Fosse and Jack Heidemann), Hendrick suddenly and without explanation refused to talk with the media, declining all requests for interviews.

It earned for him the nickname, "Silent George," and his aloofness more than once created problems between him and Manager Ken Aspromonte.

But it didn't prevent Hendrick from playing well; in his four seasons with the Indians, he averaged 23 homers and 75 RBI.

There were no tears shed when he was traded in 1976 to San Diego (for Johnny Grubb, Fred Kendall and Hector Torres).

Before the next season was half over, Hendrick was dealt again, to St. Louis, and he spent six more good - but still silent - years with the Cardinals, who then traded him to Pittsburgh in 1985.

From there he went to the California Angels for whom he played three more seasons and retired in 1988, later becoming a coach for the Angels.

George Hendrick

Hendrick's career stats are not Hall of Fame caliber, but impressive enough to command great respect, as well as a multimillion salary based on today's standards: a .278 batting average, 267 home runs and 1,111 RBI in 18 major league seasons.

Initially, upon his retirement, Hendrick faded into obscurity in Southern California. Nobody seemed to care where. Then, a few years ago, Hendrick made a surprise appearance at an Indians' old-timers' game at the Stadium.

And, believe it or not, "Silent George," the guy with a so-called personality problem, could not have been friendlier.

Or more talkative.

"I guess part of the problem was that I was very young and didn't know how to handle it, the attention and all that stuff," Hendrick began his explanation.

But there was something else, and finally Hendrick talked about it.

"Right after I came to the Indians I was interviewed by a writer from Dallas after I'd had a pretty good game against (Texas Rangers pitcher) Lloyd Allen," he said.

"I was quoted saying some pretty nasty things about Allen, things that I didn't say. I apologized to Allen and found out that he and the writer didn't get along, and that the writer used me to put Allen down.

"I decided then that I wouldn't trust anybody in the media, and the way I handled it was to not speak to you guys, not even say hello.

"I was rude, and if I offended you, I'm sorry. Please tell the other guys."

When it was time to leave the clubhouse and go to the field for the game, Hendrick smiled, extended his right hand and said, "It was a pleasure talking to you."

It also was a pleasure talking to him. Finally.

Fritz, Mike, Susanne and Marilyn

They kept following each other like a pair of traveling salesmen from town to town. And what they had to sell far outweighed the talent in their left arms.

They were an oddity, an almost sad curiosity.

Mike Kekich/Fritz Peterson

They were Fritz Peterson and Mike Kekich, who will be remembered, not necessarily for their pitching, but as pitchers who traded wives, children, houses and even family dogs while they were teammates with the New York Yankees in 1973.

Peterson arrived in the big leagues first, in 1966, and went 12-11 for the Yankees.

Kekich, signed by Los Angeles and hailed as "another Sandy Koufax," made it to the Dodgers in 1968, when he went 2-10 as a rookie. Then he was traded to the Yankees.

In New York the pitchers became close friends. Too close. Many think their wife-swapping ruined Kekich. His relationship with Marilyn Peterson and her two sons didn't last.

It was different with Peterson after he married Susanne Kekich. They had a daughter to go with Susanne's two daughters from her marriage with Kekich, and they found religion.

"I now have peace of mind," Peterson said two years after exchanging families. "Everything is falling into place for us."

Less than a year after they traded wives, Kekich was dealt to the Tribe (on June 12, 1973) for minor league pitcher Lowell Palmer and cash.

But Mike didn't stay long with the Indians, nor did he pitch well for them, going 1-4.

Kekich was released the following spring, a few days before training camp ended - perhaps, as was speculated, because then-General Manager Phil Seghi was negotiating a deal for Peterson and didn't want to bring the pitchers together again.

It was a contention that Peterson sloughed off. "Our relationship is amicable," Peterson said when asked about his new wife's former husband.

Whatever, Peterson came to Cleveland on April 27, 1974, in a package with three other Yankee pitchers - Steve Kline, Fred Beane and Tom Buskey, at the expense of first baseman Chris Chambliss and pitchers Cecil Upshaw and Dick Tidrow.

It was not one of the Tribe's best trades.

Peterson went 9-14 and 14-8 the next two seasons, leading the Indians in victories, and with a 3.94 earned run average in 1975, though it would be his last productive season.

The following winter Peterson got into a contract hassle with the Tribe and, on May 28, 1976, with an 0-3 record, was sent to Texas for pitcher Stan Perzanowski.

Once again Peterson followed in the footsteps of Kekich, who had joined the Rangers in 1975, but didn't stay the season.

Peterson didn't last long either. He won one game for Texas in 1976, but his left shoulder, ravaged by over 2,200 innings of pitching in the big leagues, was ruined and his baseball career ended then.

Fritz and Susanne Peterson settled in Barrington, Ill. where they launched a new career, this one in Christian work and tried to live down their earlier notoriety, while Kekich faded into obscurity.

Jim Piersall did things baseball players usually don't do.

Once he ran the bases backwards. Another time he shot an umpire with a squirt gun.

And he almost never shut his mouth.

When Piersall was acquired by the Indians from Boston (on Dec. 2, 1958 for first baseman Vic Wertz and outfielder Gary Geiger) he was baseball's version of the "Tasmanian Devil," a funnel cloud of ejections, strange behavior and controversy.

The hyperactive center fielder wasn't just a bomb waiting to go off. He *was* a bomb that kept exploding.

One night at Yankee Stadium, Piersall made a sensational diving catch in center field to rob Mickey Mantle of a hit. After the catch, Piersall pulled himself into a sitting position and laughed long and hard at the fabled Yankee star.

Once during another game in New York, two fans jumped the outfield fence and ran toward Piersall. He saw then coming and charged at them. The two men quickly changed direction and scampered back to the stands.

Piersall almost caught them and even tried to kick one in the rear. Fortunately he missed.

Jim Piersall

When Piersall was in the minor leagues, he complained once about the dust on home plate, but was ignored by the umpire. So, in his next at-bat, Piersall cleaned the plate with a stream of water from a squirt gun. Then, for good measure - but not good sense - Piersall squirted the umpire between the bars of his mask.

Piersall wasn't comfortable unless there was a five-alarm five blazing around him. There was reason for this.

He broke into the big leagues in 1950 with the Red Sox and, during his time in Boston, Piersall suffered a nervous breakdown. Pushed to be a perfect player by a demanding father, Piersall couldn't stand the strain.

The details of the breakdown were made public in a book by Piersall entitled *"Fear Strikes Out,"* which was made into a movie starring Tony Perkins.

In Cleveland, Piersall's behavior figured in the firing of managers Joe Gordon and Jimmy Dykes. When Tribe General Manager Frank Lane traded Gordon to Detroit for Tigers manager Dykes in 1960, Cleveland newspapers called Piersall the "winner" of a conflict with Gordon.

Piersall hit for his highest average, .322, in 1961, and wasn't directly implicated when Dykes was fired by General Manager Gabe Paul with one game left in the season.

But subsequent events made it clear that Piersall was considered a negative influence on the team.

"I think I did as much with him as anyone could have," Dykes was quoted then. "But (Piersall) can make it awful tough for any manager. You've got to pamper him and you've got to be tough with him. It's a problem."

Piersall was traded to the Washington Senators for pitcher Dick Donovan, outfielder Gene Green and infielder Jim Mahoney on Oct. 5, 1961.

It probably was not coincidental that the deal was made only three days after Mel McGaha was hired as the Tribe's new manager.

Baseball's last 'Iron Man' pitcher

Though he was a pitcher who won just 21 games and lost 26 in a six year major league career, Emil "Dutch" Levsen almost certainly will never be forgotten, thanks to a remarkable performance on Aug. 28, 1926.

Emil (Dutch) Levsen

Then a 28-year old right-hander for the Indians, Levsen pitched - and won - two complete games in a double header against the Boston Red Sox in Fenway Park, allowing but four hits in each.

Not only has Levsen's performance never been duplicated, it hasn't even been attempted - perhaps wisely.

Levsen was assigned both games by then manager Tris Speaker in order to save the Tribe's seven-man pitching staff, according to the Cleveland *Plain Dealer's* account of the double header.

"Levsen's feat allowed Speaker to save George Uhle for the homecoming game with the (St. Louis) Browns at Dunn Field (later renamed League Park) tomorrow," it was reported.

That was the year Uhle led the American League with a 27-11 record; Levsen was 16-13, Joe Shaute 14-10, and Sherry Smith 11-10, while three other pitchers were a combined 18-29.

Surprisingly, the Indians almost won the pennant in 1926, finishing second with an 88-66 won lost record, only three games behind the New York Yankees.

Henry P. Edwards, *Plain Dealer* sports editor, wrote this about Levsen's iron man stint:

"To Emil Levsen, graduate of Iowa State, goes the credit of performing the most unusual feat of modern pitching, that of working both ends of a double header, each of nine innings, and winning them both as he did today, when he hurled the Indians to two triumphs over the Boston Red Sox, 6 to 1 and 5 to 1.

"In displaying wonderful skill and courage to successfully demonstrate that the 'Iron Men' of the old days had nothing on him, Levsen worked his powerful right arm with such precision that the Red Sox gathered only eight hits off him in the two contests, four in each.

"Three of the hits of the first game were flukes, and happened to be bunched just right to allow Boston to escape a shutout, while one of the four in the second affair also was a scratch.

"The red-faced boy from Iowa, strange as it may seem, did not strike out a batsman in either game. His control, however, was excellent, and he made the Red Sox hit the ball where it could be handled easily by his colleagues, who never faltered through the double bill."

Also strange as it may seem - though perhaps because of his 18 inning performance against the Red Sox - Levsen never was a winning pitcher after that 1926 season. His record was 3-7 with a 5.49 ERA in 1927, and when it fell to 0-3 in 1928, he was released.

Levson, who died in 1972 at the age of 74, compiled a 21-26 won lost record, in his five-plus seasons in the major leagues, all with the Indians.

As a footnote to Levsen's iron man feat, the *Plain Dealer* also reported after the double header: "When the Red Sox lost the second game to Levsen, they also lost a day off (today), which is an off day on the schedule, as (manager) Lee Fohl informed them that, because they lost, they must report for a workout instead of going fishing."

The first time he saw it, Ted Williams laughed and asked the umpire, "What the hell is that?"

But he didn't laugh for long.

And, quickly what he saw became a challenge.

Which is exactly what Lou Boudreau had in mind - what he really *hoped* would happen - when he envisioned and then deployed the Indians in their famous "Williams Shift."

It was July 14, 1946, in the second game of a double header between the Indians and Red Sox in Boston's Fenway Park.

Williams had hammered three homers in the first game, and Boudreau was desperate to stop him.

What Boudreau did was move himself from shortstop to the position normally occupied by the second baseman, who was Jack Conway in that game.

Conway dropped back to short right field, and third baseman Ken Keltner moved behind second base.

Only the left fielder, who was George Case, covered the left side of the field, playing in so he was only about 30 feet behind the infield.

The center fielder, Pat Seerey, shaded toward right, while right fielder Hank Edwards and first baseman Jimmy Wasdell were positioned normally.

Lou Boudreau

"I laughed, but I was flattered," Williams would say later, when he also would admit his attitude then was wrong.

Ostensibly, the object was to force Williams to hit the ball to left field.

"The charts we kept showed that 95% of Williams' hits against us - and he got many of them - would be into right field," said Boudreau.

"That's what gave me the idea of the shift … to make him hit the ball to left. I even hoped that he would bunt so we could hold him to a single or a double.

"I knew Ted Williams. I knew his thoughts were on being the greatest hitter in the game of baseball, and to me, he came very close to it," added Boudreau.

"I knew his disposition, too. I knew what it meant to Williams to battle a challenge. He tried to go through the shift. He was that type of individual.

"It was important to him to face up to a challenge, and to beat it, when hitting was involved."

Boudreau proved to be right.

Rather than slap the ball to the opposite field, or even to bunt along the unguarded third base line, Williams usually swung away, disdainful of the shift – but often unable to find a hole.

Which Boudreau's charts confirmed.

"After we instigated the shift we were 37% better in retiring Williams than we were prior to the shift," the former manager of the Indians said.

Arguably the greatest hitter of all-time, Williams didn't make many mistakes when he had a bat in hand.

But he did when confronted with the "Williams Shift."

How Cleveland lost Cy Young

Cy Young

The Indians have had their share of superstars - Napoleon Lajoie, Tris Speaker, Earl Averill, Bob Feller and Lou Boudreau among them - but none was greater than the first: Denton True (Cy) Young.

Unfortunately, Young who could have pitched Cleveland to many championships, was traded away in what was the first - and perhaps still is - the strangest deal in baseball history.

Nicknamed "Cy," which was short for "cyclone" because of the velocity of his pitches, Young originally pitched in Cleveland from 1890 through 1898. Then the city's professional baseball team, a member of the National League, was called the "Spiders."

Young returned near the end of his career, in 1909, nine years after Cleveland had become a charter member of the American League, but gained most of his fame pitching for the Boston Red Sox

Born in the picturesque little Ohio township of Gilmore, about 100 miles south of Cleveland off what is now Interstate-77, Young was baseball's all-time winningest pitcher with a 511-316 won-lost record in 22 seasons.

The legendary 6-2, 210-pound right-hander was traded to St. Louis, another National League team, after winning 25 and losing 13 games for the Spiders in 1898. It was a strange deal because it was made by Cleveland owner Frank DeHaas Robison, who traded Young and several other of the Spiders' best players to … himself.

That's right. Himself. Here's how.

Robison, a Cleveland businessman who'd owned the Spiders since 1889, bought the St. Louis franchise in 1898. It made him the owner of two teams in the same league, which was allowed in those days.

Obviously, Robison wanted his St. Louis franchise to be dominant, so he loaded it with the best players, sending the worst to Cleveland.

The Spiders were so badly weakened they were referred to as the Cleveland "Misfits." The franchise subsequently folded, making room for the Cleveland "Blues" to come to life under the ownership of Charles W. Somers when the American League was formed in 1901.

Somers brought Young back to Cleveland by purchasing the 42-year old pitcher for the then-exorbitant price of $12,500. By then, Young's fast ball no longer was compared to a cyclone. He won only 29 and lost 29 games the next 2 1/2 seasons, and was released by the Indians in August 1911 when his record was only 3-4.

However, the years before he returned to Cleveland were something else for Young, who was elected a charter member of the Hall of Fame in 1937, and died in 1955 at the age of 88 at his home in Newcomerstown, Ohio.

In his remarkable career, Young hurled three no-hitters, one a perfect game, set a record for pitching 23 consecutive hitless innings in 1904, won 30 games in five seasons and 15 times won at least 20.

It's little wonder that baseball named its annual award for pitching excellence in honor of Cy Young, who would've made Cleveland a dominant team to start the century.

The defused 'Bogalusa Bomber'

There never was any doubt about Charlie Spikes making it, and making it big.

He was the No. 1 choice of the New York Yankees in the 1969 amateur draft, and the key man in the Indians' six-player trade on Nov. 27, 1972, in which all-star third baseman Graig Nettles and catcher Gerry Moses were sent to the Bronx Bombers.

Which proves again how inexact the "science" of baseball scouting can be.

Charlie Spikes

"Charlie is capable of hitting .275-.280, with 40 to 50 homers a year for a lot of years," Indians General Manager Phil Seghi said without fear of dissent.

Interestingly, it was one of the first big deals made by Seghi who, earlier that year, was promoted to general manager when Gabe Paul resigned to become president of the Yankees and, of course, engineered the acquisition of Nettles.

In addition to Spikes, the Indians also received catcher John Ellis, infielder Jerry Kenney and outfielder Rusty Torres.

But it was Spikes, who grew up in Bogalusa, La. and was nicknamed the "Bogalusa Bomber," the Indians wanted as desperately as Paul wanted Nettles.

Unfortunately, the deal was a disaster for the Tribe - though not for the Yankees.

Oh, in his first two seasons in Cleveland, Spikes showed signs of living up to Seghi's lavish prediction; he hammered 23 homers (though his average was only .237) in 1973, and 22 (with a .271 mark) in 1974.

But then something happened.

"I don't know what it was," Spikes admitted in a 1979 article, a year before his major league career ended. "My stroke left me. I don't know why."

Neither did the Indians, when Spikes' average fell back to .229 and .237, and his home run production dropped to a total of 14 in 212 games the next two seasons, 1975 and 1976.

Then, after playing only 32 games in 1977, when he hit .232 with three homers, the Indians traded Spikes to Detroit for shortstop Tom Veryzer.

After playing in 10 games in 1978, Spikes was released by the Tigers.

Atlanta gave the once "can't-miss" prospect another chance in 1979, and Spikes responded with a .280 average, but only three homers in 66 games. After 41 games in 1980 - when he struck out 18 times in 36 at-bats and failed to hit even one homer - the Braves also quit on the "Bogalusa Bomber."

By then there was no doubt Charlie's stroke was gone. In 2,039 major league at-bats, Spikes struck out 388 times, or once every 5.25 trips to the plate. "I kept trying to find my stroke, but I never did," he said. "Maybe it was the injuries, the times I got hurt. I don't know."

Nobody does, though Frank Robinson had a theory. "I always wondered if Charlie's problems began when he got hit in the face with a pitch in winter ball (March 1976)," the former Tribe manager speculated.

Whatever, Spikes' career never came close to expectations, that's for sure.

And to make matters worse, none of the other three players the Indians received with Spikes did much either, while Nettles enjoyed 11 productive seasons in New York.

The squire who wouldn't take 'no'

Baseball men kept saying "no" to Gene Woodling. No, as in, "No, you can't hit," and, "No, you don't fit in our plans."

But Woodling, a.k.a. "the Squire of Remsen Corners" in Medina County outside Cleveland, steadfastly refused to accept rejection.

Gene Woodling

And because he did, Woodling enjoyed a 17 year major league career that began in the Indians farm system and didn't end until 1962, when he played 81 games and hit .274 for the New York Mets at age 40. What's more, Woodling finished with a career batting average of .284 and cashed five World Series checks.

He represents one of the few – and one of the biggest - mistakes made by Bill Veeck, who owned the Indians from 1946-49.

Veeck traded Woodling to Pittsburgh in December 1946 for aging catcher Al Lopez. Veeck didn't want Lopez to catch; he was more interested in Lopez as a potential manager to replace Lou Boudreau. In that respect the deal for Woodling wasn't bad.

Lopez played only one season for the Indians, but took over in 1951 as manager and probably was their best ever. Woodling flourished, too, after leaving Cleveland - though he established impressive credentials before his departure.

Signed by the Indians out of Akron East High in 1940, Woodling won three minor league batting championships in four seasons. He made it to the varsity for a brief trial in 1943 before going into the service for two years during World War II.

Woodling spent most of 1946 on the Indians bench watching George Case, Hank Edwards and Felix Mackiewicz play the outfield, and batted .188 in 61 games. "I think I spent the season keeping track of Bob Feller's strikeouts," he quipped in a 1955 newspaper article.

Things didn't get much better for Woodling after he was traded for Lopez, but a year later there was drastic improvement. "I went to San Francisco in the (Class AAA) Pacific Coast League and became a good hitter, a real good hitter," Woodling said of his demotion by the Pirates. He hit .385 and won the PCL batting championship.

The New York Yankees purchased Woodling in 1949 and he helped them win the pennant each of the next five years.

When the Yankees finished second to the Indians in 1954, they decided to bolster their pitching staff and Woodling was included in one of baseball's biggest trades. He and eight others went to Baltimore for Bob Turley, Don Larsen, Billy Hunter and five other players. .

Six months later, in June 1955, the Indians tried to correct their original mistake by getting Woodling back, with $15,000, for Dave Pope and Wally Westlake. Woodling proceeded to prove again the Indians had been wrong. He hitt.321 and won the "Man of the Year" award in 1957.

But then Frank Lane did it again. He traded Woodling back to Baltimore, with Dick Williams and Bud Daley to reacquire Larry Doby and Don Ferrarese.

But Woodling still wasn't finished. The Squire of Remsen Corners played five more years - all of them productive and when he finally retired, nobody could doubt that he'd proved that all those naysayers of long ago had been wrong.

If he were playing for the Indians today, Al Milnar would command a salary in the $5 million or $6 million range. Perhaps even more.

Unfortunately for Milnar, who grew up on Cleveland's near East Side, things were different when he was one of the best left-handed pitchers in baseball.

That was 1940, the year Milnar went 18-10 and the Indians almost won the American League pennant.

It earned for Milnar a 1941 contract for $13,000, the largest salary he ever made in eight seasons in the big leagues.

"Those days we weren't smart enough to have agents," Milnar was quoted in a 1986 interview.

It was midway through the 1942 season that Milnar, whose family name was spelled "Mlinar," before he changed it, came within one out of hurling a no-hitter against the Detroit Tigers. Doc Cramer broke it up with two out in the ninth.

Baseball's owners apparently weren't too smart then, either.

Milnar was signed by the Indians off the Cleveland sandlots in 1933, but didn't make it to the major leagues until 1936, despite compiling an outstanding minor league record.

When Milnar was only 19 in 1933, he pitched an exhibition game against the Indians and struck out 18 batters.

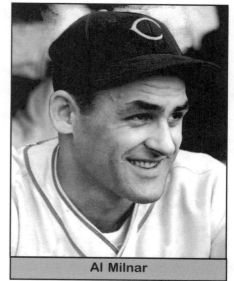

Al Milnar

And he won a total of 46 games in 1934 and 1935 for New Orleans, then the Tribe's top farm club in the Class A Southern Association, but to no avail.

"Now they bring up a guy if he's 1-3," Milnar said with resignation, not rancor, in that 1986 newspaper story.

Milnar went 14-12 with the Indians in 1939. During that season he was granted a $200 bonus by then-vice president Cy Slapnicka after outdueling future Hall of Famer Lefty Gomez to beat the New York Yankees, 2-1, in 11 innings.

That victory over Grove was called by Milnar, "My greatest thrill in baseball."

For whatever reason, Milnar's career went downhill after his 18-victory season in 1940. His record slipped to 12-19 in 1941, and to 6-8 in 1942.

It was in 1941 that Milnar became the answer to a trivia question for having given up the final hit, on July 16, in Joe DiMaggio's record-setting 56 game hitting streak.

When Milnar had won only one game and lost three by Aug. 27, 1943, the Indians sold him to the St. Louis Browns for the then-waiver price of $7,500. He went 1-2 in three games with the Browns, and shortly thereafter Milnar entered the Army for World War II.

It cost him the 1944 and 1945 seasons - which apparently ended Milner's chances for a successful comeback.

Milnar returned in 1946, but his fast ball was gone. He pitched only 14 2/3 innings for the Browns and Philadelphia Phillies, and called it quits with a 57-58 career record. He managed in the minors for a couple of years, but then got out of baseball.

Thereafter, sadly, Milnar, the local boy who made good, was virtually forgotten despite having been one of the best pitchers in baseball, if only for a year or two.

The 'calmest man in baseball'

Alva Bradley, who owned the Indians from 1928 until he sold the franchise to Bill Veeck on June 21, 1946, always said that, while he hired a manager, "the public fires him."

So it was that Bradley hired Roger Peckinpaugh in 1928, and again in 1941, after the public had fired Peckinpaugh's predecessors, Jack McCallister and then Oscar Vitt.

Roger Peckinpaugh

Peckinpaugh, the first and one of the best of many Cleveland sandlotters signed by the Indians after he was a star at East High School, stepped into an especially difficult situation when he replaced Vitt.

The Indians had staged a rebellion against Vitt during the 1940 season, and it was that revolt that was blamed for their losing the pennant to Detroit on the final weekend.

When Peckinpaugh was hired, Associated Press columnist Larry Hauck wrote: "The turbulent Cleveland Indians will play next season for the calmest man in baseball, Roger Peckinpaugh. He is one of those persons who counts to a thousand, not 10, before acting."

Unfortunately, it took more than serenity for the Indians to win under Peckinpaugh in 1941, just as it did during his first 5 1/2 years as Tribe manager, until "the public" fired him on June 9, 1933.

Then Bradley said, in announcing the appointment of Walter Johnson to lead the Tribe, "There is no man for whom I have a higher personal regard than I have for Peckinpaugh. But this team lacks pop. It plays loosely. And as I have said before, we only hire the manager, the public fires him."

Under Peckinpaugh, the Indians finished seventh in 1928, climbed to third place in 1929, then fell back to fourth, where they wound up each of the next three seasons, 1930-32, and were lodged in that same position when he was fired in 1933. The Tribe also finished fourth in Peckinpaugh's second tour of duty in 1941, giving him a 5 1/2 year managerial won - lost record of 490-481 (.505).

Peckinpaugh, a shortstop, played 17 years in the major leagues, beginning in 1910 with the Indians.

They traded him to New York on May 20, 1913, and eight years later Peckinpaugh led the Yankees to their first-ever pennant.

It wasn't until after he was dealt to Washington in 1922, however, that Peckinpaugh enjoyed his greatest success. A light but timely hitter, Peckinpaugh was selected Most Valuable Player of the American League in 1925 when he batted .294, helping the Senators win a second consecutive pennant.

It also was in 1925, against Pittsburgh in the World Series, that Peckinpaugh suffered his greatest embarrassment. He committed eight errors, still a major league record for a seven game series.

Nevertheless, Peckinpaugh was one of the greatest shortstops of his day, and retired with a .259 lifetime average.

Though Bradley gave Peckinpaugh a two-year contract in 1941, the public - once again - fired the manager after the Indians tied for fourth place with a 75-79 record.

This time, however, Bradley kicked Peckinpaugh upstairs, to be the Indians' general manager, a position he held the next 4 1/2 years, until Veeck came in and took over himself.

And the new manager hired by Bradley was Lou Boudreau, then only 24, who would, in seven years, lead the Indians to one of their greatest seasons.

If they'd had him sooner, there's no telling how many pennants the Indians might have won before and after their first one in 1920.

But Edgar Rice, better known as "Sam," didn't arrive in Cleveland until 1934, after he'd been released by the Washington Senators for whom he'd played 2,307 games over a span of 19 years.

Rice hit .300 in 13 of those seasons with the Senators, was an excellent base stealer and an exceptional outfielder. At one time he held the American League record for total chances in the outfield: 478 in 1920.

Rice, then 44, played only that one season for the Tribe, batting .293, and retired, even though his 98 hits in 1934 gave him a career total of 2,987, a mere 13 shy of 3,000, a level that only 24 players in the history of baseball have reached (including Cal Ripken Jr., who is certain to do so in 2000). However, Rice didn't seem to care, perhaps because, in those days, scant attention was paid to such records.

It certainly didn't matter to Hall of Fame electors as Rice was voted into the shrine in 1963, one of 25 players who once wore Cleveland uniforms to be so honored.

Sam Rice

Rice took a circuitous route to the Hall of Fame, as outlined by historian Lee Allen shortly after his induction.

"Rice got off to a much later start than most players. Born on a farm near Morocco, Ind., Rice worked in the wheat fields in the Dakotas and Minnesota, served as a railroad section hand and bottled whiskey at the Green River distillery in Louisville.

"Eventually Rice drifted to Norfolk, where he enlisted in the Navy and was assigned to the USS New Hampshire.

"He made the ship's baseball team and did his first playing at Guantanamo Bay (Cuba), then saw service in Mexico, helping restore order after a political assassination created havoc. On leave at Petersburg, Va. at age 24, Rice tried out with the local team as a pitcher and looked so good that Doc Lee, who owned the club, bought him out of the Navy.

"When the Virginia League blew up in 1915, Lee, who owed (Washington Senators owner Clark) Griffith $800, sent him Rice in lieu of the money, and Sam reported to the Senators as a pitcher.

"But his ability to hit was well known. Early in 1916, he made nine pinch hits in 11 tries, three of them off Elmer Myers of the Athletics, who told Rice, 'You'd better quit pitching.' Rice did, and embarked upon a career as an outfielder and hitter that few could match."

From 1919 through 1930, Rice never appeared in fewer than 141 games. He seldom struck out - only 275 times in 20 years and usually took only one swing, his batting eye was that keen.

Often compared in personality and style to Hall of Fame second baseman Charley Gehringer, Rice went to bat 600 or more times in eight different seasons, and retired with a lifetime average of .322. He batted .300 or better 14 times including .350, his best season, in 1925.

Because Rice retired while playing for the Indians, they claim him as one of their Hall of Famers. Too bad they couldn't have claimed Rice before it was too late to take full advantage of his enormous ability.

The failed return of 'Rocky'

The date was March 10, 1966, and Frank Lane, who was then working as a scout for Baltimore, smiled as he talked about the deal the Orioles had just made with the Indians.

"The fans in Cleveland will love the guy they're getting," said Lane. When asked why, Lane replied, "Because he's a dead ringer for Rocky Colavito."

Lou Piniella

Lane had good reason to know about both – Colavito's looks and the emotions of Tribe fans. Six years earlier, when Lane was then the Indians general manager, he traded the popular Colavito to Detroit for Harvey Kuenn, and most of the fans in Northeastern Ohio never forgave him for the dastardly deed.

That "guy" Lane predicted the fans would come to love was Lou Piniella, acquired for minor league catcher Camilo Carreon.

And while it was true that Piniella physically resembled Colavito, he didn't hit like the former tribe slugger and fan favorite – at least not in the opinion of the brass – and he went back to the minors each of the next three seasons after trials in spring training.

Totally frustrated by his inability to make it with the Indians, and embittered when they returned him to Portland of the Class AAA Pacific Coast League again in 1968, Piniella tearfully talked of quitting baseball.

"I don't know what else I can do to prove I'm good enough," said Piniella, who'd hit .308 at Portland in 1967, but was demoted after just six games and five at-bats without a hit in April of 1968. He didn't quit, of course, and reluctantly returned to Portland for, as he vowed, "one more year." It turned out to be all that Piniella needed.

Despite his acknowledged great potential – and physical resemblance to Colavito – Piniella was left unprotected by the Indians when the American League expanded at the end of the 1968 season, and he was claimed in the draft by the then-Seattle Pilots.

A week before the 1969 season began, the Pilots traded Piniella to the Kansas City Royals, the AL's other expansion team, and it was with the Royals that Piniella really began to resemble Colavito – especially at the plate. Not only did he make it with the Royals, Piniella won the AL "Rookie of the Year" award after hitting .282, and embarked upon an 18 year major league career.

Piniella subsequently was traded to the New York Yankees in 1973, for whom he hit a career high .330 in 1977, helped them reach the World Series four times, and retired as a player after the 1984 season with a lifetime .291 average in 1,747 games.

Then "Sweet Lou," as he came to be nicknamed, turned to managing the Yankees in 1986 and 1987, and the latter half of 1988, compiling a won-lost record of 417-224, before moving to the radio booth, though only briefly.

Piniella took over as manager of the Cincinnati Reds in 1990, led them to the National League pennant and a four-game sweep of the highly favored Oakland Athletics in the World Series. He managed the Reds through 1992, then returned to Seattle in 1993 as the skipper of the Mariners, the team that succeeded the Pilots in 1977.

Not bad for the kid who wasn't considered good enough to play for the Indians – even though he looked a lot like Rocky Colavito.

Vic Wertz is best remembered for making an out, and for a message scrawled in lipstick across his bald pate.

Both happened in 1954, the season the Indians won an American League record 111 games and the franchise's third pennant.

But there's so much more to remember about Wertz, a hard-hitting outfielder-first baseman without whose contributions the Indians could not have dominated the league as they did that season.

Vic Wertz

Wertz is the guy who hit a 460 foot drive to center field at the Polo Grounds in the eighth inning of the first game of the 1954 World Series against the New York Giants.

It would have been a three run homer in any other major league park, including the old Municipal Stadium in Cleveland.

But not at the Polo Grounds.

Willie Mays, the Giants' center fielder, turned at the crack of the bat and ran - and ran and ran - finally catching the ball over his shoulder with his back to the plate.

Film of the catch is shown regularly at World Series time, and was one of the 20 "greatest moments" in baseball history in a recent poll in *USA Today*.

Mays' sensational play choked off a Tribe rally, maintained a 2-2 tie, and enabled the Giants to win, 5-2, on a 10th inning pinch homer – a home run that popped over the 260-foot right field fence - by Dusty Rhodes. The Giants went on to sweep the World Series.

Wertz also is famous as the centerpiece of the Indians' party upon clinching the pennant on September 18, 1954.

Lettered in lipstick across the top of Wertz's bald head - and photographed for posterity - were the words, "We're In."

But more than Mays's catch and the message celebrating the pennant, Wertz, who died in 1983 at age 58, should be remembered as one of the most courageous players to wear a Tribe uniform.

He was acquired June 1, 1954 from Baltimore for journeyman pitcher Bob Chakales in one of Hank Greenberg's best deals.

Though Wertz had played only the outfield prior to joining the Indians, Manager Al Lopez promptly installed him at first base. It turned out to be a master stroke.

However, disaster struck the following season. Wertz contracted polio on August 26, 1955, and was hospitalized for 20 days.

The Indians floundered and finished - without Wertz - in second place, three games behind New York.

It was feared Wertz would never play again.

But he did, and very well.

Wertz made a remarkable comeback in 1956, hitting .264 with 32 homers and 106 RBI, and was voted the Indians' "Man of the Year" by Cleveland baseball writers.

He went on to play seven more seasons for a 17 year total in the big leagues, and retired in 1963 with a lifetime average of .277 and 266 homers.

The Indians' 'odd couple'

They were the odd couple of broadcasting: Jimmy Dudley and Bob Neal.

The two talented broadcasters worked elbow-to-elbow for nearly 20 years – but they were antagonists, not partners.

Jimmy Dudley

Each blamed the other's professional jealousy for their mutual problem, and Dudley probably best summarized their relationship when he was quoted in a newspaper article in 1979: "Neal thought he should be No. 1, and I knew I was No. 1."

In many respects they were similar, which may have been the basis of their problem. Whatever, while they were an excellent team on the air, they had absolutely no relationship off the air.

Dudley came to the Indians' airwaves first. He initially teamed up with Jack Graney in 1948, the year the Indians won their second pennant and first since 1920.

When Graney retired be was replaced by Neal in 1954, the year the Indians won their third pennant.

Except for a couple of years when Neal switched to television, the two worked together - and often intentionally antagonized each other on the air - until Dudley was fired after the 1967 season. Five years later Neal also was fired.

But neither man mellowed in retirement. Dudley, who lived in Tucson, Ariz. and was inducted into the Baseball Hall of Fame as a broadcaster a few months before his death in 1998, was the radio voice of the Seattle Pilots in 1969. But when that franchise moved to Milwaukee, Dudley was terminated. Neal, who had health problems in his later years, moved to San Diego after he was fired, and died in 1983.

Dudley's favorite memory was of the 1954 Indians, who won an American League record 111 games. "That team not only was the best I ever covered, it also was the best group of guys," he said in 1994, the 40th anniversary of the Indians' third championship season. They did everything together, on and off the field. They won together and lost together, though they didn't lose often.

"The 1948 team also was great to cover because, not only was it a good team, it also was a bunch of good guys.

"But there wasn't the same degree of camaraderie in 1948 as in 1954."

Neal, who did play-by-play of Browns games during their early years, also got some network assignments, one of which turned out to be one of the most famous games in baseball history - Don Larsen's perfect game in the 1956 World Series.

"I had the first 4 1/2 innings, and all my dramatic talents were wasted," Neal was quoted in 1979. "My partner, who was Bob Wolff, and I had a hell of an argument in the booth. I said the listeners had a right to know Larsen was pitching a no-hitter, but Wolff said he didn't want to jinx him."

It was never made clear who prevailed - other than Larsen.

During Neal's illness, Dudley expressed sympathy for his former partner, but said nothing had changed in their relationship.

"No, I never hear from him," Dudley said about Neal.

And Neal would have said the same about Dudley.

It is a story that sadly resembles that of the late Ernie Davis, the 1961 Heisman Trophy winner who was expected to become an immediate star with the Cleveland Browns, but died of leukemia before he ever played a game in the NFL.

Though Walter Bond arrived with much less fanfare than Davis, the 6-7, power-hitting outfielder-first baseman, came up to the Indians in 1960 after three solid minor league seasons.

As reported in the Cleveland *Press*, "The big rookie set the Cactus League on fire (in spring training) with his tremendous home runs, triples and doubles ... and it was after one of those games that Manager Joe Gordon announced, 'I've got to keep this kid on the ball club when we open the season.'"

Gordon did, but Bond batted only .221 in 40 games in 1960 and was demoted, first to Toronto of the Class AAA International League, and then Vancouver of the Class AAA Pacific Coast League.

Bond got another chance with the Tribe in 1961, reporting to spring training with what he called a "new temperament."

"Last year when I came to Cleveland I forgot that I was just playing baseball," he was quoted in the *Plain Dealer*. "I guess I was the most publicized rookie of the spring and that made it hard. I

Walter Bond

kept getting letters and phone calls from people who blamed me because Rocky Colavito was traded (in April 1960). They said Frank Lane never would have traded Rock if he thought I wouldn't be able to fill (Colavito's) shoes.

"Well, I can't blame those fans. Rocky was a popular man. But I didn't trade him."

Despite his high hopes – and the Indians' high expectations – Bond failed again. He opened the 1961 season with the Tribe, but hit just .173 in 38 games, and was optioned to Salt Lake City in the P.C.L, where he played in 1962, this time batting .320.

It earned him another shot with the Indians, and in the final 12 games of the season, Bond hit .380 with 19 hits in 50 at-bats, including six homers and 17 RBI, but had to quit after playing 12 games.

And again he was expected to win a regular job with the Tribe the following season.

However, on May 15, 1963 it was revealed that Bond had leukemia. The disease was diagnosed during the winter of 1962-63 when Bond, serving as an Army reservist, was to undergo a hernia operation. At first it was thought that he had what was then called only "a low blood count," and was given a medical discharge.

But, despite the disease, Bond still wouldn't give up. He insisted on trying again in 1963, and the Indians sent him to Jacksonville (Fla.) of the International League. For awhile, Bond showed signs of being recovered. However, the disease proved to be only in remission. Bond batted .276 and when the season ended the Indians sold his contract to Houston.

Bond played for Houston in 1964 and 1965, hitting .254 and .263, respectively, and in 1966 was traded to Denver (of the Class AAA Pacific Coat League) where he hit .316. It earned him another shot in the major leagues in 1967, with Minnesota, but after 10 games, in which he hit .313, Bond had to quit again. This time for good. Five months later, on Sept. 14, 1967, Bond died in Houston.

Oh, how 'The Crab' could hit

Jesse Burkett's nickname was "The Crab," for obvious reasons.

He had a "testy disposition," and was a very "sullen fellow," wrote the former sports editor of the Cleveland *Press*, the late Franklin Lewis.

Jesse Burkett

But, oh, how "The Crab" could hit.

Burkett batted .409 for the old Cleveland Spiders in 1895, and .410 the next year.

The Cleveland franchise at that time was a member of the 12 team National League, the only "major" professional baseball league then in existence since the demise of the American Association in 1892, and the Players League in 1891. He was elected to the Baseball Hall of Fame in 1946.

Burkett was a teammate of the legendary Cy Young and, in fact, was with Young as part of a trade that cost Cleveland several of its all-time best players in 1899.

The Cleveland franchise was then owned by a man named Frank DeHaas Robison, described by historians as "a wealthy street car magnate."

What Robison did, in effect. was trade Burkett, Young, and several other of the Spiders' best players to himself.

Robison, who had owned the Spiders since 1889, also bought the St. Louis franchise in 1898, giving him two teams in the National League which. of course, would not be allowed now. But baseball was different then - at least off the field - and Robison decided he wanted the St. Louis team to be dominant.

Thus, he transferred the best players to St. Louis, while assigning the worst to the Spiders.

And there was no doubt that Burkett, along with Young, was among the best in the game at that time, his nasty disposition notwithstanding.

Only 5-8 and 155 pounds, Burkett - "The Crab" - played 16 seasons, through 1905, won three NL batting championships, and retired with a .338 lifetime average.

After ending his playing career, Burkett bought the minor league Worcester, Mass. team in the old New England League.

True to his nature, Burkett regularly lost his temper at the ineptitude of his players and, even at the advanced age of 50-plus, would grab a bat and enter the game as a pinch hitter.

"'I'll show you blind-eyed bums how to hit that ball,' and then Burkett did," it was reported by the late Cleveland *Plain Dealer* sports columnist James E. Doyle in a 1962 interview with a man who'd played for Burkett's team.

"'The old boy still had his wonderful batting eye, and no hitter ever had more of what he called 'the old confeedence, but, of course, he couldn't run anymore ... he just waddled.'"

Had Burkett and Young been allowed to remain in Cleveland, it's probable the team would have won a pennant - perhaps several - long before the Indians finally did in 1920.

As it was, Robison's old Spiders won only 20 games and lost 134 in 1899. The franchise was dormant in 1900, and baseball returned to Cleveland under the ownership of Charles W. Somers when the American League was formed in 1901.

A unique 'run-of-the-mill' game

It is one of baseball's most obscure records, and happened in one of the strangest games in history.

On June 9, 1908, the Cleveland Naps (who became the Indians in 1915) played the Boston Red Sox at League Park and nothing like it has happened in the major leagues since then.

The published report of the game is almost as "unique."

Here's how the Cleveland *Plain Dealer* described that game played in the eighth year of the formation of the American League, as every man in the Cleveland lineup made a hit and scored a run in the same inning, the fifth.

"It was a run-of-the-mill game halfway through the contest. Boston enjoyed a 2-1 lead through the first four innings, as the Naps went to bat.

"But then it became a game that is unique in major league history. In that fifth inning each player in the Cleveland lineup made a hit and scored a run (Nig Clarke actually scored two runs but he still had only one hit as he scored his second run of the inning after reaching base as the result of a Boston error).

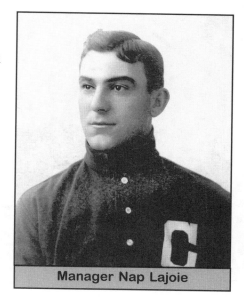

Manager Nap Lajoie

"Clarke started the Naps fifth with a single. In trying to advance Clarke with a sacrifice, Bill Hinchman popped to Andy McConnell. Piano Legs Hickman singled and so did Joe Birmingham. On Cavvy Cravath's wide throw to the plate, Clarke scored and Hickman and Birmingham reached second and third. Heinie Berger drove a single past Harry Lord and Hickman and Birmingham crossed the plate.

"Josh Clarke followed with another single and when Bill Bradley also hit safely, Berger scored.

"At that point James (Deacon) McGuire, the Boston manager, decided he had seen enough of his pitcher, George Winter, and brought in Ralph Glaze.

"George Stovall greeted the new pitcher with a base hit that registered Josh Clarke. Nap Lajoie, the Cleveland player-manager and second baseman, threw his bat at a wide one for a hit that filled the bases.

"Danny Sullivan in right muffed Nig Clarke's long fly and Bradley and Stovall were able to score.

"Hinchman got his hit for the inning. It was to center field for a home run (the only extra base hit of the inning), driving in Lajoie and Nig Clarke.

"Glaze then got Hickman and Birmingham to end the inning as a '10' was hung on the scoreboard. The fact that each team scored four more runs in the last three innings is of little importance."

As it turned out, however, those 10 runs Cleveland scored in the fifth were necessary as the Naps won the game, 15-6.

It was not considered a "crucial" game for the Naps because it was still early in the season. However, they wound up with a 90-64 record, one-half game behind the Detroit Tigers who won the pennant because they played - and lost - one less game due to a rain-out that wasn't rescheduled.

Lajoie, who played 21 years and compiled a lifetime batting average of .338 before he retired in 1917, got three hits that day, as did Birmingham and Stovall. Lajoie, who took over as Cleveland's manager in 1905, stepped down at midseason in 1909, though he remained on the team as a player.

Ironically, the man who replaced him as manager was James McGuire - the same James McGuire who managed the Red Sox in 1908 and was fired by them shortly after that unique "run-of-the-mill game."

'Good old Joe Earley'

It was truly a Golden Year for baseball in Cleveland.

There hasn't been a baseball season like 1948 since then, not even 1954 when the Indians won 111 games, but were swept in the World Series by the New York Giants, or even 1995 and 1997, when they also won American League pennants, but again failed to win the world championship.

Joe Earley poster

Lou Boudreau and Bill Veeck were civic heroes in 1948, and household names were Ken Keltner, Joe Gordon, Dale Mitchell, Eddie Robinson, Gene Bearden, Jim Hegan and any of the 15 or 20 other players who wore Tribe uniforms that season.

Children who were too young to stay up late, got up early just to find out who won the Indians game the night before.

Housewives ironed and washed dishes and scrubbed floors to the accompaniment of Jack Graney and Jimmy Dudley as they screeched into microphones over radio station WJW.

Husbands read the sports pages while dinner got cold - if they didn't stay downtown late to go to a ball game.

And grandmothers who didn't know a strike from a double play rejoiced when the Indians won, and were remorseful - with the rest of the family - when they lost. Some even cried.

And Veeck, called "the Barnum of Baseball" with good reason, came up with what might have been his best promotion: to honor the fans for their devotion to the team.

Veeck picked a guy named Joe Earley, named him "Mr. Average Baseball Fan," and showered him with gifts before a night game in September.

Earley was chosen as the result of a letter he wrote to the Cleveland *Press* in which he suggested that fans ought to get some recognition for their support of the Indians. After all, he pointed out, it had been 28 years since their last championship.

Veeck, master showman that he was, seized the opportunity.

In his book, "Veeck as in Wreck," the late owner of the Indians called the night for Earley "the gag that reaped us the most publicity."

He explained, "We started by announcing we were giving Earley a house done in early American architecture. Out came an outhouse.

"We announced the presentation of an automobile, fully equipped. Out came one of those old Model T cars, filled to the scuppers with gorgeous women.

"After the fun was over, the real gifts came. A new Ford convertible, followed by a truck filled with gifts; refrigerator, washing machine, luggage, wristwatch, clothes, console, everything any quiz show subsequently thought of. Everything, to be frank, we could talk the local merchants into contributing to the cause."

The non-gag gifts were worth more than $15,000, including $5,400 in cash that Earley turned over to the Cancer Fund. Everybody went home happy. More importantly, the fans returned to the Stadium often. Indians attendance that season - 2,620,627 - was a major league record that stood until 1962. It was the culmination of what truly was the first "Golden Year" in Cleveland, thanks to Veeck, who died in 1986 at the age of 71.

Of the more than 150,000 regular season games that have been played in the major leagues in baseball's modern era (since 1901), only13 have been perfect – i.e., 27 batters retired without anyone reaching base – and two of them were pitched by players wearing Cleveland uniforms.

They were Addie Joss, who beat the Chicago White Sox, 1-0, on Oct. 2, 1908, and Len Barker, who also was perfect in defeating the Toronto Blue Jays, 3-0, on May 15, 1981.

One other perfect game – nine innings from the first pitch to the last – was thrown in the World Series by Don Larsen of the New York Yankees, who beat the Brooklyn Dodgers, 2-0, on Oct. 8, 1956.

The other 11 members of the exclusive, perfect game fraternity:

Cy Young, for the Boston Pilgrims (Red Sox), over Philadelphia, 3-0, on May 5, 1904;

Charles Robertson, Chicago, 2-0, over Detroit, April 30, 1922;

Jim Bunning, Philadelphia, 6-0, over the New York Mets, June 21, 1964;

Sandy Koufax, Los Angeles, 1-0, over Chicago, Sept. 9, 1965;

Catfish Hunter, Oakland, 4-0, over Minnesota, May 8, 1968;

Mike Witt, California, 1-0, over Texas, Sept. 30, 1984;

Tom Browning, Cincinnati, 1-0, over Los Angeles, Sept. 16, 1988;

Dennis Martinez, Montreal, 2-0, over Los Angeles, July 28, 1991;

Kenny Rogers, Texas, 4-0, over California, July 28, 1994;

David Wells, New York, 4-0, over Minnesota, May 17, 1998; and

David Cone, New York, 6-0, over Montreal, July 18, 1999.

Not considered "perfect" games by *The Sporting News* in its *Complete Baseball Record Book*, and not included in the above list were games pitched by Ernie Shore of the Boston Red Sox, who retired 27 consecutive batters after replacing Babe Ruth, who walked the first batter he faced, then was ejected by the umpire, in a game on June 23, 1917, in a 4-0 victory over Washington; Harvey Haddix of Pittsburgh, who was perfect for 12 innings, but lost, 1-0, in the 13th against the Milwaukee Braves, May 26, 1959; and Pedro Martinez of Montreal, who pitched nine innings without allowing a runner to reach base before Bip Roberts doubled in the 10th in the Expos' 1-0 victory over San Diego, June 3, 1995.

Fifteen no-hitters (including those by Joss and Barker) have been thrown by Cleveland pitchers in the 20th century. The other 13:

Earl Moore (though he lost, 4-2, in the 10th, to Chicago, May 9, 1901; Robert Rhoads, 2-1, over Boston, Sept. 18, 1908; Joss, 1-0, over Chicago, April 20, 1910 (in addition to his perfect game); Ray Caldwell, 3-0, over New York, Sept. 10, 1919; Wes Ferrell, 9-0, over St. Louis, April 29, 1931; Bob Feller, 1-0, over Chicago, April 16, 1940; Feller, 1-0, over New York, April 30, 1946; Don Black, 3-0, over Philadelphia, July 10, 1947; Bob Lemon, 2-0, over Detroit, June 30, 1948; Feller, 2-1, over Detroit, July 1, 1951; Sonny Siebert, 2-0, over Washington, June 10, 1966; Dick Bosman, 4-0, over Oakland, July 19, 1974; and Dennis Eckersley, 1-0, over California, May 30, 1977.

There also have been 11 no-hitters pitched against the Indians, by:

Charles Bender, Philadelphia, 4-0, May 12, 1910; Tom Hughes, New York (who gave up a hit in the 10th and lost in the 11th, 5-0, Aug. 30, 1910; Joe Benz, Chicago, 6-1, May 31, 1914; Leslie Bush, Philadelphia, 5-0, Aug. 26, 1916; Vernon Kennedy, Chicago, 5-0, Aug. 31, 1935; Monte Pearson, New York, 13-0, Aug. 27, 1938; Allie Reynolds, New York, 1-0, July 12, 1951; Dave Morehead, Boston, 2-0, Sept. 16, 1965; Dean Chance, Minnesota, 2-1, Aug. 25, 1967; Dave Stieb, Toronto, 3-0, Sept. 2, 1990; and Jim Abbott, New York, 4-0, Sept. 4, 1993.

The 'All-Century' Indians

It's only one man's opinion, and while there's no contest at some positions, there undoubtedly are varying sentiments concerning the players who belong on the Indians "All Century" team.

That's especially true considering the success the Indians enjoyed in the final five seasons of the 1900s, when they dominated the American League Central Division from 1995-99, won the franchise's fourth and fifth pennants in 1995 and 1997, and came within one out of capturing the world championship in 1997.

Al Lopez

Napoleon Lajoie, who played for Cleveland from 1902-14, and was the team's player-manager from 1905-09, is named by some historians as having been the best position player in the history of the franchise.

It's hard to believe, however, that Lajoie played second base better than Robbie Alomar did in 1999.

And, at least until Omar Vizquel reached his peak the last couple of seasons of the 20th century, Lou Boudreau (1938-50) was considered the best shortstop in Tribe history.

Another old-timer who long was regarded as one of the game's best all around catchers, Steve O'Neill (1911-23), also was pushed for his place on the team by Sandy Alomar Jr., at least until Alomar was hampered by a succession of injuries in 1998 and 1999. Jim Hegan (1941-42, 1946-57) is another who merits consideration, though he was not as consistent a hitter as O'Neill and Alomar.

Few will dispute that Bob Feller (1936-41, 1946-56) deserves the distinction of being called the best pitcher in Indians history. Bear in mind that Cy Young earned his fame and most of his 511 victories with other teams in the National League, including 241 with the old Cleveland Spiders from 1890-98, before returning to Cleveland in 1909, near the end of his career, and pitched for the Naps 2 ½ seasons, going 29-29.

Other right-handed pitchers who merit mention: Addie Joss (1902-10), Stan Coveleski (1916-24), Jim Bagby Sr. (1917-22), George Uhle (1919-28), Wes Ferrell (1928-33), Mel Harder (1928-47), Bob Lemon (1946-58), Early Wynn (1949-57), Mike Garcia (1949-59), and Gaylord Perry (1972-75) – though none was better than Feller, nor meant more to the franchise than the man nicknamed "Rapid Robert."

Sam McDowell (1961-71), who many believe could have been one of baseball's all-time greatest left-handed pitchers if not for an admitted and well-publicized drinking problem, still was the best southpaw the Indians ever had.

Others who deserve consideration: Herb Score (1955-59) whose career was cut short by eye and shoulder injuries, Gene Bearden (1947-50) who had one sensational season, pitching and winning the 1948 pennant-playoff game, and Vean Gregg (1911-14) who had three consecutive 20 victory seasons, but mysteriously lost his stuff and was traded away.

Certainly, Tris Speaker (1916-26), who also was an Indians' player-manager (1919-26) belongs on the All-Century team as its center fielder, and the left fielder (though he played center) is Earl Averill (1929-39), who is given the honor over Charley Jamieson (1919-32) and Albert Belle (1989-96).

The right fielder would be "Shoeless Joe" Jackson (1910-15), had he played longer for Cleveland – and not been banished from baseball after he was traded to the Chicago White Sox because he allegedly participated in the gambling conspiracy to fix the outcome of the 1919 World Series. Jackson was one of eight White Sox players barred from baseball.

Instead of Jackson, Cleveland's All-Century right fielder is either Larry Doby (1947-55, 1958), though he also played center, Manny Ramirez, who broke in with the Indians in 1994 and had a career year in 1999, or fan favorite Rocky Colavito (1955-59, 1965-67).

The choice here is Hall of Famer Doby, because of his better all-around ability, and the fact that Ramirez hasn't played long enough for the Tribe.

Hal Trosky (1933-41) probably was the team's best first baseman, though Andre Thornton (1977-79, 1981-87) deserves mention, and so do George Burns (1920-21, 1924-28), Luke Easter (1949-54), and Jim Thome, who started as a third baseman with the Indians in 1991, and switched to first base in 1997.

Another close race for honors is at third base where Al Rosen (1947-56) is the choice over Ken Keltner (1937-44, 1946-49), Bill Bradley (1901-10), and Buddy Bell (1972-78). But all four were great players.

Lou Boudreau

The leading candidates as the Indians' All-Century manager are Speaker, Boudreau, Al Lopez (1951-56), and Mike Hargrove (1991-99) – and it isn't coincidental that they were the four men who led the team to its five pennants (1920, 1948, 1954, 1995 and 1997).

Speaker resigned under pressure; Boudreau was fired by then-General Manager Hank Greenburg; Lopez retired (but returned to manage the Chicago White Sox); and Hargrove was dismissed by General Manager John Hart.

Lopez, whose winning percentage, .617 (570-354) was the best in Tribe history, is the choice, though Boudreau's teams won the most games (728-649), followed closely by Hargrove (723-589), while Speaker (616-520), O'Neill (199-168) and Lajoie (397-330) warrant consideration.

Thus, the Indians "All-Century" team, at least in the eyes of this observer:

First Base: Trosky - 11 seasons, 1,347 games, .302 average, 228 home runs, 1,012 RBI.
Second Base: Lajoie - 21 seasons, 2,480 games, .338 average, 82 home runs, 1,599 RBI.
Third Base: Rosen – 10 seasons, 1,044 games, .285 average, 192 home runs, 717 RBI.
Shortstop: Boudreau – 15 seasons, 1,646 games, .295 average, 68 home runs, 789 RBI.
Center Field: Speaker – 22 seasons, 2,789 games, .345 average, 117 home runs, 1,529 RBI.
Left Field: Averill – 13 seasons, 1,668 games, .318 average, 238 home runs, 1,164 RBI.
Right Field: Doby – 13 seasons, 1,533 games, .283 average, 253 home runs, 970 RBI.
Catcher: O'Neill – 17 seasons, 1,590 games, .263 average, 13 home runs, 537 RBI.
Right-Handed Pitcher: Feller – 18 seasons, 266-162 won-lost record, 3.25 ERA, 2,581 strikeouts.
Left-Handed Pitcher: McDowell – 15 seasons, 141-134 won-lost record, 3.17 ERA, 2,453 strikeouts.
Manager: Lopez.

BOB
LEMON
23-7

EARLY
WYNN
23-11

MIKE
GARCIA
19-6

BOB
FELLER
13-3

AL
LOPEZ
MANAGER

CLEVELAND
Indians
1954
BIG FOUR

Dick
Dugan

The best of the Indians ...
... in the Hall of Fame

Twenty-six men who once wore Cleveland uniforms are in the Baseball Hall of Fame, and two others with Cleveland ties also are among the game's immortals, having earned their way into the shrine through front office positions.

The former players, and the year in which they were elected:

Second baseman Nap Lajoie, 1937
Outfielder Tris Speaker, 1937
Pitcher Cy Young, 1937
Outfielder Ed Delahanty, 1945
Outfielder Jesse Burkett, 1946
Pitcher Bob Feller, 1962
Pitcher John Clarkson, 1963
Outfielder Elmer Flick, 1963
Outfielder Sam Rice, 1963
Pitcher Stan Coveleski, 1969
Shortstop Lou Boudreau, 1970
Pitcher Satchel Paige, 1971

Pitcher Early Wynn, 1972
Pitcher Bob Lemon, 1975
Outfielder Earl Averill, 1975
Outfielder Ralph Kiner, 1975
Shortstop Joey Sewell, 1977
Pitcher Addie Joss, 1978
Outfielder Frank Robinson, 1982
Pitcher Hoyt Wilhelm, 1985
Pitcher Gaylord Perry, 1991
Pitcher Hal Newhouser, 1992
Pitcher Steve Carlton, 1994
Pitcher Phil Niekro, 1997

Outfielder Larry Doby, 1998

Al Lopez, who was elected to the Hall of Fame in 1977, managed the Indians from 1951-56, leading them to the pennant in 1954, and later managed the Chicago White Sox from 1957-65 and again in 1968 and 1969.

Billy Evans, general manager of the Indians from 1927-35, was elected to the Hall of Fame in 1973, and Bill Veeck, who owned the Indians from 1946-49, and later owned the St. Louis Browns and Chicago White Sox, was elected in 1991.

The Hall of Famers who spent most of their playing careers in Cleveland were Averill, Boudreau, Coveleski, Doby, Feller, Flick, Joss, Lajoie, Lemon, Sewell, Speaker and Wynn. Also identified primarily as having played in Cleveland: Perry and Paige, though both also played extensively for other teams, including Paige's long career in the Negro League.

Young, winner of 511 games in 22 years, pitched for the Cleveland Spiders in the National League from 1890-98, the St. Louis Cardinals and Boston Pilgrims from 1899-1908, and for the Cleveland Naps from 1909-11, and the Boston Braves in 1911;

Burkett was a longtime National League star who played for the Spiders from 1891-98;

Rice wore a Cleveland uniform in 1934;

Kiner played most of his career with Pittsburgh, winding up with the Indians in 1955;

Robinson established his Hall of Fame credentials with four other teams before coming to the Indians as major league baseball's first black manager from 1975-77;

Wilhelm pitched for the Tribe in 1957 and 1958;

Newhouser finished his career with the Indians in 1954 and 1955;

Carlton won most of his games in the National League before pitching for the Indians in 1987, and Niekro also closed out his career with the Indians in 1986 and 1987.

Cleveland Municipal Stadium

The Tribe's most memorable games

April 24, 1901   Cleveland pitcher "Wild Bill" Hoffer starts the first game ever played in the American League and loses to the White Sox, 8-2, in Chicago.

May 23, 1901   Cleveland beats Washington, 14-13, scoring nine runs in the ninth inning after the first two batters are retired.

October 2, 1908   Addie Joss pitches the second perfect game (of the 13) in baseball's modern era to beat Chicago, 1-0, at League Park, in a game the Cleveland *Plain Dealer* calls "the greatest baseball game ever played" in its editions the next day.

April 11, 1912   "Shoeless Joe" Jackson goes 3-for-5 with two stolen bases to lead Cleveland (then called the "Naps") to a 3-2 victory over Detroit in front of more than 19,000 Opening Day fans at League Park.

July 11, 1914   Babe Ruth makes his debut as a major league pitcher for the Red Sox and beats the Indians, 4-3, in Boston.

July 10, 1920   Tris Speaker makes a record-tying 11th consecutive hit in the Indians' 7-2 victory over the Senators in the first game of a double header in Washington.

October 10, 1920   Bill Wambsganss, the Indians' second baseman, makes the only unassisted triple play in a World Series game, Jim Bagby Sr. becomes the first pitcher to hit a home run in a World Series, and Elmer Smith hits the first grand slam in a World Series game as the Indians beat Brooklyn, 8-1, in Game 5, en route to their first world championship.

October 12, 1920   Stan Coveleski beats Brooklyn, 3-0, at League Park in the seventh and deciding game as the Indians win their first World Series.

May 17, 1925   Speaker gets his 3,000th career hit, a double in the fourth inning off Tom Zachary in the Indians' 2-1 loss to Washington at League Park.

August 28, 1926   Emil "Dutch" Levsen pitches two complete game victories for the Indians against the Red Sox in Boston, allowing four hits in each (an achievement that has never been duplicated).

July 10, 1932   Johnny Burnett gets nine hits in the Indians' 18-17 loss to the Philadelphia Athletics in an 18 inning game at League Park.

July 31, 1932   80,184 fans see the Indians play the first game at the Stadium as Mel Harder loses to Hall of Famer Lefty Grove and Philadelphia, 1-0, on an eighth inning single by another future Hall of Famer, Mickey Cochrane.

The Tribe's most memorable games

September 7, 1935   A bases loaded line drive off the bat of Joe Cronin in the ninth inning of the first game of a double header in Boston ricochets off the forehead of Indians third baseman Sammy Hale into the glove of shortstop Bill Knickerbocker, who throws to second baseman Roy Hughes for the second out, and Hughes' relay to first baseman Hal Trosky completes a triple play to help Mel Harder win his 18th game, 5-3.

August 23, 1936   Bob Feller makes his first major league start at age 17 and strikes out 15 batters in a 4-1 victory over the St. Louis Browns at League Park

October 2, 1938   Feller strikes out a record 18 batters, but loses to Harry Eisenstat and Detroit, 4-1, in the first game of a double header at the Stadium.

April 16, 1940   Feller pitches the only Opening Day no-hitter in baseball history to beat the White Sox, 1-0, in Chicago.

September 27, 1940   The Indians lose what would have been their second pennant as Detroit and rookie pitcher Floyd Giebell beat Feller, 2-0, on Rudy York's home run at the Stadium in the third-last game of the season.

July 16, 1941   Joe DiMaggio gets three hits, two singles off Al Milnar in the first and third innings, and a double off Joe Krakauskas in the eighth, extending his consecutive game hitting streak to 56 as New York beats the Indians, 10-3, at League Park.

July 17, 1941   The Indians, in a 4-3 loss to New York at the Stadium, end DiMaggio's 56 game hitting streak on the pitching of Al Smith and Jim Bagby Jr., and the flawless fielding of third baseman Ken Keltner and shortstop Lou Boudreau.

July 14, 1946   Player-manager Boudreau, who got five extra base hits and drove in four runs in an 11-10 loss to the Red Sox in the opener of a double header in Boston, implements the "Williams Shift" against Ted Williams in the second game, which the Red Sox also win, 6-4.

July 5, 1947   Larry Doby makes his Indians debut as the American League's first black player, striking out as a pinch hitter in a 6-5 loss to the White Sox in Chicago.

August 8, 1948   Boudreau limps off the bench and delivers a key pinch hit against New York reliever Joe Page to lead the Indians to a double header sweep at the Stadium, 8-6 and 2-1.

The Tribe's most memorable games

October 4, 1948   Boudreau hammers two homers to help rookie southpaw Gene Bearden beat the Red Sox, 8-3, in Boston as the Indians win an unprecedented one-game playoff for their third pennant.

October 11, 1948   Bob Lemon, with relief help from Bearden, beats the Braves, 4-3, in Game 6 in Boston as the Indians win their second World Series.

September 29, 1954   Willie Mays makes a sensational catch to rob Vic Wertz of an extra base hit at the Polo Grounds as Bob Lemon loses Game 1 of the World Series, which sets the stage for the New York Giants to sweep the Indians, 5-2, 3-1, 6-2, and 7-4.

August 13, 1958   Rocky Colavito pitches three hitless innings in the second game of a double header as the Indians lose, 3-2, to Detroit at the Stadium

June 10, 1959   Colavito hits four consecutive home runs, one off Jerry Walker, two off Arnold Portocarrero, and another off Ernie Johnson as the Indians defeat the Orioles, 11-8, in Baltimore.

July 13, 1963   Early Wynn wins his 300th major league game with relief help from Jerry Walker as the Indians beat the Athletics, 7-4, in the second game of a double header in Kansas City.

April 8, 1975   Frank Robinson, making his debut as major league baseball's first black manager, hits a first inning home run off Doc Medich as the Indians beat New York, 5-3, at the Stadium.

May 15, 1981   Len Barker pitches the eighth perfect game in the major leagues' modern era to beat Toronto, 3-0, at the Stadium.

October 3, 1993   The Indians play their final game in Cleveland's Municipal Stadium in front of 72,390 fans, and lose, 4-0, to Jason Bere and Chicago.

April 4, 1994:   The Indians play their first game at Jacobs Field and beat Seattle, 4-3, in 11 innings in front of a capacity crowd of 41,459 fans as reliever Eric Plunk is the winning pitcher.

October 17, 1995   The Indians beat the Mariners, 4-0, in Seattle in Game 6 of the A.L. Championship Series to win their fourth pennant.

October 15, 1997   The Indians beat the Orioles, 1-0, in Baltimore in Game 6 of the A.L. Championship Series to win their fifth pennant.

"I had my bad days on the field, but I didn't take them home with me. I left them in a bar along the way." – **Hall of Fame Indians pitcher Bob Lemon**

"Gaylord Perry is an honorable man. He only uses the spitter when he needs it.
 – **former Indians president Gabe Paul**

"You don't need a stable of superstars. It's amazing what mileage you can get with players who play together." – **former Indians manager Frank Robinson**

"I ain't what I used to be, but who the hell is?" – **Hall of Fame pitcher Dizzy Dean**

October 15, 1899 Cleveland Spiders end the season with a 20-134 record; still the worst in the history of baseball, and the franchise is dropped by the National League.

February 21, 1900 Byron "Ban" Johnson visits Cleveland banker Davis Hawley to offer him a franchise in the new American League of Professional Baseball. Hawley refers Johnson to Charles Somers and John Kilfoyl who agree to bankroll the franchise, which has been moved from Grand Rapids, Mich. to Cleveland and nicknamed "Lake Shores."

April 24, 1901 The newly nicknamed Cleveland "Blues" (from "Lake Shores") lose their first game, 8-2, to the White Sox in Chicago in the American League's inaugural game.

1902 Nickname of the Cleveland franchise is changed from "Blues" to "Bronchos."

June 3, 1902 Bronchos acquire second baseman Napoleon Lajoie and pitcher Bill Bernhard from the Philadelphia Athletics.

1903 Nickname of the Cleveland franchise is changed from "Bronchos" to "Naps," in honor of star second baseman Napoleon Lajoie.

October 27, 1904 Napoleon Lajoie replaces William Armour as the third field manager of the Cleveland franchise.

October 2, 1908 Addie Joss pitches the second perfect game in baseball's modern era (since 1901), beating the Chicago White Sox, 1-0, in Cleveland.

March 17, 1908 Charles Somers rejects an offer to acquire Ty Cobb from Detroit in a trade for Elmer Flick, as proposed by Tigers manager Hughie Jennings.

October 6, 1908 The Naps finish second to Detroit by one-half game because they have played (and lost) one more game than the Tigers.

August 21, 1909 Napoleon Lajoie is replaced as manager of the Naps by James McGuire, but remains as the team's second baseman.

July 19, 1910 Cy Young wins his 500th game with a four-hitter as Cleveland beats the Senators, 5-2, in 11-innings in the second game of a double header in Washington.

July 30, 1910 The Indians ("Naps") purchase "Shoeless Joe" Jackson from New Orleans of the Class A Southern Association where he had been assigned by the parent Philadelphia Athletics (the deal was part of the July 23, 1910 trade in which Bris Lord was sent to the Athletics in exchange for Morrie Rath).

Tribe timeline

April 14, 1911   Addie Joss dies of tubercular meningitis.

July 24, 1911   A team of American League all-stars beats the Indians ("Naps"), 5-3, in a benefit game for Addie Joss' family, at League Park

July 11, 1914   The Indians lose, 4-3, to the Boston Red Sox, as Babe Ruth makes his debut as a major league pitcher in a game in Boston.

January 16, 1915   Nickname of the Cleveland franchise is changed from "Naps" to "Indians."

August 20, 1915   The Indians trade "Shoeless Joe" Jackson to the Chicago White Sox for outfielders Larry Chappell, Braggo Roth, pitcher Ed Klepfer and $31,500.

February 21, 1916   The Indians are sold by Charles Somers to a group of investors headed by James C. "Sunny Jim" Dunn for $500,000.

April 8, 1916   The Indians acquire outfielder Tris Speaker from the Boston Red Sox for pitcher Sam Jones and infielder Fred Thomas (and $55,000) in what many believe was the best trade ever made by the franchise.

July 18, 1919   Tris Speaker becomes the Indians' ninth manager (and fourth player-manager), replacing Lee Fohl.

August 17, 1920   Indians shortstop Ray Chapman dies after being hit in the head by a pitch from Carl Mays of the New York Yankees.

October 3, 1920   The Indians win their first American League pennant with a 98-56 record, finishing ahead of the Chicago White Sox by two games.

October 10, 1920   Indians second baseman Bill Wambsganss makes the only unassisted triple play in World Series history, Jim Bagby becomes the first pitcher to hit a home run in a World Series, and Elmer Smith hits the first grand slam in a World Series as Cleveland beats Brooklyn, 8-1, in Game 5.

October 12, 1920   The Indians beat Brooklyn, 3-0, to win the seventh and deciding game of the World Series.

November 17, 1927   The Indians are sold by the widow of James Dunn to a group of investors headed by Alva Bradley for $1 million.

May 13, 1929   The Indians and New York Yankees become the first teams to wear numbers on their uniforms in a game at League Park won by Cleveland, 4-3.

July 31, 1932 Cleveland Municipal Stadium, built at a cost of $3 million, is opened and the Indians lose the first game, 1-0, to Lefty Grove and the Philadelphia Athletics.

July 8, 1935 69,831 fans see the American League beat the National League, 4-1, in the third All-Star Game (and first of five to be played in Cleveland).

April 16, 1940 Bob Feller of the Indians pitches the only Opening Day no-hitter in baseball history, beating the White Sox, 1-0, in Chicago.

June 13, 1940 A contingent of 10 Indians present owner Alva Bradley with a petition demanding that Manager Oscar Vitt be fired, causing the team to be called the "Cleveland Cry Babies."

September 27, 1940 Bob Feller and the Indians lose to Floyd Giebell and the Tigers, 2-0, in the third last game of the season, clinching the pennant for Detroit.

October 28, 1940 Indians owner Alva Bradley fires Manager Oscar Vitt and replaces him with Roger Peckinpaugh.

November 25, 1941 Lou Boudreau, the Indians' 24-year old shortstop, replaces Roger Peckinpaugh as the 15th manager of the Indians, the fifth to serve as player-manager, and the youngest manager in baseball history, giving rise to his nickname as the "Boy Manager."

July 16, 1941 Joe DiMaggio gets three hits, two singles off Al Milnar in the first and third innings, and a double off Joe Krakauskas in the eighth inning, extending his consecutive game hitting streak to a record 56 as New York defeats the Indians, 10-3, at League Park.

July 17, 1941 Joe DiMaggio's record consecutive game hitting streak is stopped at 56 at the Stadium as the New York Yankees beat the Indians, 4-3, in front of 67,468 fans.

April 14, 1942 Lou Boudreau makes his debut as major league baseball's youngest manager in a 5-2 Opening Day victory over the Tigers in Detroit.

July 7, 1942 An American League all-star team beats a team of U.S. servicemen all-stars, 5-0, in front of a crowd of 62,094; the game is played at the Stadium for the benefit of the War Relief Fund.

June 22, 1946 The Indians are sold by Alva Bradley to Bill Veeck for $1.9 million.

Tribe timeline

July 5, 1947	Larry Doby becomes the American League's first black player, and second (to Jackie Robinson) in the major leagues, when he strikes out as a pinch hitter in his debut against the White Sox in Chicago.
September 13, 1948	Pitcher Don Black suffers a brain aneurysm while batting in a game against the St. Louis Browns in Cleveland and never pitches again.
October 3, 1948	The Indians lose to Detroit, 7-1, to end the season in a tie for the pennant with the Red Sox, both with 96-58 records.
October 4, 1948	Gene Bearden pitches a five-hitter for his 20th victory, and Lou Boudreau hits two homers as the Indians beat the Red Sox, 8-3, in Boston to win the franchise's second pennant in the first-ever playoff game in baseball history.
October 11, 1948	Bob Lemon is the winning pitcher as the Indians beat the Boston Braves, 4-3, in the sixth and deciding game of the World Series.
November 21, 1949	The Indians are sold for $2.2 million to a group headed by Ellis Ryan, which begins a succession of ownerships that subsequently include Myron H. Wilson (1952-56), William Daley (1956-62), Gabe Paul (1963-66), Vernon Stouffer (1966-72), Nick Mileti (1972-75), Alva "Ted" Bonda (1975-78), F. J. "Steve" O'Neill (1978-86), Richard and David Jacobs (1986-2000), and Larry Dolan.
December 19, 1952	The Indians are sold to a group of Clevelanders headed by Myron H. Wilson.
July 13, 1954	A crowd of 68,751 sees Al Rosen, playing with a broken right index finger, hit two home runs to lead the American League to an 11-9 victory over the National League in the second All-Star Game played in Cleveland, taking a 13-8 lead in the series.
September 9, 1954	The Indians become the first Cleveland baseball team to win 100 games when they defeat Philadelphia, 5-4, as the winning run scores in the 11th inning on a bases loaded walk to Hal Naragon.
September 18, 1954	Early Wynn wins his 22nd game as the Indians beat the Tigers, 3-2, to clinch their third pennant.
September 25, 1954	Early Wynn raises his record to 23-11 with a two-hitter to beat the Tigers, 11-1, in the second last game of the season, giving the Indians an American League record 111th victory.
October 2, 1954	New York Giants beat the Indians to sweep the World Series, 3-0, 3-1, 6-2, and 7-4.

February 29, 1956	William R. Daley, Hank Greenberg and Ignatius O'Shaughnessy purchase the Indians for $3,961,800 from a group headed by Myron H. Wilson.
May 7, 1957	Indians pitcher Herb Score is struck in the right eye by a line drive off the bat of the New York Yankees Gil McDougald; he recovers but is never a big winner again.
November 20, 1962	Gabe Paul forms a syndicate that buys the Indians from William R. Daley, Ignatius O'Shaughnessy and others for a reported $6 million.
July 9, 1963	Willie Mays of the New York Giants sparks the National League to a 5-3 victory over the American League, cutting the A.L.'s lead in the series to 17-16-1, in the third All-Star Game played in Cleveland.
August 28, 1970	Indians first baseman Tony Horton suffers a nervous breakdown, attempts suicide, and never plays again.
September 25, 1971	The Indians lose to Baltimore, 6-4, in 11 innings at the Stadium for their first 100 loss season since 1914.
March 22, 1972	The American League approves the sale of the Indians by Vernon Stouffer to Nick Mileti for $9,750,000.
April 7, 1973	A record Opening Day crowd of 74,420 at the Stadium sees the Indians beat Detroit, 2-1.
August 29, 1973	Alva "Ted" Bonda replaces Nick Mileti as chief executive officer and principal owner of the Indians.
October 3, 1974	Frank Robinson is hired by the Indians as major league baseball's first black manager, the 28th Indians manager, and their sixth player-manager.
April 8, 1975	Frank Robinson, baseball's first black manager, hits an Opening Day home run in his first at-bat off Doc Medich to lead the Indians to a 5-3 victory over the New York Yankees at the Stadium.
February 3, 1978	F.J. "Steve" O'Neill becomes principal owner of the Indians and Gabe Paul returns from the New York Yankees to be president and general manager of the team.
May 15, 1981	Len Barker pitches the eighth perfect game in baseball's modern era (since 1901), beating the Toronto Blue Jays, 3-0, in Cleveland.
June 12, 1981	The second player strike in major league baseball history begins; it lasts 50 days.

Tribe timeline

August 9, 1981
An all-time record crowd of 72,086 for the fourth All-Star Game of five played in Cleveland sees the National League beat the American League, 5-4, giving it a 33-18-1 lead in the series.

November 13, 1986
Richard E. and David H. Jacobs buy the Indians from the estate of F.J. "Steve" O'Neill for a reported $45 million.

December 11, 1986
The American League approves the sale of the Indians to Richard E. and David H. Jacobs.

April 9, 1987
Future Hall of Famers Phil Niekro and Steve Carlton team up to beat the Blue Jays, 14-3, in Toronto (Niekro pitched five innings for his 312th career victory, and Carlton pitched four scoreless innings in relief); it is the first time that two 300 game winners pitched for the same team in the same game.

October 6, 1991
The Indians' 7-4 loss to the Yankees in New York is their 105th of the season, breaking the franchise record of 102 defeats set in 1914 (51-102), and equaled in 1971 (60-102), and 1985 (60-102); it marks the fifth time in 90 years the club has lost 100 games (the 1987 team had a 61-101 record).

March 22, 1993
Pitchers Steve Olin and Tim Crews are killed, and pitcher Bob Ojeda is severely injured in a boating accident in Clermont, Fla. during spring training.

November 4, 1993
Pitcher Cliff Young is killed in a truck accident in Willis, Tex.

October 3, 1993
The Indians lose, 4-0, to the Chicago White Sox in the final game played at Municipal Stadium.

April 4, 1994
The Indians beat Seattle, 4-3, in the first regular season game played at Jacobs Field; it is the Indians first season as a member of the American League Central Division which also includes Chicago, Milwaukee and Kansas City.

July 15, 1994
Albert Belle is caught using an illegal (corked) bat in a game against the White Sox in Chicago during the Indians 3-2 victory and is suspended by A.L. President Dr. Gene Budig for 10 games (the suspension is later reduced to six games).

July 25, 1994
Mike Hargrove's contract as manager of the Indians is extended for two more years, through 1996, with a club option for 1997.

August 10, 1994
A 5-3 victory over the Blue Jays in Toronto proves to be the final game of the season, which is halted by a players strike with the Indians finishing in second place with a 66-47 record in the A.L. Central Division, one game behind the Chicago White Sox; the strike is finally settled and play resumes April 27, 1995.

September 8, 1995   The Indians beat Baltimore, 3-2, at Jacobs Field to clinch the American League Central Division championship; the victory gives them an 86-37 won-lost record and a 22 ½ game lead over Kansas City with 21 games remaining.

September 15, 1995   A crowd of 41,833 fans at Jacobs Field gives the Indians an attendance total of 2,634,139 for 66 dates (with five home games remaining), breaking the franchise record of 2,620,627 set in 1948; the Indians lose the game to Boston, 6-3.

October 1, 1995   A 17-7 victory over Kansas City at Jacobs Field gives the Indians a final 100-44 won-lost record, their first 100 victory season since 1954 and second in franchise history; they finish with a 30 game lead over Kansas City in the American League Central Division and the crowd of 41,819 at Jacobs Field gives the Indians a new season attendance record of 2,842,725.

October 6, 1995   The Indians beat the Red Sox, 8-2, in Boston in the third and deciding game to sweep the best-of-five American League Division Series.

October 17, 1995   The Indians beat the Mariners, 4-0, in Seattle in the sixth and deciding game of the best-of-seven American League Championship Series to win their fourth A.L. pennant.

October 28, 1995   The Indians lose to the Braves, 1-0 (on a home run by David Justice off Jim Poole), in Atlanta in the sixth and deciding game of the best-of-seven World Series.

September 10, 1996   The Indians beat California, 7-5, in front of 42,181 fans at Jacobs Field, raising the season attendance total to 2,852,882, breaking the 1995 record of 2,842,725 with 11 home dates remaining.

September 17, 1996   The Indians beat the White Sox, 9-4, in Chicago, to clinch a second straight A.L. Central Division championship; the victory gives them a 91-59 won-lost record and a 12 game lead over Chicago with 11 games remaining.

September 25, 1996   A crowd of 42,469 for the season's final game, a 6-3 victory over Minnesota at Jacobs Field, gives the Indians another record attendance total of 3,318,174; it also is the 79th consecutive capacity crowd of 1996, raising to 131 the number of sellouts in a row, dating back to June 12, 1995, and gives the Indians a 99-62 record and a final 14 ½ game margin over second place Chicago.

October 5, 1996   The Indians lose to Baltimore, 4-3, in 12 innings at Jacobs Field in the fourth and deciding game of the best-of-five American League Division Series.

Tribe timeline

May 13, 1997 Mike Hargrove's contract as manager of the Indians is extended for two more years, through 1999, with a club option for 2000.

July 8, 1997 Sandy Alomar Jr. hits a seventh inning, two-out, two-run homer off San Francisco southpaw Shawn Estes to break a 1-1 tie and give the American League a 3-1 victory over the National League in front of 44,945 fans at Jacobs Field in the 68th All-Star Game, the fifth played in Cleveland; Alomar Jr., one of three Indians on the A.L. team (David Justice and Jim Thome also were selected) is voted the game's Most Valuable Player; the A.L. victory cuts the N.L. lead in the series to 39-28 (one game in 1961 ended in a 1-1 tie because of rain).

September 23, 1997 The Indians clinch a third straight A.L. Central Division championship with a 10-9 victory over New York at Jacobs Field; it gives them an 84-71 won-lost record and a 7 ½ game lead over Chicago with six games remaining.

September 27, 1997 A crowd of 42,854 at Jacobs Field sees the Indians beat Minnesota, 10-6, giving them another season attendance record of 3,318,943, breaking the old mark of 3,318,174 set in 1996, with two home dates remaining.

September 28, 1997 The Indians lose their final game to Minnesota, 5-1, in front of a crowd of 42,940, raising their final season attendance record total to 3,404,750; it was the 211th consecutive sold out game at Jacobs Field, dating back to June 12, 1995, surpassing the major league record of 203 set by the Colorado Rockies in 1997.

October 6, 1997 The Indians beat New York, 4-3, at Jacobs Field in the fifth and deciding game of the best-of-five American League Division Series.

October 15, 1997 The Indians beat the Orioles, 1-0, in Baltimore to win the sixth and deciding game of the best-of-seven American League Championship Series.

October 26, 1997 The Indians lose to the Florida Marlins, 3-2, in 11 innings in Miami in the seventh and deciding game of the World Series.

August 21, 1998 Mike Hargrove's contract as manager of the Indians is extended for one year, through 2000, with a club option for 2001.

September 16, 1998 The Indians beat Minnesota, 8-6, at Jacobs Field to clinch a fourth consecutive A.L. Central Division championship; the victory gives them a 12 ½ game lead over Chicago with 12 games remaining, making them the seventh team in major league history to be in first place every day of the season.

September 20, 1998   Another capacity crowd of 43,082, the 292nd consecutive game the Indians have sold out at Jacobs Field since June 12, 1995, sees the Indians end the home season with a 5-3 victory over Kansas City; the crowd boosts the final attendance total to another record 3,467,299, breaking the 1997 mark of 3,404,750; the victory, raising the team's final won-lost record to 89-73, is the 624th (with 526 losses) for the Indians under Mike Hargrove, making him the second winningest manager, behind Lou Boudreau (728-649) in club history.

October 3, 1998   The Indians beat the Red Sox, 2-1, in Boston in the fourth and deciding game to win the best-of-five American League Division Series.

October 13, 1998   The Indians lose to the Yankees, 9-5, in New York in the sixth and deciding game of the best-of-seven American League Championship Series.

September 8, 1999   Despite losing to Texas, 3-0, the Indians clinch their fifth consecutive A.L. Central Division championship during a flight to Chicago as the White Sox were losing to Anaheim, 6-5; it left the Indians with a 23 ½ game lead over Chicago with 23 games remaining.

October 3, 1999   Another capacity crowd of 43,012 at Jacobs Field for the Indians final game of the regular season, a 9-2 loss to Toronto, raises the attendance total to 3,468,448, breaking the 1998 record 3,467,299; it was the Indians' 373rd consecutive sold out game, dating back to June 12, 1995, and gave them a final won-lost record of 97-65.

October 11, 1999   The Indians lose to the Red Sox, 12-8, in Boston in the fifth and deciding game of the best-of-five Division Series.

October 15, 1999   Mike Hargrove is fired as the Indians' 36th manager after leading the team to five consecutive A.L. Central Division championships and two pennants (1995, 1997) since replacing John McNamara on July 6, 1991; Hargrove's teams won 721 games (losing 591), the second most victories (to Lou Boudreau's 728) in franchise history.

November 1, 1999   Charlie Manuel, the Indians hitting instructor since 1994, and previously in 1988 and 1989, is hired to replace Mike Hargrove as the team's 37th manager.

November 4, 1999   Richard Jacobs, who has owned the Indians since 1986, announces that he is selling the franchise to Clevelander Larry Dolan for a reported $323 million, about $278 million more than Jacobs paid for the club 13 years earlier.

January 19, 2000   Major League owners approve the sale of the Indians to Larry Dolan.

February 7, 2000   Indians shareholders approve Larry Dolan's purchase of the franchise.

Index

Index

Index